Praise for *The Right Side of History*

"I'm glad to add my voice to this book by Adrian Brooks—a book celebrating a tradition of radical and progressive LGBT activists who have agitated for America to fulfill its originally stated goals by granting full equality to its citizens as 'one nation under God, indivisible, with liberty and justice for all.'"

> —Father Daniel Berrigan,
> priest, counterculture peace activist, and poet

"*The Right Side of History*'s fundamental premise: Queer activism is an act of patriotism, and radical Queer activists are, and have always been, central to the struggle for a more perfect union. To read this book is to join our Queer ancestors as they dance, riot, write, organize, sew, sashay, and howl their way through American history."

> —Katie Gilmartin, author of *Blackmail, My Love*

Praise for Adrian Brooks's memoir, *Flights of Angels*:

"*Flights of Angels* is a no-holds-barred story set within the larger framework that defined the era, the country, and especially its urban centers.... Brooks is certainly honest, and he recreates a unique era that was ultimately shattered by the passage of time and devastation of AIDS. Nicoletta's striking photographs enhance this unusual text."

> —*Library Journal*

THE RIGHT
SIDE OF
HISTORY

THE RIGHT SIDE OF HISTORY

100 YEARS OF LGBTQI ACTIVISM

ADRIAN BROOKS

FOREWORD BY JONATHAN D. KATZ, PhD

CLEiS
PRESS

Published in the United States by Cleis Press,
an imprint of Start Midnight, LLC,
375 Hudson Street, Twelfth Floor, New York, New York 10014.

Printed in the United States.
Cover design: Scott Idleman/Blink
Cover photograph: iStockphoto
Text design: Frank Wiedemann

First Edition.
10 9 8 7 6 5 4 3 2 1

Trade paper ISBN: 978-1-62778-123-7
E-book ISBN: 978-1-62778-131-2

Library of Congress Cataloging-in-Publication data is available.

"Bayard Rustin: Offensive Lineman for Freedom" by Patricia Nell Warren previously published in *Outsports,* February 15, 2009.

*"Until the lions have their own historians,
the history of the hunt will always glorify the hunter."*

—Chinua Achebe

for
Josephine Baker
and Bayard Rustin

CONTENTS

Foreword

by Jonathan Katz

Most history is a forced march forward, a succession of events in which the past births the present and the present, the future. But this ever-forward motion to the regular, staccato drumbeat of years fails to account for the far messier story of queer history, which has a tendency to circle back, to move in serpentine ways, to avoid—in every sense—the straight path forward. For example, the 1920s were in every way more accepting than the 1950s, but at the same time, black America and white America had two very different visions of queerness, as did the upper crust and the working class. There is, in short, no graph paper detailed enough to catch the mystifying leaps, backtrackings, and repetitions that are queer American history—or, better, American history queered.

The Right Side of History abandons the grand, synthetic master narrative for a sequential series of revealing close-ups: snapshots of some of the countless personalities that shaped America, even as America did her level best not to acknowledge them or their queerness. It brings to life a diverse cast, stretching from the Edwardian period to today, alive to the many differences beyond sexuality that have animated some of its best known and least known figures—including those who, by virtue of race, gender, or class, were effaced even in our own chronologies.

The book is willfully cacophonous, a chorus of voices untamed. Covering the years from the freewheeling turn-of-the-century Bohemianism of Isadora Duncan and the 1924 establishment of the nation's first gay group—the Society for Human Rights—it also includes the organization and gay activism of labor unions in the 1920s and 1930s, the 1950s Civil Rights Movement, the 1960s anti-war protests, the sexual liberation movements of the 1970s (and more contemporary issues such as marriage equality), and queers at the forefront of the contemporary peace and social justice movement, from antiwar protests to Palestinian rights. The book shows how LGBT and intersex folk have always been at the forefront of progressive social evolution in the United States, artistically, spiritually, and politically. It references such celebrated heroes and heroines as Abraham Lincoln, Eleanor Roosevelt, Bayard Rustin, Harvey Milk, and Edie Windsor, all having played parts in the nation's steady advance toward full equality. Equally, the book honors some whose names aren't recorded in books, from participants in the Names Project (now a national phenomenon memorializing 94,000 people who have died of AIDS) to the current underground anonymous agitprop artists—Bay Area Arts Queers Unleashing Power—who take their politics to the street. Among its many contributors are some of the pioneering voices in queer history itself.

Adrian Brooks is one of these. For almost fifty years and on five continents, from his start as a 60s hippy, anti-war, and civil rights activist, then, as radical gay lib poet and theater performer in the 70s, and as a novelist and nonfiction writer on to the present day, he's been directly involved in the vanguard or an astute observer to a huge slice of the history related here.

Central to the tale this book tells is the role of queer people in the spasmodic expansion of civil rights and civil liberties in a country that has promised a lot more than it has delivered. Of course, socially marginalized ourselves, we queers have long had reason to identify with other marginalized populations. But there is something beyond empathy in our tendency towards progressive politics.

For many of us, queerness was an elected identity. We could have lived like countless others who swallowed our differentness and aped a life that was foreign to our nature. Instead, the people whose voices fill this book elected to cast themselves out of the social norm, to willfully bear a stigma that is only now lifting. So many were convinced that they would—through sheer force of will—create a more just, equitable, and open America. There is power in that—and pleasure, to be sure. But mostly there is a deep, ethical commitment to the founding ideals that this nation honors as much in breach as in act. In holding fast to a centuries-old promise, queer Americans have regularly reminded their fellow citizens that free can be a verb. And in the pages of this book, that radiant vision still shines even as a dream of freedom, once considered unattainable, is achieved and a blistering history is righted.

Introduction

by Adrian Brooks

In many cities around the world, Pride is kicked off by a V-shaped wedge of dykes on bikes. They flex their biceps and gun the engines of Harley-Davidson motorcycles before thundering off to the cheers of the crowd.

In San Francisco, a parade starting at the Bay heads toward the Castro District—the first U.S. neighborhood where it was safe to be gay and visible. Here, a huge rainbow flag flies over a painted wooden village.

Particularly today—June 29, 2013—the mood is joyful. The U.S. Supreme Court has just struck down the Defense of Marriage Act, clearing the way for marriage equality. San Francisco's population of 837,000 has swelled to almost double that number as 1,500,000 tourists and reinforcements flood the spectacle. But in cities and towns from Los Angeles to Boston, many millions of others have also gathered to celebrate.

They are legion: proud parents, Gray Panthers, people of color, children, transgender people, and bisexuals. There are hilarious images, outrageous costumes. Masons; Lions; Veterans of Foreign Wars; Elks; Boy Scouts; representatives of gay churches, synagogues, temples, and mosques; gay farmers; firefighters; police; and pom-pom wielding cheerleaders are all elements of a tremendous unity. These are the largest LGBT events in the world. In London, Berlin, Sydney, New York, and San Francisco, the crowds are even larger than Woodstock. Hundreds of thousands of marchers, plus hundreds and hundreds of thousands of wildly enthusiastic supporters, wave flags and rainbow banners as musicians entertain. Politicians express an unqualified endorsement as they salute the nation's founding principles of life, liberty, and the pursuit of happiness, as well as equality for all. Naturally, these include full legal rights: to adopt children, to serve openly in the military, and to marry.

Such gains didn't occur in a vacuum or vault into existence without terrific effort. There were victories, but losses, too. Yet even for us fortunate ones, it was a long road to get here: to this time, this place. And while such commitment must be renewed by young people coming into their own, again and again, generation after generation—*for the work is far from finished*—the path spools back to our foundations.

In the 19th century, Walt Whitman was tarred as *obscene* for celebrating "the comrade's long dwelling kiss." Emerson's journals reveal his inchoate passion for a fellow at Harvard. Thoreau swoons for "Boys... bathing at Hubbard's Bend...[their skin] a pale pink, which the sun would soon tan." And besotted with the splendid (but heterosexual) Nathaniel Hawthorne, Melville confessed, "The soft ravishments of the man spun me around in a web of dreams...the more I contemplate him; and further and further, shoots his strong New England roots into the hot soil of my Southern soul."

Even revered leaders invite query. After living with 22-year-old Abraham Lincoln in 1831—a year during which they shared a small bed, Billy Greene called Lincoln's thighs "as perfect as a human being['s] could be." From 1837 to 1841, Lincoln lived with a handsome merchant, Joshua Speed. They, too, had a double bed; thereafter, Lincoln ended some of his letters, "Yours forever." And whenever his wife was away from September 1862 to April 1863, Lincoln shared his bed (and a nightshirt) with Army Captain David Derickson, a fact that provoked Washington gossip. Was it to distance with humor, then, or was it to tease his critics that our 16th president wrote a poem with these lines?

> For Reuben and Charles have married two girls,
> But Billy has married a boy.
> The girls he had tried on every side,
> But none he could get to agree;
> All was in vain, he went home again,
> And since that he's married to Natty

Lincoln's sexuality may never be conclusively untangled, but the first woman to run for President (in 1872) was a fearless advocate of free love. In an 1871 speech, Victoria Hull stated:

> I have an unalienable, constitutional and natural right to love whom I may, to love as long or as short a period as I can; to change that love every day if I please, and with that right neither you nor any law you can frame have any right to interfere. And I have the further right to demand a free and unrestricted exercise of that right, and it is your duty not only to accord it, but as a community, to see I am protected in it. I trust that I am fully understood, for I mean just that.

* * *

By the 1890s, anarchists central to the creation of labor unions—such as the bisexual Emma Goldman—deemed it "unethical" for the state to interfere with private behavior. But upon being praised for defending Oscar Wilde after his 1895 conviction for committing "crimes against nature," Goldman declared stoutly, "No daring is required to protest against a great injustice."

From that groundswell, and at each successive step of progression—in wresting power from an entrenched few to deliver the vote to women, the right for Labor to organize, full enfranchisement to racial and ethnic minorities, and, *yes*, equality before the law—our people were in the forefront as the 20th century progressed. As such, we advanced—sometimes tentatively, sometimes bravely, but always positive we were mobilizing on the right side of history.

One doesn't have to speculate to see why "the lowest of the low," the reviled engaging in "the love that dare not speak its name," or the born-different identify with others oppressed by a patriarchal system, which denied us voice. But a quixotic quality as ephemeral as "gay humor," or some stubborn insistence on being seen and being heard, wouldn't let us collude with those seeking to will us away, persecute us into oblivion, or shame us into permanent despised status—marginalized and acceptable only if we were talented social lubricants, or utilized by straight society for our entertainment value.

Long before Josephine Baker adopted twelve children of different ethnicities for her "rainbow tribe," queer folk functioned on all levels, some mighty, some obscure. But all yearned for that which lay "out there," beyond the confines imposed, past a pact of silence allowing us to live (albeit shamed lives) as long as we'd accept the implication that we were, somehow, "less than," tolerated as long as we remained meek, non-threatening, and in our place.

Sometimes we had allies without realizing it. That fact, too, can't be too much of a surprise, since living in the closet persisted as the only way to survive for some. But even such history as ours was kept shrouded, and often cloaked by denial.

Queer folk are used to having their truths suppressed or ruled inadmissible. That goes hand in glove with the millennia of second-class status; we too often accepted this rank distinction as fate until/unless we woke up and hit a critical moment of recognition, which triggered the actuality of personal liberation. And so it is with full equality.

The striving for "a more perfect union" promised by our Constitution has been—and continues to be—exhaustive. But our freedom is no trickle-down liberation bestowed by generous benefactors upon us, ever-so-grateful for their largesse. Far from it. It moves from the street up. It thrums with the energy of dynamic meeting places: from bars and bookstores, influential public spaces and, now, the Internet. And from grass-roots populism, change infiltrates the marble corridors of U.S. federal power and spreads to places like Russia and parts of Africa where "differentness" is so viciously persecuted.

When describing Stonewall, Rita Mae Brown told me about passing the infamous Women's House of Detention: a big red brick building at Greenwich Avenue and West 10th Street. Overcrowded and deemed unsafe by the early 60s and later razed in 1971, it housed prostitutes who thronged caged enclosures high above the street and shouted to boyfriends and husbands below. On that historic night in June 1969, which is to LGBT folk what the Boston Tea Party is to the American Revolution, the penned-up women set their mattresses ablaze, banged tin cups against the bars of their cages, and screamed, *"I want to be free! I want to be free!"*

Freedom...that universal and eternal human longing. As Martin Luther King said, "The arc of the moral universe is long, but it bends towards justice."

Yes.

For myself, Quaker childhood instruction infused with Gandhi's non-violent philosophy was further informed by the ripple effect of Rosa Parks's refusal to move to the black section of a public bus in 1955. The influence of George Fox (the founder of the Society of Friends) on Voltaire, his impact on Gandhi, and his illumination of Dr. King thanks to Bayard Rustin is a clear line of descent. But I didn't get traction until 1966, when I first began protesting the war in Vietnam and was swept up in the Civil Rights crusade.

From the inspiring frisson of those immense shaping forces, a natural, fluid progression led to my plunge into radical gay lib culture—and the discovery of my own core identity in 1972.

The history of past movements may seem quaint or old-fashioned in 2015, yet much still remains undone even when marriage equality is on a roll to becoming national law. It isn't simply fighting the ongoing plagues of racism, alienation, or ageism. The trans community faces jarringly disproportionate rates of violence and discrimination. Unemployment is four times the national average and highest among trans women of color, already burdened by galling racial and economic inequalities coupled with systematic injustice. Many are forced into sex work as their only way of survival. And that entails the jeopardy of visibility.

As Pride parades unfold, of course, one sees ribald drag queens. It's a stereotype that less-than-well-informed critics have of gay men: that we want to be women. But even the gaudiest cross-dresser isn't attempting gender traverse. With its trashy vulgarity, drag is the broadest of Restoration Comedy—political satire and street theatre, as well as a deliberately chosen foil: to engage, to use humor and exaggeration to invite straight people to consider their own norms with a slanted eye and see what we rebel against in defiance of sexual imaging, *which limits and constricts them too.* The childlike willingness to splash out so colorfully or make fun of ourselves is a bawdy cue inviting response, welcoming participation. And since many have been emboldened at the sight of such hilarity and even come out as a result, it's also dead serious.

In a different way, billboards lining the San Francisco parade route highlight our concerns. For adding an unpredictable edge to the proceedings, one spots the sly urban handicraft of a contemporary underground, anonymous, and anarchist agitprop group: *Bay Area Art Queers Unleashing Power.*

With fidelity to the spirit of the anti-war 60s and gay liberation/feminist 70s, these self-anointed Robin Hoods take power: they reinterpret commercial advertisements and put their own spin on billboards to advocate for the rights of undocumented workers, non-intervention in Syria, opposition to Israeli apartheid tactics on the occupied West Bank and in Gaza, and the rejection of legislation curbing the right to assemble in public places under the guise of being intended to prevent loitering. Defacing anti-Muslim ads put on city buses by outside right-wing Christian zealots, BAAQUP blasts religious and racial stereotypes, supports the "Teach Peace" program, pushes for improved health care and human rights *for all,* and declares its solidarity with former army activist and prisoner of conscience Chelsea Manning.

The simple fact is: queers have been in the vanguard—and remain engaged—in that onerous, often lonely-making route, which so often begins in the streets and works through grassroots populism in successive waves of interlocking, overlapping concern for advancing to a greater, finer, wider, more compassionate and indivisible Whole. It's part of who we are. But the reality of being American requires that a commitment to our founding principles must be renewed by personal discovery with each generation—actively, not passively—if the country is to remain true to its stated goals. It's far too easy to proclaim concern about, or glib fidelity to, LGBTQI issues only. The actual challenge is comprehensive: a fair and telling yardstick for evaluating self-anointed spokespersons or would-be community leaders. And in an era of buzz and wannabes, this fierce but subtle necessity has never been more urgent.

The distance traversed thus far represents our mounting, shared success. But every generation builds on the struggles of brave forebears to achieve the heretofore unimaginable: an even greater felicity, just as the patriots of 1776 initiated and as the framers of the Constitution intended. In fact, it's the same renegade spirit that imbues Pride parades today as the rainbow flag flies high.

PART I

◇◇◇◇◇

Before Stonewall

Chapter 1

The Divine Discontent
of Isadora Duncan

by Adrian Brooks

Baring her breasts and waving a bright scarf, Isadora announced her bisexuality to a horrified Boston audience and shouted, "This scarf is red! And so am I!"

It was 1922.

It's doubtful if anyone could trump Isadora Duncan as an artistic genius, free spirit, and influence on 20th century arts. As a theorist, choreographer, and performer, she elevated dance to the status of major art: one of its transformative exponents.[1] But the beautiful Romantic and self-described freedom fighter was even more.

By 1900, Isadora was advocating liberation of the body and its unity with a holistic Self, the full equality of the sexes, free love, and social and political revolution. As a radical, she saw not just dance but movement itself as emblematic of spiritual truth—the vehicle to a greater harmony and union with pantheistic Divinity. Freewheeling and impulsive, idealistic, courageous and iconoclastic, Isadora smashed all prior concepts of art, as well as those of the female artist. Her destiny was to stir, startle, shock, outrage, liberate, inspire, and illuminate while in pursuit of a dream, one which she achieved for others, if not, ultimately, for herself.[2]

Isadora advocated principles that proved to be 100 years ahead of their time. But her passionate crusading was more than "the divine discontent without which no artist can hope to succeed."[3] It revealed a fire—as timeless as her wish to inspire—to discover and create, and, also, to challenge and confront the Philistines.

Still, to understand her more fully, one must spool back to her roots.

When Isadora was born in 1877, the Victorian Age was at its zenith. Dominated by men, it upheld the status quo. Women knew their place. Convention was equated with beauty. Novelty was fine…but mustn't go too deep. Even so, women—"the dangerous ones"—had dreams of equality.

Soon after Isadora's birth in San Francisco, her father lost his money, and Isadora was raised in poverty. But, as she later stated, her spirit was unperturbed: "As a child, I danced on the sea beach beside the waves…. My art was already in me when I was a little girl." Thus inspired, she was teaching dance by the age of six. When she was twelve, her parents divorced, and Isadora's mother moved the family to Oakland. As a teen who already distrusted marriage and male domination, Isadora dropped out of school, drawn to spontaneous movement, fantasy, and improvisation. After traveling around the United States, she worked for a New York theatrical entrepreneur but quickly became disenchanted with established form. She moved to London, where upon encountering the Elgin Marbles at the British Museum she had an epiphany.

Dance was rigid, formal, and ritualistic in 1898—not a mode of personal expression. But inspired by classical Greek art and her lifelong love of the sea, Isadora devised a radical new approach: "What we are trying to accomplish [is] to blend together a poem, a melody, a dance—so that you will not listen to the music, see the dance, or hear the poem, but live in the scene."

Her time in London laid the groundwork for a vision based in naturalism, fluidity, and an organic sense of herself as an instrument or conduit. As her friend and biographer Sewell Stokes said, "Nothing mattered when Isadora danced except her dance. A spiritual vitality…deified the body it animated. Her dance, one felt, had been in that room since the beginning of time; a beautiful vibration that was eternally avoiding imprisonment."[4]

Choreographer Frederick Ashton observed, "Anyone of any age could duplicate *what* she did but not *how* she did it. It was incredible. She could also stand still—and often did—but it was an alive stillness."[5]

In 1900, she arrived in Paris. Performing on bare stages in tunics emphasizing her lyricism and to the minimal accompaniment of Chopin piano preludes, she reduced dances to a single gesture: the wave of an arm, the rhythmic abstract repetition of a step. But as dancer, choreographer, and teacher Hanya Helm said, "Isadora traveled on ether to the moon."[6]

In addition to revolutionary breakthroughs such as sinuous movements, a theory of fall and recovery, ebbs and flows, contraction and release, and dynamism, Isadora issued strident pronouncements, especially about ballet. "Toe walking deforms the feet; corsets deform the body," she insisted, adding, "Nothing is left to be deformed and there is not much of this in the women who dance modern dances."

The opinionated radical was among "the first to see the linkage between dance and the human spirit, to recognize that dance rhythms are created by gravity." Yet even while winning acclaim for performances related to character, situation, and theme, her primary interest was in education: bringing up children to celebrate beauty and live in affiliation to a deeply felt dream of the perfect life. For Isadora, art was a decidedly non-commercial mission; her calling was to illuminate life by connecting movement to emotion, and emotion to truth. And freedom.

Dancing barefoot, leaping, bounding, skipping, and using her arms as expressive instruments, Isadora insisted that the core or source of dance lay in the solar plexus, "the crater of motor power," not in the over-trained legs or tight muscle structure required by classical ballet. As she explained in words that paralleled her passionate commitment to revolutionary politics, "all movement is governed...by attraction and repulsion; resistance and yielding. Primary or fundamental movements...must have within them the seeds from which will evolve all other movements, each to give birth to others in an unending sequence of still-higher expression, thoughts, and ideas." Furthermore, she declared, "True movements are not invented, they are discovered."

By 1902, Isadora was a star in Paris. In 1905, she went to Russia for the first time and "gave an irreparable jolt to the Imperial Ballet," profoundly influencing its dancers and choreographers. As a critic wrote, "she was the first to dance the music and not *to* the music."[7]

On her other trips to Russia in 1907 and 1908, the dominant dance culture of Europe collided with Isadora's revelation. Her art was female centric; there was no place for men, only art and children. As choreographer Agnes de Mille said, "Isadora cleared away the rubbish. She was a gigantic broom." De Mille's opinion was echoed by Ted Shawn. The dancer, teacher, and choreographer stated: "There was an inner strength so great that one felt the Valkyries themselves were charging. She was heroic."

Duncan's personal life was equally radical. While refusing to marry—seeing marriage as a bourgeois institution—she had a son with the visionary English stage designer, Gordon Craig, in 1906. In 1910, her affair with an American millionaire, Paris Singer, resulted in a baby girl. After both of her children died in a freakish 1913 car accident, she had a third child with an Italian sculptor. Their baby survived only a few hours.

After that tragedy, Isadora became involved with the great actress Eleonora Duse, and conducted a passionate affair with writer Mercedes de Acosta (later a lover of Marlene Dietrich and Greta Garbo). Writing de Acosta, Isadora said, "Mercedes, lead me with your little hands and I will follow you—to the top of a mountain. To the end of the world. Wherever you wish."

Back in Russia in 1922, where the new Bolshevik government had promised her a state school for dance (a project she sought eagerly, though it never materialized), Isadora married Symbolist poet Sergei Esenin, a wedding being the only way to get him an exit visa. She didn't speak Russian, and the poet, who was eighteen years her junior, spoke no French. Moreover, according to some, the only English that he knew when they married was a single sentence: "We make love like tigers."

Their union was explosive. The blond, bisexual poet was sulky and dishonest; jealous of her fame, he felt that a dancer's notoriety was fleeting, while a poet's was eternal—even though Isadora was a world star. Worse than his jealousy was his abuse. Esenin beat up Isadora during epic battles that resulted in furniture being smashed up, running around hotel hallways naked, evictions, alcoholic rants, and tumultuous reconciliations. And, convinced of his genius and jolted by their impossible passion out of a fixation on the death of her children, Isadora was madly possessive.

Arguing over the existence of God, Isadora agreed with Bolsheviks that the concept of God was old and silly. "My Gods are Beauty and Love!" she told Esenin. Pointing to their bed, she said in Russian "*Vot bog! (This is God!)*"

On an American tour, Isadora's enthusiastic Communism—she'd become a citizen of Russia and now proclaimed the ideals of a new world order of justice, equality, and free love—triggered a firestorm of protest. The tour zigzagged between fiasco and the artistic triumph of a capacity crowd at Carnegie Hall. Even so, the uproar over the outrageous politico reached crescendo in New England. There, Isadora was seen as a walking, talking bomb-thrower and anarchist.

Jeered by appalled Bostonians shocked by her feminism, her sexuality, her marriage to a far younger (Communist) foreigner—she tore off her clothes. Exposing her body, she declared nudity "beautiful," scolded the audience for being so repressed, and refused to buckle to howls of righteous condemnation. "I am an artist. Who are they?" she scoffed dismissively. "Women in hats."

She did not stop there. Quoted for saying that many Americans seemed to have forgotten that the United States began with a revolution, she added that she and her husband were both revolutionists. Newspaper headlines screamed about this "dangerous and erratic woman." The mayor of Chicago called her "a Bolshevik hussy." In Indianapolis, the mayor classified her with nude dancers and warned that she might end up arrested.

Heavier, now, at forty-five, Isadora wasn't always sober when dancing but she continued to exert her magic. As Sol Hurok, the tour producer, said, "She didn't really have to move. In *Marche Slav*...she just stood with her hands tied together. She moved just slightly yet somehow she told the story of a people's revolt against slavery." But if Isadora used the stage for enthusiastic dances, Esenin used it for drunken orations (in Russian). Even so, his health was failing. As their relationship floundered, they returned to Europe and separated.

Her 1923 Russian tour was a phenomenal success. Invited to honor Lenin at his funeral, Isadora astounded her audience by dancing to *Ave Maria*. By that time France viewed Communism with suspicion, but naïve and impulsive, Isadora lived riotously—extravagantly—and planned ahead for the establishing of a French school for 1,000 children brought from Russia. Yet nothing gelled. And bookings fell by the wayside.

Now in debt, Isadora continued to carry on luxuriously in 1924. Though she found money "filthy...[and] filled with germs," she needed it to survive. Isadora lived on the run, ducking creditors, sending hotel or restaurant bills to friends, imploring rescue, announcing that she was "starving," and performing only on rare occasions. Still, even as her life became what future generations might call process art or a performance piece, she remained the unreformed, pluperfect Bohemian dedicated to a credo of living for the moment, irrespective of consequences. Her career may have tanked but Isadora was still a trailblazer, blasting cultural consciousness from the late Victorian era into the modern age. Dance had taken its rightful place as a major art. Implicit in that fact was the coequality of women and the centrality of sex.

An episode from her 1905 visit to Russia captures her philosophy and her spirit at a time when classic Russian ballet reigned supreme and Anna

7

Pavlova was its prima ballerina. Isadora and Pavlova liked each other, but couldn't have been more different.

Once, when departing from dinner, Pavlova explained that she had to retire early to get up and do her exercise routine. Isadora, who was just warming up for a night of carousing, told Pavlova that she was missing all the fun. Pavlova replied that she was taking care of her instrument while Isadora was ruining hers through neglect.

"That may be true," Isadora admitted. "But look what you've done to your body. You're a very great artist, but you're not a woman any more."

By 1925, Isadora's life had spun out of control. She plunged into reckless affairs and often had to beg for money. She went to parties in order to eat. But whatever her overindulgences, no one could accuse her of not being a woman. Or not living life to the hilt. Yet even then, this self-anointed freedom fighter could astonish.

In January 1927, Janet Flanner wrote in the *New Yorker*: "In the three summer programs which Isadora recently gave in her studio in Nice…her art was seen to have changed. She treads the boards but little now, she stands almost immobile or in slow splendid steps with slow splendid arms moves to music, seeking, hunting, finding. By an economy (her first) she has arrived at elimination. As if the movements of dancing had become too redundant for her spirit, she has saved from dancing only its shape." Flanner goes on, "Great artists are tragic. Genius is too large; and it may have been grandeur that proved Isadora's undoing—the grandeur of temporary luxury, the grandeur of personal ideals. She is too expansive for personal salvation. She has had friends. What she needed was an entire government. She had checkbooks. Her scope called for a national treasury. It is not for nothing that she is hailed by her first name only as queens have been."[8]

In the summer of 1927, Isadora gave her last performance in Paris. After the recital, the critic was forced to admit that "Isadora had lost none of her popularity" judging by "the overwhelming applause." But what happened on September 14 added further luster to her legend.

Hot for a handsome mechanic in the South of France, Isadora finally met him when he came to pick her up in a Bugatti convertible. She jumped into the car, wearing a billowing red scarf like those she used in performance and often wore offstage. Draping it around her neck, she told friends: *"Au revoir mes amis. Je vais à la gloire. (Goodbye, friends. I'm going to glory)."* But when the driver hit the gas, the scarf snagged in the spokes of a wheel. As the car shot forward, her neck was broken. She died instantly.

In London, a dance critic eulogized, "Thanks to her, we are not afraid of nudity." The *San Francisco Chronicle* headline ran, "Something Mighty Fine About Isadora." A New York columnist spoke for the world, "We knew that this woman was one in a million...one of the greatest dancers we have ever seen or were ever likely to see." The Copenhagen *Politiken* said, "Her violent death seems almost natural, symbolic. In some ways, it seems this life had to end like this. In the realm of the arts, she now belongs to the great fallen ones."

A great peer weighed in. Ruth St. Denis said, "To reject her genius is unthinkable," while a direct beneficiary of Isadora's legacy, Martha Graham, observed, "her influence is stronger today than when she was living."

The legend of the Bohemian artist-lover-political pagan revolutionary *extraordinaire* lives on—the untamed and radical bisexual free spirit who so believed in art, activism, and a fusion of individual consciousness to a greater unified Whole. As Isadora said, "If my art is symbolic of...any one thing, it is symbolic of the freedom of women and her emancipation from hidebound conventions." And upon finishing her 1927 autobiography just shortly before her death, she cried, "Adieu, Old World! I hail a New World."

ENDNOTES

1 Other dance pioneers include: Loie Fuller (1862-1928), Ruth St. Denis (1879-1968), and Hanya Holm (1893-1992).

2 Walter Terry. *Isadora Duncan: Her Life, Her Art, Her Legacy* (New York: Dodd, Mead and Company, 1963), 149.

3 Terry, 138.

4 Ibid., 88.

5 Ibid., 154.

6 Ibid., 159.

7 Ibid., 40-41.

8 Isadora Duncan. *My Life* (New York: Boni & Liveright, 1927).

Chapter 2

Henry Gerber's Bridge to the World

by Hayden L. Mora

If a prophet can be defined as one "who advocates or speaks in a visionary way about a new belief, cause, or theory,"[1] Henry Gerber fits the bill. He was born in 1892 in Germany, and, despite facing the structural violence of poverty, xenophobia, and homophobia, he came to the United States in 1913 as part of a massive influx of European immigrants. Upon arriving, he encountered a country that historian Marc Stein describes as being in the midst of, "several major social, cultural, and political transformations, [including] large-scale urbanization, industrialization, immigration, and migration."[2] Social movements—many influenced (and often led) by anarchists, socialists, and communists—strove with workers' movements to redefine the relations of power between labor and capital, even as the gulf between the rich and poor reached unprecedented proportions. The suffragette movement challenged institutionalized misogyny, resulting in the jailing of hundreds, who were force-fed and violently attacked as they worked for the national enfranchisement of women. Booker T. Washington, W.E.B. Du Bois, and others led the charge for civil rights even as the extrajudicial killings of black men and women in the South raged on.

Nowhere was persuasive change more evident than in Chicago, where Gerber settled. As Stein writes, "Many residents, wage laborers, immigrants, and migrants spent less time with their families, more time in single-sex environments, and more money on leisure activities. The expanded world of commercialized amusement, bars, restaurants, and dance halls encouraged the pursuit of pleasure."[3] These conditions created new spaces for same-sex attraction and love to be discovered and expressed. In these spaces and others, homosexuality and homosexual activity was neither invisible nor truly public.

According to Xavier Mayne's 1908 account of the situation, the bathhouse culture of same-sex liaisons was already well established in Chicago and other major U.S. cities.[4] But both state and the anti-vice reform efforts were radically increasing their attempt to define and regulate "deviant sexual behavior." Two years before Gerber's arrival, the Chicago Vice Commission (a committee formed to deal with female prostitution) reported surprisingly large amounts of male homosexual activity. In fact, the committee claimed to have found whole groups and colonies of these homosexuals. They concluded their report by suggesting that the state enforce harsher penalties for crimes already in the books (such as sodomy) and suggested stripping offenders of citizenship.[5]

In A Queer History of the United States, Michael Bronski explains the terror and intimidation for people who were different: "These attacks, always in coded language that never mentioned 'fairy,' 'pansy,' or 'homosexual,' were primarily aimed at homosexual men. Waves of 'sex panics' spread across the country," and several states passed laws that, "allowed the courts to incarcerate 'sexual psychopaths' for undetermined periods of time in mental institutions."[6] Bronski further writes:

These laws were broadly written, and the definition of "sexual psychopath" always remained vague so that it could be applied as indiscriminately as possible. Sexual psychopath laws, clearly influenced by social purity concerns, almost always presumed children being victimized. The terms *child molester, homosexual, sex offender, sex psychopath, sex degenerate, sex deviant,* and sometimes even *communist* were used and became interchangeable in the mind of the public. The conflation of vague "sexual deviancy" with homosexuality and child molestation set up what was to become a widely accepted myth: that male homosexuals were innately driven to seduce or sexually assault male children. This myth was a strong influence in shaping the public discussion of homosexuality well into the twenty-first century.[7]

In 1917, some say that Gerber was sent to a mental institution because of his homosexuality. When WWI broke out, he was given a choice: to be interned as an enemy alien, or to serve in the army. He enlisted and went to Germany. There, he encountered a society far more integrated and open than the United States. Gerber then contacted Magnus Hirschfeld, who founded the Scientific Humanitarian Committee in 1897. The SHC was a highly organized group that had published several magazines and had led a campaign to repeal a section of the German penal code criminalizing same-sex relations. With "Justice through science" as its motto, the committee argued that the law made homosexuals easy prey for blackmail and urged understanding.[8] They also suggested that criminalization weakened the strength of the state.

After the war, Gerber returned to the United States determined to begin organizing gay men along similar lines to Hirschfeld's organization. At the time, individuals caught engaging in same-sex activity faced fines, imprisonment, chemical castration, and institutionalization. Gerber wrote, "I thought to myself that if I succeeded I might become known to history as deliverer of the downtrodden." And, "If I succeeded in freeing the homosexual, I, too, would benefit."[9] In 1924, Gerber founded the Society for Human Rights, the first same-sex advocacy group in the United States. The group's mission stated their purpose:

> [T]o promote and protect the interests of people who...are abused and hindered in the legal pursuit of happiness, which is guaranteed them by the Declaration of Independence, and to combat the public prejudices against them.... The Society stands only for law and order; it is in harmony with any and all general laws insofar as they protect the rights of others, and does in no manner recommend any acts in violation of present laws...[n]or the public welfare.[10]

In that one mild-sounding paragraph, Gerber had asserted that gay men were persons protected by the promise of the rule of law, that it was those who would abuse and hinder the homosexual in the pursuit of their legal, guaranteed rights who were the true criminals. Additionally, he'd positioned homosexual rights as an extension of the founding documents.

Unlike anarchists and communists, who positioned sexual liberation as being at odds with a capitalist democracy, Gerber offered a liberal vision of sexual freedom, which embodied rather than challenged the values of the country. Even the manner in which he founded the organization—a formal request for state sanction—spoke to this approach when he outlined the primary tactics of the Society for Human Rights in a three-point plan:

- "[E]ngage in a series of lectures pointing out the attitude of society in relation to their own behavior and especially urging against the seduction of adolescents.

- "Through a publication...we would keep the homophile world in touch with the progress of our efforts.

- "Through self-discipline, homophiles would win the confidence and assistance of legal authorities and legislators in understanding the problem: that these authorities should be educated on the futility and folly of long-prison terms for those committing homosexual acts."[11]

These tactics—broad-based public education and community-building through lectures, publications, and advocacy with legislators and legal authorities to change policy—would be used by LGBTQ organizations as major strategies and tactics from that point on to the current day.[12]

Gerber enlisted seven friends as initial members of his Society for Human Rights. In an early example of interracial cooperation and cross-cultural support, African-American Minister John T. Graves served as president of the organization. Soon Gerber began to struggle, however. He was a visionary, but lacked organizational skill. Moreover, he met with indifference from all but "the poorer gays." When he sought financial support from wealthy gay white men, he was rebuffed. His efforts to enlist the support of opinion leaders among medical professionals and sex education advocates were also blunted. They demurred, unwilling to risk their reputations. Reflecting on this experience, Gerber wrote:

The first difficulty was in rounding up enough members and contributors so the work could go forward. The average homosexual, I found, was ignorant concerning himself.

Others were fearful. Still others were frantic or depraved.

Some were blasé. Many homosexuals told me that their search for forbidden fruit was the real spice of life. With this argument, they rejected our aims. We wondered how we could accomplish anything with such resistance from our own.[13]

Although SHR membership excluded bisexuals, unbeknownst to Gerber and other members one vice-president was married. When his wife found out about the organization, she reported it to the police in the summer of 1925. A detective and reporter woke Gerber at 2:00 a.m. one morning. Upon being let in, the detective asked, "Where's the boy?" The *Chicago Examiner* headline read: "Strange Sex Cult Exposed."[14]

Arrested as a "degenerate," Gerber was tried three times. Ultimately, the charges were dismissed, but Gerber had gone bankrupt paying for his defense. In the end, the SHR was ruined, Gerber lost his job, and (in a telling sign of the paranoia of the era) not one of Chicago's rich gay men came to Gerber's aid or offered support for a cause dedicated to their own welfare and security.

Embittered by the increasing regulation of sex and sexuality, and by the perceived apathy of other gay men, Gerber had lost much of his idealism. Later in life, however, he founded a pen-pal group called the Dill Pickle Club, which historian Chad Heap identifies as one of the critical ways in which the construction of the Chicago lesbian and gay community (and, by extension, the national community) took place.[15] Further, Gerber struck up a correspondence with several gay men around the country, with whom he continued to debate ideas about organizing gay men in the United States.

Accounts vary, but it seems likely that Gerber met Harry Hay in 1929 in Los Angeles, twenty years before the formation of the Mattachine Society. Still, there is little doubt that Gerber was the movement's godfather. Although his organization was short-lived, he foresaw its necessity, and while few prophets succeed in their lifetime, Gerber had sought to push against the inertia of the status quo—to act heroically even when others were seized by fear or consumed by self-interest and cynicism.

As an activist and organizer, I've spent 15 years working on campaigns; and as a member of the labor movement, an out trans man from a working class background, and as a radical critic of power, I'm acutely aware of the ways in which contributions to social progress are often obscured. Considering the continuing injustices and the profound consequences that

14

so many queers globally face while members of our community still stand by (and others pay with their lives), I can relate to Gerber's demoralization. Yet as I write this from inside of the Washington, D.C. office of the Human Rights Campaign, the largest LGBTQ advocacy organization in the United States, radical changes have occurred. In a sense, one by-product of Gerber's idealism is a reminder to all of us to believe in our visions and our work as part of a bridge to the world that we believe in, even if we cannot always see the way forward. Hold on to our own.

ENDNOTES

1 Oxford Dictionary

2 Marc Stein, *Rethinking the Gay and Lesbian Movement* (New York: Routledge Press, 2012), 50-51.

3 Ibid., 51.

4 Ibid., 41.

5 Ibid., 44.

6 Michael Bronski, *A Queer History of the United States* (Boston: Beacon Press, 2012), 142.

7 Ibid.

8 "Dr. Magnus Hirschfeld," Hirschfeld-Eddy-Stiftung, accessed January 23, 2014, http://www.hirschfeld-eddy-stiftung.de/en/foundation/about-us/names/magnus-hirschfeld/

9 Jonathan Ned Katz, "Henry Gerber: Gay Pioneer," in *Out and Proud in Chicago: An Overview of the City's Gay Community*, ed. Trace Baim (Boston: Agathe Publishing, 2008), 36.

10 Jonathan Ned Katz, *Gay American History: Lesbians and Gay Men in the U.S.A.: A Documentary* (New York: Crowell, 1976), 386-387.

11 Vern L Bullough, *Before Stonewall: Activists for Gay and Lesbian Rights in Historical Context* (New York: Harrington Park Press, 2002), 28.

12 David Bianco, *Gay Essentials: Facts for Your Queer Brain* (Los Angeles: Alyson Books, 1999), 136-137.

13 Katz, *Gay American History*, 388.

14 Katz, "Henry Gerber," 36.

15 Chad Heap, "Gays and Lesbians in Chicago: An Overview," in Baim, *Out and Proud*, 10.

Chapter 3

The 1934 Longshoremen's Strike

by Adrian Brooks

San Francisco was the wildest city in America from its inception. Founded by Gold Rush miners in 1849, its first buildings were bars, brothels, and bathhouses. But when union organizers brought West Coast commerce to a halt in 1934, gays weren't just engaged; they were central.

At the time, neither the Golden Gate nor the Bay Bridges had been built. With no direct road links to the north or to Oakland, the city's economy relied on its waterfront. But politics was central to its identity. Its dockworkers had organized in 1853, and sailors formed their trade's first union in 1866.[1] As the labor capital of the West, internationally known for union activism, "at the turn of the century, [San Francisco] was the first port city in the world to be known as 'a closed-shop.'"

Bay Area democratic activism, interracial community, and worker rights movements got their start back then while gay culture centered on the waterfront bars. But uniquely for the United States, the raucous city was the only place where the Puritan work ethic and traditional religious morals were never dominant. Pleasure was not frowned upon.

Labor unions had tried to organize longshoremen and sailors in various ways since the 1920s. Their militant newspaper—*The Water-*

front Worker—pressed their most urgent demands, including: more men on each gang, lighter workloads, and the right to form their union. But employers fought back by using race as a tactic: they hired black strike-breakers, deliberately turning race against race as "scab labor."

The 1933 National Recovery Act—one part of FDR's plan to help the United States out of the Depression—led to a huge growth of membership in the coal miners' union. Soon, thousands of longshoremen moved west. But, once hired, they organized "slowdowns," in order to try to win better working conditions.

In 1934, the California Congress of Industrial Organizations' vice president was Frank McCormick. His lover was labor organizer Stephen Richard Blair of the National Union of Marine Cooks and Stewards (NUMCS). A sign in the NUMCS union hall declared that, "Race-bating, Red-baiting, Queer-Baiting is Anti-Union." The importance of this was not lost on Harry Hay, an activist who was swept up in, and transformed by, the strike. Hay had attended the Southern California Labor School. In 1934, he'd become lovers with actor Will Geer. As a result of their relationship, Hay began to see homosexuals as a distinct and oppressed class.

Shipping companies and docks had required longshoremen to go through a hiring hall after a series of failed Communist-infiltrated strikes. Now, as thousands of new workers poured into the Bay Area, unions demanded a closed-shop job security. When their employers insisted on an open shop as a precondition for holding arbitration, the unions refused to negotiate.

In May every longshoreman in every West Coast port walked off the job. The seamen's unions, including the Marine Cooks and Stewards, joined them. Strikebreakers were housed on moored ships and in walled compounds and brought to work under armed guard. When strikers attacked one such stockade in San Pedro, two of them were killed. Other battles broke out in San Francisco, Oakland, Portland, and Seattle.

As David F. Selvin writes in *A Terrible Anger: the 1934 Waterfront and General Strikes in San Francisco,* opponents of the Roosevelt administration included not only William Randolph Hearst's mighty newspaper chain but major Republican voices such as the *San Francisco Chronicle,* the *Oakland Tribune* and the foremost anti-union advocate, the *Los Angeles Times.*

Respected journalist Lorena Hickok reported to President Roosevelt's aide and advisor Henry Hopkins. Since 1932, Hickok had been Eleanor

Roosevelt's lover—the recipient of passionate letters in a relationship that continued throughout their lives (as is documented by the thousands of letters they exchanged).

For example, ER to LH on March 9, 1933, soon after moving to the White House and unpacking: "My pictures are nearly all up & I have you in my sitting room where I can look at you most of my waking hours. I can't kiss you (in person) so I kiss your picture good night and good morning." And LH to ER on December 5, 1933: "Most clearly, I remember...the feeling of that soft spot just northeast of the corner of your mouth against my lips."[2]

The activist first lady not only served as FDR's ears and eyes; she was also his moral conscience and social goad. As such, the president wasn't only hearing about the situation on the west coast from Hopkins; his wife was up to date.

Hickok revealed that "newspaper publishers have been getting together in more or less secret sessions and laying plans to rid [California] of Communists, but privately to fight Roosevelt." This attitude was not confined to press barons who opposed the New Deal—a program that they reviled as Socialism in disguise. As Selvin declares, "Waterfront employers shared the anti-FDR outlook. Roosevelt and his Secretary of Labor...were intent on unionizing 'all industry,' the shipowners' lawyer...contended; 'to accomplish this they used their governmental power to favor the unions in every labor controversy....' 'Labor was given all the breaks,'" another said. "And to my way of thinking [the federal government] didn't hesitate to use any methods to build up organized labor."

Teamsters supported the strikers by refusing to handle "hot cargo"— goods unloaded by strikebreakers. Longshoremen countered the divide-and-conquer tactics of bosses by opening their union to black workers. For the first time, black leaders called for black workers not to break a strike but to join it. Allan Berube writes in *My Desire for History*, "For these stewards of color, the idea of solidarity with white workingmen is a huge act of faith. They are staking their futures on the outside chance that if the white unions win this strike, white men will treat them as equals and come to their defense when they are attacked.... But they are taking the risk anyway."

Gay stewards of many races are working in the strike kitchens. "The Marine Cooks and Stewards Union sets up strike kitchens on all the waterfronts. In San Francisco, the 'Maritime Palace' kitchen serves 15,000 meals a day."

Realizing the situation was dangerous, FDR wanted the strike to end. Still, he delayed. Then, on July 5—"Bloody Thursday" —employers tried to reopen the San Francisco port by force. Early in the day, police tear-gassed crowds; mounted officers charged people, strikers fought back. Later that day, another scuffle occurred at the corner of Mission and Stuart Streets. A car came into the intersection. A man got out and fired into the crowd.[3]

"Blood ran red in the streets of San Francisco yesterday," one reporter writes in the *Chronicle*. "One thousand embattled police held at bay five thousand longshoremen and their sympathizers.... The furies of street warfare raged for hour piled on hour. Hundreds were injured or badly gassed. Two were dead, one was dying, 32 others shot and more than three score sent to hospitals."[4]

The police called what ensued a "general riot," claiming that two inspectors had been surrounded by a mob shouting, "Kill them." They further asserted that officers had been pelted with bricks and rocks. "Feeling that their lives were in danger, the officers fired shots from a shotgun and several shots from their revolvers at...men who were trying to overturn [their] car." Witnesses testified that they saw no bricks thrown until after the shots were fired. One added that, in response to threats to overturn the car, the officer shouted, "If any of you sons-of-bitches want to start something, come on."

The California National Guard moved in to restore order. Wearing steel helmets, carrying rifles with bayonets, and standing with machine guns in place, they were deployed on the city's docks. Federal troops at the Presidio Army Base were placed on alert. Strikers marked chalk outlines where the dead men had lain, lay flowers, and printed the words "ILA men killed—shot in the back," and "Police murder." Police scattered the crowd and kicked the bouquets into the gutter.

If the violence had stunned the city, "the funeral left people astounded. Rewrite men in the newspapers' city rooms struggled to match words to the spectacle. Observers and participants alike strove to understand the emotions generated."[5]

On July 8, thousands of strikers, their families, and their supporters participated in a funeral march; it went down Market Street. The event stretched for one and a half miles.

The route of that procession starting at the Bay and heading to City Hall is exactly the same route that Pride Parades would take decades later. And it is the same distance that marchers from the Castro District to City Hall would travel in future demonstrations as they moved along Market Street, heading west to east.

Harry Hay was one whose life was transformed by witnessing the shooting and the funeral. As a resident of Los Angeles, he was well aware of the climate of fear and the brutal intimidation that gay people had to endure. The terrors included being entrapped, beaten, blackmailed, mugged, exposed in the press, and publicly humiliated. In addition, there were other real threats, such as losing one's job and one's family. Rather than endure the shame, many chose suicide.

"I was committed from then on, man," Hay later said. "The commitment was not an intellectual thing to start with. It was a gut thing. You couldn't have been part of that and not have your life completely changed."[6] Increasingly, political activism began to define Hay's life. Later he joined a Marxist study group through which he started to understand the theory of class struggle.[7]

"A stupendous and reverent procession," the *Chronicle* reported. "While the entire city gasped...these two men...were given the most amazing funeral San Francisco has ever seen.... Here they came as far as you could see in a silent orderly march, a mass demonstration of protest...a mighty show of strength that amazed the citizens who packed the sidewalks and pressed out onto the street."

The Labor Council's newspaper said that the public and press "universally" agreed. "The crowds were immediately awed into silence...and amazement was written upon faces as the magnitude of the demonstration of respect dawned upon them."

"It was as if, for the first time, the people of the city had come face to face with the strikers—the 'radicals and communists,' who the newspapers, heads of state and local government, and employers had warned were fomenting a revolution," Selvin continues.[8] "It was as if, for the first time, the people of the city saw them, literally saw them, not as bloody-minded, bomb-throwing revolutionaries but as ordinary, everyday workers, protesting exploitation, seeking redress of their grievances."

The impact was immediate and immense. Dozens of unions voted for a general strike. The mayor of San Francisco declared a state of emergency. Over the next two weeks, food deliveries were sporadic while more unions voted to support the Longshoremen. An American Civil Liberties Union lawyer was kidnapped and beaten. The National Guard blocked Jackson Street with machine guns mounted on trucks. Backed up by police, they also conducted vigilante raids on strikers' organizing centers while a police spokesperson suggested that those raids may have been staged by Communists in order to get publicity. In Hayward (a city south of Oakland), a scaffold with a noose dangling from the beam was erected in front of City Hall. It boasted a sign saying, "Reds, beware."

By October, with the standoff paralleling the post-WWI chaos in Germany, which led to the rising menace of Hitlerism, sanity and conciliation prevailed. Each side could claim victory: employers won a nominal win by insisting on an open shop, but workers won lighter loads, work ceilings of 120 hours a month, fines imposed on any boss for "slandering colored brothers," and the firing of strikebreakers. Soon, they also won a pay increase just shy of $1.00 an hour, which they had demanded.

Ultimately, the balance of power swung towards the longshoremen. Even so, pitting employers and big business against unions, which Hearst papers accused of trying to "Sovietize" the port, exposed ugly divisions. Altogether, six people had been killed in the 82-day period from May 6, 1934 to July 17, 1934. Beyond raw figures, however, the strike marked an important pivot for unions, and with telling consequences, Harry Hay was radicalized. His direct experience, fused with his trenchant Marxism, drove him to establish the Mattachine Society in 1950 and, years later, to declare a quasi-spiritual gay crusader identity. Hay's period of direct activism was brief. Nevertheless, he became widely known as the father of the gay liberation movement by setting out a political framework for it, and giving it coherent utterance.

The result of the strike was that "with astonishing vigor, workers grasped the hope and, increasingly, the reality of a new day. They left behind the dilapidated, impoverished state to which the 1920s and the...Depression had brought them and acted from a new awareness of common grievances and common purpose, a newly organized class identity. They reached toward a revised...pattern of industrial relations that stretched across the land...until it was frustrated and nearly dismantled under...Ronald Reagan. Over that half-century, millions...won new economic status. They powered the astonishing waves of labor organization and collective bargaining...that brought down the high citadels of anti-unionism. In countless ways, workers responded vigorously to the hope, the encouragement, and the dream of dignity and self-worth...to win a just place in American society."[9] Labor organizers saw possibilities for radical transformation and solidarity with the working class, while gay people started to see out of their closets.

ENDNOTES

1   William Camp, *San Francisco: Port of Gold* (New York: Doubleday, 1947), 279, quoted in Carolyn L. Cartier, Alan A. Lew, *Seductions of Place* (New York: Routledge, 2005), 140.

2   Roger Streitmatter, *Empty Without You: The Intimate Letters of Eleanor Roosevelt and Lorena Hickok* (New York: The Free Press, 1998).

3   David F. Selvin, *A Terrible Anger* (Detroit: Wayne State University Press, 1996), 14.

4   Allan Bérubé, *My Desire for History: Essays in Gay, Community, & Labor History* (Chapel Hill: University of North Carolina Press, 2011), 305-306.

5   Selvin, 15.

6   Daniel Hurewitz, *Bohemian Los Angeles: and the Making of Modern Politics* (Oakland: University of California Press, 2007), 241.

7   Bérubé, 306.

8   Selvin, 16-17.

9   Ibid., 18.

Chapter 4

The Cradle Will Rock

by Eric A. Gordon

The Cradle Will Rock by Mark Blitzstein—a classically trained musician who did for the United States what Kurt Weill did for German music—was a zesty, exuberant, sophisticated, optimistic, and funny appeal to the working class, as well as a warning to the middle class not to get stranded on the wrong side of history.[1]

The show concerned union organizers fighting the corruption of a Big Boss—"Mr. Mister"—and how working class solidarity wins the day. *Cradle*'s characters weren't stereotypes; they were eccentric and engaging cartoon figures drawn from the world of agitational propaganda, with real-world counterparts most people in the audience would recognize. Skewering the rich who preached liberalism while always ready to "Send for the Militia" (the title of one of Blitzstein's contemporaneous nightclub sketches), he made hypocrites cringe.

In the scene, with its two gay characters, the composer seemed to be saying to other gays, "Don't let a sense of inferiority about homosexuality cloud your social and political consciousness."

Cradle delighted in a variety of dance tempos, croon numbers, and an urban folk style. Its satire and parody echoed Gilbert and Sullivan and revealed the influence of Brecht and Weill. Still, it was a thoroughly American work—not just in the music, but also in speech patterns representing the panorama of social classes. A high point of left-wing culture in the "Angry Thirties," it broke all the rules of a standard Broadway musical, featuring a new kind of "untrained" singing by actors. It situated the battle against America's reactionary elements squarely within the historical continuum of justice-seeking.

The show's opening night turned into the most electric moment in the nation's theatrical history. Underscoring this was a constellation of shaping forces.

Officially, the Depression began in October 1929. It grew slowly, but by the time Franklin D. Roosevelt was elected President in 1932, the situation was disastrous. Unemployment stood at almost 25 percent. Strife between labor and management frequently caused deadly violence. The Ku Klux Klan was powerful and even staged a huge march in Washington. There was a large, active, and unapologetic fascist movement in the United States. As the Thirties unfolded, Hitler came to power, and the civil war in Spain pitted Republicans (who represented democracy) against fascists, backed by Germany and Mussolini's Italy. Nazi encroachment of Europe loomed. France and England embraced neutrality, desperate to avoid catastrophe, even if it meant appeasing Hitler. People wondered if the United States could survive.

To save capitalism FDR instituted programs, which represented core socialist beliefs from twenty years earlier: a minimum wage, a 40-hour work week, unemployment insurance, and assistance to the needy. The first New Deal programs provided financial reforms and emergency relief for states and cities. By the mid-thirties, the government had become the largest employer in the country. The Works Progress Administration (WPA) and Social Security provided for the poor in hundreds of ways, from highway and dam construction to small-scale assistance.

The Federal Theater Project (FTP), a part of the WPA, provided jobs for thousands, and created a national theater movement. Founded in 1935 and directed by Hallie Flanagan, it was based in New York and employed luminaries like Orson Welles (soon to direct *Citizen Kane*) and Marc Blitzstein. But as it tackled previously taboo topics, such as anti-Semitism, syphilis testing, and housing inequity, it aroused Republican ire.

Flanagan decided to stage *Cradle*. Produced by John Houseman and directed by Welles, the play was slated to open at the Maxine Elliott Theater on June 16, 1937. But in a blatantly political decision, an announcement from Washington came on June 10: WPA funding was being cut by 30 percent. As such, Federal Theater shows were instructed not to premiere until July 1, well after the date set for *Cradle*. The government wanted to avoid any inference of scapegoating, but *Cradle* was the only show so affected. No other openings were scheduled. The abuse of power in New York was mirrored in Chicago, where conflict between police and strikers resulted in the infamous Memorial Day massacre at Republic Steel. Eighty-four were hurt and ten killed. Of the dead, seven were shot in the back.

As *Cradle* approached its premiere, pickets and protests massed on Broadway. Cast and crew all belonged to unions. If they violated the shutdown, they could be expelled from the FTP and never work again. But the rules were explicit: They weren't allowed onstage. Moreover, in an unprecedented display of censorship and interference with its own arts program, the government resorted to force.

Police and armed troops surrounded the Maxine Elliott Theater, preventing actors from removing anything. *Cradle* had no home, no cast permitted to perform, no musicians allowed to play, no props, no sets… nothing but instinctive will. Stymied in Washington by officials declaring helplessness, Welles returned to New York. Welles, Houseman, and Blitzstein went ahead with plans for what was billed officially as their final dress rehearsal on June 15. The producers made sure that everyone who was anyone would be at the Maxine Elliott Theater for what might be their last chance to see *The Cradle Will Rock*.

The next morning, press agents announced that the show was cancelled. Simultaneously, producers called the same newspapers and organizations to say that the show would definitely go on, and to await further notice. Armed guards still stood at the doors of the Maxine Elliott. When one actor tried to leave, they seized his toupee!

Actors Equity apprised Welles that while actors couldn't appear onstage, nothing could prevent them from entering the theater and performing their parts from the interior of the house. That is what Welles proposed, not knowing how many—if any—would be prepared to argue this technicality. In addition, the musicians' union (hostile to perceived Communists) declared that, as an "operatic" work, *Cradle* would require additional musicians if it played a Broadway house, and its producers would have to pay Broadway scale. Clearly, the orchestra would have to go home; the only way the work could go on would be if Blitzstein alone sat at the piano.

If the show could proceed without sets, costumes, lights, an orchestra, and (likely as not) without a cast, the one thing it couldn't do without was a piano. The show's technical assistant borrowed a battered instrument and got it into a passing truck. She handed the driver five dollars and told him to keep driving around the block.

Reporters started gathering late in the afternoon. Joining them were hundreds of ticketholders. To pacify them, a few cast members sang songs from the show while producers assured the press and public that the show would go on. But where?

As one theater after another was found unavailable or unsuitable, despair descended. Finally, close to eight o'clock, a theater broker stood up. For hours, he'd been timidly begging to be heard, but was ignored. It seems that all along he had been offering the Venice Theater on Seventh Avenue between 58th and 59th streets. Why wouldn't it do?

In an instant, the one hundred dollar rental fee lay in his hands. As legend goes, it was raised from the press corps hungrily awaiting the next act of this unbelievable but all too real drama. Yes, the Venice would do just fine!

With 1,742 seats, the Venice held more than twice the audience of the Elliott and word spread quickly among friends. By subway, private car, and taxi, people traveled the twenty blocks north to the Venice. But mostly they went on foot, a whole audience marching uptown on a warm late spring night, gathering more support along the way.

When the technical assistant called, she was directed to West 58th Street. The truck arrived; firemen from a neighboring station hoisted the piano onto the stage. Blitzstein promptly had its front ripped off so it would produce more tone.

The Venice had seen better times. The lighting man discovered a single working spotlight, and the theater's principal activity was an Italian variety show. Stage rear, a huge backdrop depicted the Bay of Naples in gaudy colors, Mount Vesuvius smoking off to one side. Over the edge of the box hung an Italian fascist flag. Someone ripped it down, and the audience cheered.

By ten of nine, every seat was filled. Reporters and cameramen lined the aisles. There was nothing left to do. No one knew what might happen. Maybe Marc Blitzstein, in his shirtsleeves and suspenders, sweating in the light of the single spotlight, would sing all the parts himself?

Welles opened with a speech tracing the history of the production, identifying the characters and describing the missing elements of his staging. Then he introduced Blitzstein, who began with the Moll's street-corner song. He got through the first two or three lines. Then, in producer John Houseman's recollection,

> Hearing the words taken out of his mouth, Marc paused. The spotlight moved off into the house, where a thin girl in a green dress with dyed red hair was standing, glassy-eyed, stiff with fear, only half audible but gathering strength with every note.
> *For two days out of seven*
> *Two dollar bills I'm given....*
> It is almost impossible to convey the throat-catching, sickeningly exciting quality of that moment. An actor wrote: "If [the actress] had not risen on cue in the box, I doubt the rest of us would have had the courage to stand up and carry on. But once that thin, incredibly clear voice came out, we all fell in line."
> *So I'm just searching along the street*
> *For on those five days it's nice to eat.*
> *Jesus, Jesus, who said let's eat?*
> A flash-bulb went off. The audience began to clap.[2]

From then on, those performers who had come to the Venice that night—and it turned out that most had, including the chorus—rose on cue. Duets took place across thirty rows of seats. Blitzstein sang eight roles. From time to time, his piano was joined by the one instrumentalist who showed up, the accordion player, who played along when he thought it would help.

When it was over, pandemonium broke out. New York had never seen such sheer theatrical defiance. Eventually, Welles quieted the audience down, informing them that they'd just shared in the creation of a historic event, which had broken down the creaky barrier between audience and stage. But no one needed a white-suited expert to tell them what they'd just experienced.

The next morning, news of the sensational, daring break appeared on front pages around the country. Unquestionably, *Cradle* was a work of searing audacity. But there's also no question that by refusing it a home, the Federal Theater did the work the greatest favor possible. Overnight, it became an established masterpiece.

Blitzstein remained a committed Leftist. He had joined the Communist Party in 1939, and with it, called for anti-lynching laws. In World War II, posted in London as a U.S. Army cultural worker, he organized a massive concert featuring a chorus of black servicemen (at a time when the Army was segregated) to combat racism. Although he left the Party in 1949, he never lost that edge. Many of his major subsequent works continued to strongly indict the capitalist system.

About as open a homosexual as one could be during his lifetime, Blitzstein committed his talents to the defense of freedom, seeing his efforts as true to the American spirit. As he said, "I am addicted to humanism." One way he acted in a countercultural manner was that he rarely focused his theater works (he wrote most of his own lyrics and books, as well as the music) on romantic love. Broadway already had plenty of those stories. He preferred to investigate social issues, a factor that made him a decidedly noncommercial figure. In one choral piece from the late 1950s—"In Twos," which was written for an interracial couple—he has two young lovers walking the streets of New York because they have no place to go and be alone together. In the years that gave us *West Side Story*, the easiest assumption might be that the couple is interfaith or interracial—but tellingly, no gender is mentioned; they could just as easily be same-gender. A Whitmanesque message to the future, perhaps? Blitzstein had, indeed, set almost a dozen Whitman texts as songs in the 1920s, some of them overtly erotic.

Summoned to testify in 1960 by the House Un-American Activities Committee, Blitzstein did not invoke the Fifth Amendment. First, he read a statement challenging the propriety of the HUAC's mandate to question him at all. Voluntarily, then, he spoke as one with nothing to hide or explain or apologize for. He claimed complete innocence of all legal or moral crime and unsettled his questioners by refusing to inform, surrendering no further details about his or anyone's activities.

"Being a philosopher is incumbent on us all," he told a Brandeis University audience in 1960. "We have no choice. If there's a single good thing that has happened because of the Bomb, it is that no one—repeat, no one—can evade the critical questions. Meaning has become a necessity."

The composer's contributions to America's music and culture moved from an early dissonant, Dadaistic style in the 1920s and early 1930s to the more populist idiom *of The Cradle Will Rock* and his follow-up working-class opera *No For an Answer*, then to sophisticated operatic and Broadway works such as *Regina*, a setting of his good friend Lillian Hellman's play *The Little Foxes*, and an adaptation of Sean O'Casey's play *Juno and the Paycock* as the tragicomic musical *Juno*. He is also well known for the work that brought him the steadiest income he ever earned: his English-language adaptation of Brecht and Weill's *Threepenny Opera*. By the 1950s, this confirmed rebel had become accepted, if not "established," in the canon of his nation's highest cultural peers.

In the years before his death, Blitzstein was working on two short operas adapting Bernard Malamud stories, a rare foray into his Jewish roots. He also did not live to complete what he felt would be his triumphal achievement, a large-scale opera about the infamous arrest and 1927 execution of the Italian-American anarchists Sacco and Vanzetti. On a working holiday on the island of Martinique in 1964, the composer was attacked by three men in a gay-bashing incident. He died at fifty-eight.

Blitzstein's legacy continues. Among his theater works, *Cradle* and *Regina* continue to see regular productions, as evidenced by a recent reception of *Cradle*. In Charles Isherwood's review in the *New York Times*, he asks:

When [will] the exploitation of the average Joe...end[?].... [Blitzstein's] answer: Right this minute!....

That's thunder, that's lightning, and it's going to surround you! *No wonder those stormbirds seem to circle around you.*

Yanking you back from Blitzstein's heady dream is an insert in the program...that rattles off a grim list of statistics about the widening gap between rich and poor and the decline of unionized labor. Did you know that the ratio of the salary of the average American chief executive to the average American worker is now 365 to 1? Mr. Mister seems to be doing pretty well. See any stormbirds circling?[3]

ENDNOTES

1   Much of this chapter relies upon information from Eric A. Gordon, *Mark the Music* (New York: St. Martin's Press, 1989).

2   John Houseman, *Run-through* (New York: Simon and Schuster, 1972), 268-269.

3   Charles Isherwood, "A Tuneful Depression-Era Howl: 'The Cradle Will Rock,' a '30s Revival at City Center," *The New York Times*, July 11, 2013.

Chapter 5

Bayard Rustin:
Offensive Lineman for Freedom

by Patricia Nell Warren

Barack Obama's election as America's first black president is a good time to refresh our memory on LGBT figures in the black civil rights movement. Bayard Rustin is an obvious choice. Rustin, who became a gay activist later in life, was a brilliant, charismatic, passionately courageous man. He was Dr. Martin Luther King's chief strategist and right-hand man.

The word "activist" rolls off our tongues easily today. But in 1920s and 1930s America, taking a stand on human rights issues automatically made you a target for the FBI. You were pegged as a communist or socialist agitator—terms used as deadly weapons against anybody who tried to challenge the status quo, whether it was race relations or unionizing or veteran's rights.

Bayard's close-knit family was rooted in eastern Pennsylvania, in the small town of West Chester. When his mother Florence was 17, she got pregnant out of wedlock. Bayard was born in 1912. Since his father never stepped forward to accept responsibility, Florence's parents, Julia and Janifer Rustin, adopted the boy as their own.

Slender, intense Julia was well educated—one of the first blacks in the county to finish high school. She worked for a prominent Quaker family and made herself visible in community service. When the NAACP was founded in 1910, Julia was a charter member. Though she belonged to the local African Methodist church, in part, Julia descended from indigenous native people of Delaware. Her family were Quakers, free people of color who had lived in Pennsylvania for generations.

From his grandmother, Bye—as he was called at home—soaked up that powerful example of community activism, as well as a keen consciousness of America's dissenter heritage. In the mid-1600s, the pacifist Friends (as Quakers called themselves) had begun streaming to the North American colonies to escape persecution in Anglican-ruled England. After the American Revolution, Quaker leaders influenced our founders' decision to adopt the First Amendment principle of freedom of conscience. Outraged by slavery, the Friends helped organize the Underground Railroad that enabled thousands of escaped slaves to get out of the South and establish themselves in freedom. That old escape route had run right through Bayard's hometown.

Ironically—in spite of all this history—segregation had seeped into Pennsylvania from the South. So West Chester was a city where many businesses and institutions enforced Jim Crow. As the only high school in the county, West Chester Senior High was uneasily integrated, with a small number of blacks among its 600 students.

Rustin was one of those rare students who did well at everything. He was a good-looking six-footer, popular with both black and white students—a straight-A student, a mainstay of the debating team, an award-winning essayist, and an outstanding singer (tenor). He even wrote poetry. In short, according to biographer John D'Emilio, he was "West Chester's version of a Renaissance man."

Most important, Pinhead—as he was nicknamed by friends—was the best athlete in the school. At first it was just tennis, track, and basketball where he beat everybody. But tennis was viewed as a pansy sport. Bayard was already aware of his attraction to other males and worried about his masculinity, so he went out for football to prove his own manliness to himself.

With his speed and smarts, a movie script might have made him star quarterback of the West Chester Warriors. Instead, Bayard chose to play offensive lineman, left tackle. In basic football strategy, all five linemen have the job of protecting the quarterback. But the two tackles have an extra-tough job, because they have to anchor the two ends of that offensive line, blocking multiple hits from opposing players and preventing them from making a blitz.

Bayard's will to use his strength and psychic force for his team's benefit made him the Warriors' Most Valuable Player. Later, a teammate remembered what it was like to run up against Pinhead in a scrimmage. He said, "I found it impossible to get by him. Sometimes, after knocking me down on my face, he would gently help me to my feet and quote a line from a poem."

Another teammate added, "He was the toughest hitter on the front line. I wouldn't have expected that of a young man whose grandmother was raising him to be nonviolent. Yet I could never hit as hard as he did."

Yet another teammate reminisced ruefully, "I never blocked him once…. His bones and his muscles were like steel…. He was tough."

By his junior year, that toughness had made Bayard an all-county linesman and won him letters in both football and track. During his senior year, 1932-33, he helped carry the track team to the state mile championship at the Penn Relays. That same year, the West Chester Warriors had a ten-game winning streak, with the local paper enthusing, "Bayard Rustin played his usual fine game at left tackle[; he is] working splendidly."

On that extraordinary team, some strong black-white friendships were born. But off campus, the boys ran into Jim Crow. All the team members were welcome at Julia's house; however, one of Bayard's best friends was a white boy whose parents wouldn't let their son invite Bayard to their home. The black team members weren't allowed in the YMCA or certain restaurants. They had to sit in the segregated balcony at the movie theater. For games out of town, black players couldn't stay at the same hotel as their white teammates. Some schools even refused to let their all-white teams play West Chester.

One weekend, just before the Warriors were to play in a neighboring town, Bayard organized his black teammates into a protest squad. They told the coach that if they couldn't have the same accommodations as their white teammates, they weren't going to play. The coach buckled—though he later retaliated by holding back some track awards that the boys had earned.

After that, Rustin led his special team of protestors all over West Chester—into stores, restaurants, the YMCA. The boys were usually thrown out, but they kept trying. One of his followers remembered later, "Bayard's determination was frightening. But we looked up to him as our leader. He was persuasive. He could sell you anything."

Eventually Bayard was arrested for the first time, for trying to sit in the white section of the movie theater.

In 1932, when Bayard graduated as class valedictorian, nobody would have predicted that he'd become a valued player in global civil rights activism. They figured he'd be a singer or a pro athlete...even a poet. But no local organizations made scholarships available for a talented black kid. So his grandmother Julia wangled him an out-of-town scholarship that sent him to Wilberforce in Ohio—one of the oldest black colleges in the United States.

By then, Bayard had already had his first sexual experiences with other boys, and he knew that he was gay. "I never felt any guilt," he said later. Indeed, he took the offensive in cruising for one-time experiences. But this was something that had to be kept hidden.

In college, Rustin started hearing about a young Indian lawyer. Mohandas Gandhi was emerging as a freedom leader, first against apartheid in South Africa, then against British colonial rule in his native India. Freedom-bent American blacks were thrilled to read about the exploits of this brown-skinned man who was fighting for people of color halfway around the world. By the end of World War II, Gandhi's organizing had united millions of peaceful but determined Hindus and Muslims, convincing the British to grant India her independence without a fight.

For Rustin, the challenge was clear—to graft Gandhi's concepts of pacifist nonviolent activism onto the Quaker pacifism that he'd learned from Julia.

In 1937, Rustin discovered New York City and fell in love with it. Initially, he lived with his aunt in Harlem, which had exploded into a center of music and arts creativity. His activist career started with work in the pacifist and labor movements.

From college onwards, Rustin's long career veered away from sports. Yet he always carried himself like an athlete—lean, graceful (yet powerful), and always elegantly dressed. His six-foot frame was impressive at the speaker's podium.

Rustin approached everything with a keen sense of strategy. Arrested numerous times for cruising and freedom protests, he survived a number of brutal beatings by police. That same toughness also carried him through incarceration. In 1944, federal authorities sentenced him to three years for refusing to serve in uniform. In 1947, after being arrested during a Freedom Ride, Rustin did 30 days in a Southern chain gang. The experience was so horrific that the exposé he wrote for a magazine stirred up a public outcry.

In the late 1940s, Rustin's prison experience prompted him to start speaking out about the cruelty and injustice facing American homosexuals. Making no secret of his sexual orientation, he was having his first real relationship with a young white man, handsome blond Davis Platt, a movement coworker. In 1947, they settled down in an apartment on 124th Street in New York City. Their place became a center for artists, writers, and activists.

"Bayard was fun to be with," said Platt later. But the relationship foundered on Rustin's penchant for cruising, and the two men broke up after a year.

By the 1960s, Rustin was working with emerging black leader Reverend Martin Luther King. Rustin had been pondering Gandhi's strategies with their foundation in Hindu spirituality. How could those principles be applied in the United States in a way that could draw support from liberal Christian spirituality, given the fact that ultraconservative white Christians usually supported Jim Crow? It was during the 1955 Montgomery bus boycott that Rustin first counseled Dr. King on nonviolent activism. By 1963, he was helping King to organize that historic March on Washington that kicked the black civil rights movement into higher gear.

Though Rustin was a compelling speaker and could have been a leader in his own right, he stayed behind the scenes. His sexual orientation had gotten negative public attention after a 1953 California arrest for "indecency." Puritanical church people started pressuring King to get rid of the "commie queer." He was booted out of the pacifist organization, the Fellowship for Reconciliation, for which he'd worked so hard.

"After that," comments historian E.P. Lovejoy, "Rustin refrained voluntarily from speaking out about [the] oppression of homosexuals because he wanted to protect the racial civil rights movement in which he had invested so much. He knew that his homosexuality, which was never secret when he was not outspoken, could be used against the movement. It was, especially by (the purportedly closeted gay) FBI Director J. Edgar Hoover and by the segregationist U.S. Senator Strom Thurmond.

"Rustin also faced enemies within the movement, chief among them Adam Clayton Powell, the U.S. Representative from Harlem. Powell sought to gain for himself a more influential position by denigrating Rustin. He threatened to leak fabricated allegations of a sexual affair between Rustin and King. Powell demanded that King distance himself from Rustin. King gave in and was rebuked by James Baldwin and others who rallied to Rustin's defense. King and Rustin worked together after that, and Rustin accompanied King to Oslo in 1964 when King received the Nobel Prize for Peace, but their friendship never fully recovered."

Intriguingly, the position that Rustin accepted in the black civil rights movement was a rerun of his positioning in high school football. Dr. King was the quarterback who carried the ball, and Rustin was his loyal left tackle.

But Rustin was not the only homosexual in King's organization. A lesbian friend of mine, Cherokee medicine woman Earth Thunder, recalls being one of the young workers in the late 1960s. As a Native American, she felt that King's "I Have a Dream" speech was meant for all people of color. She told me, "I can recollect some joyful times with Bayard in a private gathering in Harlem, probably 1968. We were resting between pushes to get ready for the August Democratic explosion. Rustin was with some other friends and they were singing. Some were in drag. But for most of the movement, (few) gay friends pushed the envelope." Put simply, they were all keeping a low profile like Rustin did.

After Dr. King was assassinated in 1968, Rustin hurled himself into work in other countries where people of color were fighting for their freedom. With his counsel, he supported native leaders in Africa, Vietnam, Laos, Cambodia, Haiti, El Salvador, and Grenada. He also worked for the freedom of Soviet Jews.

In 1977, Rustin settled into his happiest and most enduring relationship, with a younger man named Walter Naegle. He was still lean and handsome, but with hair going powerfully white. The two settled in New York's Chelsea district.

By then, anti-gay feeling in the United States had softened just enough that Rustin felt able to work openly for the LGBT cause without hurting other causes. During an effort for gay-friendly legislation in New York City, he testified at hearings and made a statement that sounds prophetic today. He said, "There are very few liberal Christians today who would dare say anything other than blacks are our brothers and that they should be treated so, but they will make all kinds of hideous distinctions when it comes to our gay brothers.... That is what makes the homosexual central to the whole political apparatus as to how far we can go in human rights."

Sadly, many in the gay community dismissed Rustin's efforts, considering him a Johnny-come-lately. One commentator described him as "gay, activist[,] but, sadly, not a gay activist."

In 1987, shortly after another trip abroad, Rustin took ill and died. He had just turned 75. Walter Naegle continues to tend the flame of his partner's achievements as executor and archivist for the Bayard Rustin estate.

For some years, Rustin was undeservedly forgotten by many in the LGBT movement. Yet today our younger activists are rediscovering him. In the late 1990s, when I was working with LGBT students in the Los Angeles Unified School District, I found that LGBT students of color were hungry to know that they had some towering historical role models like Rustin. To a black kid who was one of the school district's student commissioners at the time, I gave a copy of a biography about Rustin. He devoured the book, and told me that he cried all the way through it.

"It's just awesome," the student said, "that an openly gay black man was Martin Luther King's head guy."

Biographer John D'Emilio sums up Rustin's life in a few deft words. He says, "Rustin displayed courage under circumstances that are terrifying to contemplate. His life reminds us that the most important stories from the past are often those that have been forgotten and that from obscure origins can emerge individuals with the power to change the world."

In 2013, Bayard Rustin posthumously received a Presidential Medal of Freedom. Here are Barack Obama's words from the ceremony:

The Presidential Medal of Freedom goes to men and women who have dedicated their own lives to enriching ours. This year's honorees have been blessed with extraordinary talent, but what sets them apart is their gift for sharing that talent with the world. It will be my honor to present them with a token of our nation's gratitude....

Bayard Rustin was an unyielding activist for civil rights, dignity, and equality for all. An advisor to the Reverend Dr. Martin Luther King, Jr., he promoted nonviolent resistance, participated in one of the first Freedom Rides, organized the 1963 March on Washington for Jobs and Freedom, and fought tirelessly for marginalized communities at home and abroad. As an openly gay African-American, Mr. Rustin stood at the intersection of several of the fights for equal rights.

Chapter 6

The Kinsey Reports

by Anahi Russo Garrido

Alfred Kinsey's 1948 report on male sexuality didn't startle America—it blew the country's mind. *Time* magazine called it "the biggest thing since *Gone With the Wind*" as *Sexual Behavior in the Human Male* rocketed to the top of the bestseller list.

The report summarized interviews with 5,300 (mainly white) middle-class young volunteers who shared narratives of their sexual lives and histories. As a scientist, Kinsey brought unprecedented comprehensive academic rigor to sexuality studies.

Kinsey's predecessors, such as Richard von Krafft-Ebing (1846-1902), had focused on behavior deemed deviant and had established sex as a medical subject for doctors. The German researcher Magnus Hirschfeld (1868-1935) concluded that homosexuality was neither an illness nor abnormal, but his studies were terminated ruthlessly by the Nazis in 1933. Henry Havelock Ellis (1859-1939) had addressed homosexual behavior as prevalent—and accepted—in almost all known societies to the West, and suggested that this could be correlated to animal behavior: "less a defect than a special talent."[1]

But Kinsey's statistics were nothing short of stunning. He found out that 37% of American men had practiced same-sex sexuality *to orgasm*. By applying a fluid scale from 0 to 6 for grading answers instead of simplistic *either/or* scorings, he discovered that 10% of males were predominantly "exclusively homosexual" between the ages of 16 to 55; 8% were "exclusively homosexual" for at least three years between the ages of 16 and 55 and 4% were "exclusively homosexual" adults. Additionally, 50% reported erotic response to another man. Kinsey's study also included data on premarital sex, masturbation, sadomasochism, orgasm, oral sex, and fantasies, among other categories. To his great surprise, he found that 92% of men masturbated and that 68% had experienced premarital coitus or engaged in premarital sex by age 18.

In 1948, homosexuality and adultery were criminal, masturbation purportedly caused mental illness, and premarital sex was deemed shameful. But Kinsey showed such "perverted activities" to be prevalent, thereby torpedoing a cozy concept of manhood rigorously reinforced.

The nation reeled.

At that time, censorship laws mandated that in films even married couples had to have twin beds. Onscreen, there were no homosexuals. Interracial marriage was illegal in many states until 1967. Despite this puritanical climate, sexual norms were beginning to be questioned in the 1950s. The Beat Generation wrote about homosexuality and drug use. In 1950, Harry Hay founded the Mattachine Society, one of the first homophile organizations in the United States to protect and improve the rights of homosexuals.

Three years after that, Kinsey published another explosive work: *Sexual Behavior in the Human Female.* His 1953 report from interviews with 5,940 (mainly white) women caused an even greater uproar than had his initial report on men. Evangelist Billy Graham warned, "It is impossible to estimate the damage this book will do to the already deteriorating morals of America." But with the second publication, the proverbial cat was out of the bag.

Kinsey found that 50% of women had had premarital sex, and 55% were turned on by some form of sadomasochism. Erotic biting, even to the point of causing bleeding, was commonplace. Other findings included that 6-14% of women were bisexual, 62% masturbated, 13% had had lesbian sex to orgasm, 2-6% were mainly exclusively lesbian for some period of time during their lives, and 1-3% were exclusively lesbian as adults.

The domestic picture was revelatory. Anal sex was practiced by 11%. Before matrimony, 10% of men engaged in oral sex—afterwards 48.9%

did; similarly, 19.1% of women had performed oral sex before marriage, and 45% did so after nuptials. In the first year of marriage, 28% of men had "adulterous" sex (which did not include encounters with sex workers), while 21% of women did. At some point during their married lives, 50% of males and 26% of women had sex outside wedlock.

In 1955—two years after the report on female sexuality, the first lesbian organization in the United States was formed in 1955: the Daughters of Bilitis. And by 1957, scientists were discussing the imminent prospect of an anti-conception medication.

But what would happen if women could have sex without fear of pregnancy?

The answer came in May of 1960, with the announcement of "the Pill." The Pill freed people from having to yoke sex to an unwanted pregnancy or a shotgun wedding. The ensuing upheaval happened at mach speed. Yet, paradoxically, the Sexual Revolution had been kicked off by an unlikely-seeming radical.

Alfred Kinsey was born in Hoboken, New Jersey, on June 23, 1894, and raised in threadbare surroundings just across the Hudson River from New York City. His ancestors were Quakers, who had come from England with William Penn in 1682 but by the time Kinsey was born, his parents were Methodists and rigid adherents to the doctrine. His father was a carpenter—an inflexible man, who dominated the household through fear. Kinsey's childhood was strict and stern; pleasures were rare and suspicious.

As a child, Kinsey was often ill. Being sickly and weak made him an easy target for bullies, who saw him as "a sissy" and from whom he often had to escape. Poverty was a fact of life. Compounding his isolation, the boy often had to go to stores to beg for credit. The shame of it played a major role in his adult life, for he profoundly disliked his formative years.

But Kinsey found that one area where he could compete was at school. There, he did extremely well. Music provided a second refuge; he became an accomplished pianist. A third avenue of escape came through scouting.

In the early 20th century, scouting had an evangelical, nearly messianic quality, which also infused Methodism. The combination of Kinsey's success as a scout, his love of nature, and early bonding with other scouts helped the shy but handsome blond boy learn social skills. But sex was guilt inducing for him. While he matured early—by ten or eleven—a rampant epidemic of VD justified such terrors. By the 1930s, 500,000 new cases of syphilis were being reported every year and several major train wrecks were attributed to advanced cases. 12% of upper-middle-class women had venereal disease.[2] The word "sex" was barely mentionable.

Defying his father, who wanted him to be an engineer, Kinsey ended their relationship by choosing to study biology. He graduated from Harvard in 1916. But there was something roiling under the surface of the tall man with a charming smile. In his collecting of insects—the focus of his studies—there was something obsessive in his methodology: a need to control. Throughout his career, he chose positions where he could be as independent as possible, proselytize, and shock authority.

Kinsey married in 1921. He and his wife, Clara (who later assisted in his research), got off to an uncomfortable start sexually—a fact that caused them tension and embarrassment. In time, though, they had four children, one of whom died young. Kinsey may have been increasingly inclined towards homosexuality than heterosexuality as years passed. Still, the marriage was successful and happy. Yet, after he began his research, he had sex with students and colleagues. As Clara often joked, "I hardly see him any more at night since he took up sex."

While teaching a course on marriage at Indiana University in 1938, Kinsey was stunned to learn that many students believed masturbation could cause blindness. 19% of high school students knew that women had babies, yet they didn't realize that a man was required for the process. 91% didn't know what the word "virgin" meant; 96% didn't understand the word masturbation.

Kinsey argued that such misconceptions could be harmful and began his sexual research in 1938. To understand a landscape which seems unimaginable today, one must take a long-range view. The outlook at Indiana University, where Kinsey taught in the 1920s and 1930s, was marked by traditional views on sexuality, which linked it to traditional medical discourses that had emerged in the 19th century and had been scarred by the fears of venereal disease.[3]

As noted by Jonathan Gathorne-Hardy in *Sex—The Measure Of All Things*:

> The major cultural movement of the past two hundred and fifty years in Western Europe, and to a lesser extent in America, has been the rise of science and the parallel but opposite decline of

religion. As a result, but especially during the 19th century, sexual matters were increasingly the concern of doctors and the laboratory.

One of the extraordinary things about this century is how difficult it has proved to throw off its religion-dictated inhibitions and prohibitions. Even rightly admired figures like Freud who seemed dedicated to [this]...simply carried sin forward as neurosis from an extremely flawed, indeed non-existent empirical base. The medicalization of sex did much the same. Medicine logically requires disease; so disease had to be found in sex. Anything but common-or-garden, heterosexual, missionary position sexual intercourse to have children was at various times classified as a disease. Oral sex, homosexuality, masturbation, "back position" sex were all pathological.

It was this belief system that Kinsey set out to challenge and change, aided by funding from the Rockefeller Foundation from 1944 onward. But while Kinsey's 1948 report made him into a celebrity (at the height of his fame, thousands crowded his gatherings; nine thousand attended one such meeting), a furious backlash ensued. He often had to deal with professional groups infuriated by his work. And the puritanical venom only intensified with his 1953 report on women.

Anthropologist Margaret Mead said that Kinsey had "upset the balance between ignorance and knowledge upon which social restraint depended." Vehement criticism came from conservatives, like the Tea Party today. But no one disproved the findings—indeed, later studies reveal only slight variance with Kinsey's original research.

Kinsey's frankness only made matters difficult. In defending homosexuality he wrote: "If all [homosexual] persons were eliminated from the population, there is no reason to believe that the incidence...would be materially reduced. The homosexual has been a significant part of human sexual activity ever since the dawn of history, primarily because it is an expression of capacities that are basic in the human animal."[4] Moreover, he confronted one of America's most potent and enduring myths.

There was, he said, a type of homosexuality that was probably common among groups that are physically active: "hard-riding, hard-hitting, assertive males." He added that there is considerable homosexual activity among lumbermen, cattlemen, prospectors, miners, hunters and others engaged in out-of-door occupations. It is the type of experience that the explorer and the pioneer must have had.[5]

One Rockefeller Foundation board member, and one of Kinsey's chief critics, headed the Union Theological Seminary.[6] Kinsey was lambasted for voyeurism, exhibitionism, flawed science, corrupt research, misogyny, masochism, and for being "obsessed...and driven by his own sexual demons.... A 'deranged Nebuchadnezzar' leading women 'out of the fields to mingle with the cattle and become one with the beasts of the jungle,' peddling smut, lewd and obscene literature."[7] But then the controversy became political and influenced by the climate of the times.

After World War II, there was a strong feeling in America (especially among Republicans) of getting back to the *true* America.[8] The conservative tide was enormously enhanced by the Cold War. The Berlin airlift to surmount the Soviet blockade began in 1948. It brought...the same feelings (sometimes paranoid) a war engenders—the country must unite, nonconformity is dangerous, fears of conspiracies and enemies within.

Simultaneously, the huge growing wealth of the post-war period was shared by teenagers, and "youth means sex."[9] Once, in the mid-50s, Kerouac and a friend got drunk and drafted a letter to the President. "Dear Eisenhower. We love you—you're the great white father. We'd like to fuck you."

In 1952, Dean Rusk was appointed president of the Rockefeller Foundation. (Author's Note: As Secretary of State between 1961-1969, he would help lead the U.S. into the war in Vietnam.) In February 1954, Rusk became "extremely worried by rumors of a Congressional committee about to investigate his foundation, especially pertaining to... [the] support of Kinsey." Bowing to pressure, the Rockefellers cut Kinsey's funding.[10] Now the nonpolitical scientist found himself branded a subversive and accused of "furthering the Communist cause by undermining American values." Kinsey tried to carry on, but finding support was virtually impossible—partly due to the climate of the times and partly because soliciting money reawakened memories of his repeated humiliations as a child, when he was forced to go to stores and beg for credit.

Cut off financially, he became desperate; his health faltered in 1955, and in 1956, he died. But by then, states were repealing laws against sodomy, adultery, and fornication, using Kinsey reports as grounds for making such remarkable progress.

Political and economic factors also influenced changes in sexual cultures. As historian John D'Emilio has suggested in "Capitalism and Gay Identity," WWII soldiers massed in ports (like SF and NYC) before being shipped overseas had the possibility to explore same-sex desires. The war brought together an unprecedented number of young men. Later, when peace came, heterosexuality was reinforced. Suburbia developed— while clinging to an ideal of the happy (monogamous) couple equipped with children, a dog, and a car. In 1948, however, Kinsey's data questioned these developing ideals and proved that the myth of the virgin bride was just that: a myth.

Until then, no one had admitted it out loud. Still, Rita Hayworth stunned with her overt sensuality in *Gilda*. Seeing a "love goddess" taunting and goading provocatively shocked 1945's moviegoers. They'd never seen such raw, frontal shamelessness. They wanted more. Film noir provided it in spades, often in disturbing stories with dark sexuality.

A parallel breakthrough was the wider interest in psychoanalysis. Freud had unveiled the unconscious drives of the libido: in his view, all humans were born bisexual, but through psychological development most became monosexual. At times, Freud's findings transformed religious discourses on sin into clinical views that contributed to the demonization of particular sexual desires or practices.

Freud's methods differed from Kinsey's; he hadn't done empirical sex research. Kinsey situated the reality in a social context with heretofore unimaginable candor. Put simply: "nice girls" had premarital sex and masturbated. Normal guys—the boy next door—might not be gay, but 37% had homosexual sex. "Normal" sex included oral sex.

During the war, "Rosie the Riveter" handled jobs previously done only by men; now, women wanted emancipation and GIs were rolling home, eager to start families. Collectively, Americans were still uneasy saying "penis" and "vagina" aloud; others had no idea where—or what—a clitoris was. Although they wanted sex, a lot of that wasn't in the missionary position, or sanctified by marriage, or necessarily straight. In fact, the norm might not be the orthodox. This was too much in 1948. And so, America succumbed to reactive suspicions. Having fought war abroad, it now started hunting subversives at home.

Many purported enemies were bugaboos conjured by paranoid or sadistic megalomaniacs. During the years of blacklists and Congressional hearings on "Un-American Activities," the alcoholic Senator Joe McCarthy might not have been gay, but he was abetted by snarky homosexual Roy Cohn in trying to install a regime built on smear campaigns, tarring reputations, and tactics calculated to instill terror. As such, the American extreme right wing got its start and led the country through an uneasy rite of passage from the "joy" of victory to a new domestic fracture. An important part of the population entered a phenomenal period of prosperity, but a renewed "witch hunt" followed, targeting communists, homosexuals, and other souls labeled as "enemies" of the regime.

By turning a searchlight on America, Kinsey found startling sexual variety. But if variation was the norm, there might not be a clear right versus clear wrong; there might, in fact, be more than one way. But if this was so, *what did it mean?*

The debate would shake all prior conceptions. What a man was (or wasn't), what a woman was (or wasn't), whatever normal was (or wasn't)— all such things were suddenly grounds for inquiry. Given norms couldn't be sustained. There had to be a new way to rethink sexual discourses and practices since "their rightful place" had proved erroneous.

Kinsey was central to this pivot. In revealing the sexual lives of white (mainly middle-class) America, he initiated its demystification. What it meant was that when Johnny survived the atrocities of war and made it back home, he returned to a nation ripe for revolution in the most unlikely of all places: between its own sheets.

ENDNOTES

1   Jonathan Gathorne-Hardy, *Kinsey: Sex the Measure of All Things* (Bloomington: Indiana University Press, 2004), 55.

2   Ibid., 123.

3   Ibid., 91.

4   Ibid., 359.

5   Alfred Kinsey, et al, *Sexual Behavior in the Human Male* (Philadelphia: W.B. Saunders, 1948), 259-261.

6   Gathorne-Hardy, 395.

7   Ibid., 396.

8   Ibid., 398-399.

9   Ibid., 399.

10 Ibid., 409.

Chapter 7

Criminals and Subversives: The Mattachine Society and Daughters of Bilitis

by Victoria A. Brownworth

They were called criminals and subversives, but in 1950 they may have been the bravest people in the country: the handful of gay and lesbian civil rights activists who would change our cultural landscape years before the Stonewall Rebellion.

LGBTQ history is demarcated by Stonewall. But the activism that came before took not just courage but a keen and prescient insight. Homosexuality was viewed as both a sickness and a criminal scourge. In 1950, a Senate subcommittee issued a report, calling homosexuals a threat to national security. The rumblings of the black civil rights movement had not yet been heard in mainstream society; there was no model for gay and lesbian civil rights activists to follow or to declare themselves publicly, let alone suggest that they deserved equal treatment with their heterosexual peers. Theirs was, as Oscar Wilde had famously declaimed it on his way to prison, *the love that dare not speak its name.*

As activist Harry Hay would later be quoted in the *New York Times,* "We lived in terror almost every day." Yet in the years immediately preceding and succeeding World War II, small pockets of activism began to emerge, notably in Los Angeles and San Francisco, then jumping to New York City and Philadelphia. A coterie of gay men and lesbians, tired of the repressive circumstances under which they were forced to live, began to address their rising concerns about rampant inequality and the ever-expanding injustices against them. Two groups were formed that would change lesbian and gay history in America—the Mattachine Society, started by a small group of gay men and led by Communist organizer Harry Hay in Los Angeles in 1950, and Daughters of Bilitis, founded in San Francisco in 1955 by a young lesbian couple: Del Martin and Phyllis Lyon.

The beginning of the movement was no coincidence. Women had been given their first real entrée into independence from men throughout the war years, making it easier for closeted lesbians to leave home (where unmarried "girls" were still expected to live until they married) and share an apartment with a female "roommate." Men, returned from combat, were also granted leeway to "sow their wild oats" and "play the field," giving closeted gay men an easy excuse for not marrying. Yet society as a whole was repressive and restrictive.

Those heteronormative confines were interwoven with the sense of imminent peril being proffered by politicians about Communism, Leftism, and the American homosexual. Yet in 1950, even the Communist Party had issued a warning about the threat of homosexuality.

With its handmaidens in Congress, the U.S. State Department was intent on routing the Communists in America's midst. Homosexuality, that most "perverse" of secrets, had become inextricably linked to this fear. The same government that had rounded up Japanese Americans and interned them during World War II was now forcing registration by so-called "subversive" groups. Even the appearance of homosexuality—butch women, effeminate men—became grounds for firing and arrest.

In 1950, it was still a crime to be a gay man or lesbian with myriad sodomy and lewdness laws on the books. The criminalization of gay men and lesbians was expanding. Arrests were common. No-touching rules for same-sex couples in bars and clubs were enforced regularly by impromptu police raids. Those same raids also ensured the "three articles of clothing" rule was being upheld. It was against the law to cross-dress. Women had to be wearing at least three articles of women's clothing or face arrest. The obverse was true for men, although arrests of butch lesbians were more common than arrests of cross-dressing men. Strip-searches right in the bars or on the street outside were as commonplace as they were degrading. Concomitant with the harassment and arrests were beatings, and additionally, for lesbians, forced sodomy and rape while in lock-up. Sleazy lawyers would charge exorbitant fees to get their clients out of jail. Some would later blackmail those same clients, threatening them with exposure to families and jobs.

The misery, ignominy, and outright violence of police harassment impacted many. Even civil rights leader Bayard Rustin was arrested for "lewd acts and vagrancy" in 1953 after being arrested by police while with two other men in a car. It was an arrest that would elide him from civil rights history for decades until gay historians resurrected his involvement and importance.

In the context of post-war repression, Dale Jennings wasn't anomalous. At thirty-five, he was strong, virile, and handsome—the epitome of a war hero. A decorated veteran of World War II, he'd been stationed at Guadalcanal. The medals—Bronze Star, WWII Victory Medal, Asian-Pacific Campaign Medal, Philippine Liberation Ribbon—lay on his dresser, a reminder of his survival as well as his courage after years of service in a war 419,000 other American soldiers did *not* survive.

Jennings didn't stop fighting when honorably discharged in 1946, however. In 1953, he would be able to contextualize all that had happened to him in a speech he gave to the Mattachine Society. He was succinct as he made the link that was being forged between Communism and homosexuality. He explained that to be accused of one was to be accused of the other—and then to end up on the wrong side of the law. His prescience was astonishing. He said:

In 1953, no longer must the accusers prove their charges. The accused himself—and this will seem incredible in future times—the accused must prove himself innocent. Anyone can with impunity stand up and say, "I think that man is one of *those*." It is not really for any specific act, not on any concrete charge mind you, that one might be accused, but merely on the principle of state-of-being. This is in spite of the fact that state-of-being in normal times does not constitute a valid charge! No one can be legally found guilty of *being* a criminal or a homosexual. She or he must be accused of a *specific act of criminality* or homosexuality, and that act must be proven beyond a reasonable doubt before the accused can be found guilty. But this is not so with the suspected homosexual or his shockingly close kin, the alleged subversive. They are both so vile and low that we deny them the due process of law automatically given rapists and kidnap-murderers.

* * *

Jennings would know. Because it happened to him.

On November 11th, 1950, Jennings accompanied Bob Hull (with whom he was having an affair) and Charles "Chuck" Rowland (with whom Hull lived) to meet with Harry Hay and Hay's lover, designer Rudi Gernreich. Hay was determined to promote his ideas of a homosexual culture and concomitant activism to protect his "people." Jennings had a different perspective—he didn't see homosexuals as a group; he thought they were too disparate as individuals—but he agreed with Hay that gay men needed protection from harassment and criminalization.

That night, when Hay's wife and daughters were out of town (he had been advised by his psychiatrist to marry to cure him of his homosexuality, but it hadn't worked), would be the first official meeting of the Mattachine Society—the first successful gay rights organization in the United States.

While Hay was the official organizer, Jennings would clarify why such an organization was so desperately needed when he was arrested in April 1952 for "lewd and dissolute" behavior. Jennings had allegedly solicited an undercover police officer in a public restroom in Westlake Park (now MacArthur Park) in Los Angeles. Undercover police had been entrapping gay men for years (and continued to do so long after Stonewall). It was a common practice used by police, and the men involved—often married, like Hay, and with jobs to protect, like Jennings—quietly pled guilty.

Although Jennings had declined the offer of sex, the man had followed him home and finagled his way into Jennings's apartment. While Jennings went to get coffee, the officer signaled his partner and within minutes Jennings was handcuffed and sitting in the back of a police car with three officers discussing what would happen next. Jennings feared a beating; that was, after all, the norm—police officers regularly drove gay men outside the city limits and beat them to "help them get straight." While the officers did discuss beating him and how they would do so, what they really most wanted to know, Jennings recounted, was why he was "like *this.*"

Hay saw Jennings's arrest as a nexus for the Mattachine Society to draw attention to the unjust treatment of homosexuals by society in general and police in particular. He had been trying to start a homosexual action group for several years and had already protested police brutality against Chicanos in Los Angeles. Now one of their own, a founding member of Mattachine, was at risk: Jennings refused to plead out and his case was held over for trial.

Jennings was the first man to fight such a charge.

Jennings's arrest put the issues of criminalization of homosexuality as well as the myriad false arrests in a context activists related to easily. Desperate to have the charges dropped so they wouldn't damage his budding career as a screenwriter (Jennings was already a successful playwright and would go on to have a stellar writing career with one of his novels, *Cowboys*, turned into a film with John Wayne and Bruce Dern), Jennings called Hay, who bailed him out of jail. The day after his arrest, Jennings and Hay had breakfast together. By the end of that meal, the hardcore activist and the decorated soldier were committed to fighting the charges against Jennings and clearing his name.

Hay mobilized Mattachine to help Jennings. He established the Citizens' Committee to Outlaw Entrapment, and Long Beach attorney George Sibley, a labor attorney Hay knew from his Communist organizing days, was hired to defend Jennings in the first-ever case of its kind.

It was a surprisingly long trial, given the charges. Ten days of testimony showed the Los Angeles Police Department for the corrupt department they were and that homosexuals had been specifically targeted by the LAPD because the vice busts were easy and homosexuals were roundly despised.

Jennings and Hay got what they wanted. The jury deadlocked 11 to 1 for acquittal, so the judge acquitted Jennings of all charges. The judge and jury took the LAPD to task, stating unequivocally that the LAPD had acted with deliberate malice toward Jennings in particular and gay men and lesbians in general. The judge called entrapments and bar raids nothing short of "persecution."

For Hay, the rebuke by the court codified what he believed: homosexuals *were* a "people," a group unto themselves. Word of Jennings's acquittal spread, and the Mattachine Society membership grew exponentially. The publication of ONE magazine by Mattachine (printed in Jennings's brother-in-law's basement) also helped disseminate information on the breadth of issues that needed to be addressed by gays, notably continuing harassment by government and police.

ONE magazine would bring yet another court battle in 1954, when the United States postmaster in Los Angeles confiscated it as "obscene, lewd, lascivious, and filthy." In 1958, the Supreme Court unanimously reversed lower court rulings upholding the post office, finding in favor of ONE.

Mattachine, Hay, and Jennings ultimately altered history. Hay, with his ideas of commonality and community, and war-hero Jennings, with his outrage over being labeled a criminal and pervert, began to shape the movement that has brought LGBTQ people closer to equality than ever before.

While the Mattachine Society was growing, Del Martin and Phyllis Lyon founded the first lesbian civil rights organization in the United States in 1955. The San Francisco-based Daughters of Bilitis (DOB, named for a book of lesbian poetry written by a lover of Sappho, *Songs of Bilitis)* was formed as an alternative to bar culture. Martin and Lyon, a couple for several years when they conceived the idea, felt lesbians needed their own group separate from men, since so many lesbians wanted to be in spaces that were women-only. They asserted, "Women needed privacy, not only from the watchful eye of the police, but from gaping tourists in the bars and from inquisitive parents and families."

Though some lesbians were able to fly under society's radar—since women were still perceived as sexual only in the context of men—lesbians were still confronted with the same fears of exposure as gay men. Like many gay men, lesbians were often married with children, making fears of losing those children a significant concern. Patricia Highsmith highlighted this plight in her classic 1951 lesbian-pulp novel *The Price of Salt,* which she (a closeted lesbian herself) wrote under the pen name Claire Morgan.

In *Odd Girls and Twilight Lovers: A History of Lesbian Life in Twentieth Century America,* lesbian historian Lillian Faderman says of the founding of DOB, "Its very establishment in the midst of witch-hunts and police harassment was an act of courage, since members had to fear that they were under attack, not because of what they did, but merely because of who they were."

Like Mattachine, DOB was born out of conversations at parties among a group of lesbian couples. Del Martin and Lyon wanted to meet other lesbians without threat of arrest or exposure. They wanted a group where all women would feel welcome. In the early days of DOB, women were met at the door and told that they could give their first name—or a pseudonym—and that they had nothing to fear.

What began as a small, secret social club—the epitome of a sorority—with somewhat more modest political aspirations than Mattachine, broadened quickly into a group with chapters in Los Angeles, Chicago, and New York City. DOB also published *The Ladder,* the first lesbian magazine by and for lesbians, which continued publication until 1972. *The Ladder* published letters and articles, poems and fiction, some written by lesbians now famous in American history, from Naiad Press co-founder Barbara

Grier to novelist Valerie Taylor to award-winning playwright Lorraine Hansberry.

DOB began as a "living room"-style group. The meetings were open to all women—not just lesbians—which meant that, unlike at the bars, women could question their sexual orientation, as Lorraine Hansberry (then married to a man) would do on the pages of *The Ladder*. There were dances and discussion groups, conferences, advocacy, and research. DOB was both social and political, providing resources for women about being gay and how to access help for divorce, custody, and medical and social work concerns. It was a desperately needed venue for women trapped by the confines imposed on women in general and lesbians in particular. As Martin would later say, in being openly lesbian and forming DOB, she and Lyon were "fighting the church, the couch, and the courts." A full decade before the birth of second-wave feminism, it was revolutionary.

DOB's manifesto was short and succinct: the group's purpose was to provide as much information as possible from a library with fiction and nonfiction on "sex-variant themes" to "public discussions" on life as a lesbian in 1950s America. But DOB was also clear that things had to change for lesbians to truly be comfortable with themselves, as the mission statement abjured them to be. It also noted the group would focus on: "Investigation of the penal code as it pertains to the homosexual, proposal of changes to provide an equitable handling of cases involving this minority group, and promotion of these changes through due process of law in the state legislatures."

It would be twenty years before the American Psychiatric Association would take homosexuality out of their list of mental illnesses. It would be forty years before the decriminalization of sodomy laws, which were used most commonly against lesbians in custody battles. The founding of DOB was, for the women who did it and the women who became involved with it, an unprecedented revolutionary act.

Lesbian history has gotten short shrift in the larger context of the LGBTQ movement, but DOB was the first organization in the world solely for lesbians, and it survived for seventeen years as a flourishing lesbian civil rights group. Unlike Mattachine, Martin and Lyon were able to propel DOB up to and even past Stonewall. They saw the need to expand the straitened lesbianism they had been born into—with fear and hiding at its roots—to a consciousness that included and embraced feminism as much as the gay liberation movement and allowed women the freedom to be openly and joyfully lesbian.

But in the 1950s, to be a woman out of the kitchen was iconoclastic. DOB was watched from all sides, infiltrated early by the FBI. In 1959, DOB was made a focal point of the mayoral election when Mayor George Christopher—a Republican who had hosted HUAC hearings in the City Hall supervisor's office (and who would later lose the primary campaign for governor in 1966 to Ronald Reagan)—was challenged by Russell Wolden. Not to be outdone by Christopher's embrace of anti-Communist fervor, Wolden asserted that Christopher had made San Francisco a "haven for homosexuals."

In his campaign literature Wolden named DOB, warning, "You parents of daughters—do not sit back complacently feeling that because you have no boys in your family everything is all right.... To enlighten you as to the existence of a Lesbian organization composed of homosexual women, make yourself acquainted with the name Daughters of Bilitis."

Some could argue there was reason for concern. While the local chapters of DOB were relatively small—never more than 100 members—*The Ladder* was spreading across the country. The first issue was only 174 copies mailed to single women in the San Francisco phone book. But within a year, the mailing list had nearly tripled, and lesbians in non-urban areas with no access to lesbian culture were subscribing. DOB had provided a lifeline.

In addition, DOB had focused attention on research by and about lesbians. Rallying empathetic medical and psychiatric professionals brought more attention to the organization, while it also further broadened the scope. Soon chapters were opening outside the United States as well. DOB had tapped into an essential need of lesbians everywhere—to meet each other a in safe space and also to learn as much as they could about themselves (since the lives of women in the 1950s were still hidden from history).

The revolutionary and revelatory nature of DOB continued during one of the most repressive periods in American history. So how could lesbians come out if they believed lesbianism was a sickness and a sin? How could they meet other women if they were fearful? Martin and Lyon wanted to dispel the myths about lesbianism, as well as spread the political gospel of its viability as a way of being.

In *Contacts Desired: Gay and Lesbian Communications and Community, 1940s to 1970s,* historian Martin Meeker explains:

One of the first jobs Martin, Lyon, and others performed with that [donated] typewriter and filing cabinet was to begin producing their own newsletter and magazine. While four years separated the birth of the Mattachine idea from the publication of the first issue of the Mattachine Review, only one short year elapsed between the founding of the DOB and the appearance of the first issue of its periodical, The Ladder. And unlike the Mattachine Society, the DOB was not bound by cumbersome organizational rules regulating content and production. Indeed, the DOB was fortunate. Not only did the leaders have prior experience in publishing, but the Mattachine also offered the DOB use of its mimeograph machine. All the DOB needed was content and the time required to assemble and to print the magazine. However, other obstacles remained, not least of which was financing the publication as well as distributing it to a large enough audience so that it would eventually become self-sufficient. In summer 1956 the twenty or so active participants decided to forge ahead with a magazine designed to end the perceived isolation among lesbians. Not only would the magazine facilitate wider access to the organization, it would accomplish this by providing representations of lesbianism that ran counter to what few images circulated in the mainstream public sphere in the early 1950s, images that cast lesbians as antisocial and that thus naturalized the isolation they may have felt.

DOB's attention remained on extricating lesbians from those feelings of isolation and from believing the stories being told about them—most notably, that women without men were somehow not real women, that they were, as Freud has dismissed them, infantile creatures devoid of real sexuality. Helping women to see themselves as full human beings irrespective of men was a singular job and responsibility, which no other organization in the country—gay or straight—was doing.

Recent histories have taken a revisionist view of DOB and the Mattachine Society, arguing that they were assimilationist and apologetic at their core. And through the lens of Stonewall, perhaps they do look that way. But more than sixty years have passed since that first meeting with Hay and his buddies. Martin and Lyon remained together until Martin's death in 2008. They were the first same-sex couple to be legally married in San Francisco, just before Martin died, nearly sixty years after they met.

The smugness of revisionist history is easy to embrace, but in the era before Stonewall, when criminalization was the focal point of lesbian and gay life, that these groups existed at all seems the more stunning fact.

As Martin and Lyon would say later in interviews, "If you could only understand the fear! You just can't begin to realize the fear that was involved and how scared we were. And we [the DOB leadership] were just as scared as everybody else."

That speech Dale Jennings gave in November 1953, exactly three years after that first meeting of the Mattachine Society, illumines both Jennings's own radicalization and understanding of the role the Mattachine Society, as well as his own fight for justice played in history.

Jennings said:

Each of us here tonight is a hero, each has a place in history—if only for being here tonight. And how much more than that have we done! We are that little band that the Future will celebrate.... We most surely are leaders, historic fighting leaders!... What we have gotten, we have earned. Even our smallest victories have not been gifts. We've wrenched them from unwilling hands and now hold them only as concessions. We are despised, yet we sit here tonight in courageous defiance of a society given to lynching. The early Christians never had it so bad: their persecution ended. Ours started long before theirs, and still isn't over.... We accept the enemy's own evaluation of us when we fear.... These primitive laws must go and there is no one to erase them but us.

It was the movement that began the movement. Without these iconic men and women, how much longer would the suffering have been? These are the activists who set the stage for us, who fought back and refused to go back to the closet. These are the men and women who changed our world forever: revolutionaries, freedom fighters, risk-takers—who put their lives on the line in service to gay men and lesbians everywhere. We may never see their like again.

Chapter 8

The Beats:
Allen Ginsberg and Jack Kerouac

by Neeli Cherkovski

Before Allen Ginsberg grabbed America by the throat with his poem *Howl*, and before *On the Road* by Jack Kerouac became the talismanic refuge for young people across the country, a restless undercurrent waited to be tapped. The rebels significantly changed the gender tempo of our culture by undermining crude assumptions.

In New York, where they attended Columbia and palled around with other writers who inspired them, the laws directed against homosexuals were dreadful enough to keep almost every gay person in the shadows. "Psychosexual" laws permitted the commitment of gay men and lesbians to long terms in prison and mental institutions. Electroshock therapy was also used as a cure for homoerotic tendencies. In the process, lives were lost, careers ruined, families broken, and shame hailed down on the victims. The national outlook on sex was still occulted and under the mantle of Puritan mores.

An ethos of manly individualism was spurred on by the return of soldiers from the battlefields of World War II. It was a time of opportunity, with corresponding growth in suburban America and a congruent aging of cities. The consumer society emerged, engendering a false image of the American family as the cure-all. Yet an undercurrent of dissent existed.

Homosexuals were knitted into the fabric of the anti-Communist hysteria of the 1950s, fed by the House Un-American Activities Committee. Ginsberg followed their activities and kept files on the file-keepers. Much of the tenor of *Howl* reflects this paranoia. One best-selling book, *Washington Confidential* (1951), portrayed "lavender boys" as lurking in the shadows, intent on corrupting our youth. In Hollywood films, if homosexuality was dealt with at all, gays were portrayed as unbalanced and effeminate. Parents often felt compelled to deal with the shame they experienced upon discovering they had a sexually "abnormal" child by sending him for treatment that went far beyond therapy—one might even call it medieval. A significant number of women, unable to weather post-war constraints on gender, shared a similar fate. A rigid and myopic set of Christian values had been generalized to preserve normalcy in a nation unhinged by a terrible Depression, war, and the delirium of victory. In this climate, gay men were easily viewed as criminal.

The words in *Howl* and the spirit of male camaraderie in *On the Road* brought the voice of the cultural outsider to the fore, mainly out of the colleges and universities, but also in the big cities. Ginsberg steps into history as a social rebel and revolutionary of the word; Kerouac, with a gentler but committed openness, arrives at a new kind of maleness: one that admitted vulnerability, one accepting of so-called sexual deviance. Joined by the older William Burroughs and other bohemians centered largely in New York, these pioneers mocked Puritan values and shifted emphasis toward a new sense of comradeship that transcended what was previously considered acceptable.

Howl landed like a bombshell. Because of its intrinsically American character—fluid, with the voice of the streets—it also took on weight in a rather gentle manner, as did Kerouac's narrative of life on the road. These were rebels, not revolutionaries, who dreamed of a society without oppressive boundaries.

These men embraced their typewriters: one a poet in the tradition of Walt Whitman, the gay and gray-bearded bard of an earlier era, and the other a brooding, handsome working-class kid who wanted to write big novels reflecting his life and the lives of his friends. For them, there was no approved reading list—there was only the open road.

At the same time, two captivating young men stepped out of the silver screen to tap the sexual frustration that held the land in its grasp. Marlon Brando, in *A Streetcar Named Desire* and *The Wild Ones,* gave voice to the hidden pool of desire that smashed open the doors of Christian morality. In *Rebel Without a Cause,* James Dean gave a powerful portrayal of an adolescent in rebellion against middle-class norms and pretension. There was hardly a moviegoer—male or female—who didn't want to press against his enticing body and kiss his sensuous lips. And Marilyn Monroe would radiate enough lustful feelings to awaken the entire nation.

All of this daring from Hollywood worked on the nation's heart. Ginsberg and Kerouac focused the challenge more forcibly with their creative fervor. For Ginsberg, the inspiration came from Whitman, who spoke of "Perfect, personal candor," and Kerouac's banner read: "The unspeakable visions of the individual."

The United States had become a nation of conformists, hiding their passion behind a mantle of respectability. Innovative thinking met with suspicion. Moral guardians worked tirelessly to keep the population in check.

One sure way of doing that was to hold up the image of the homosexual as a predator intent on destroying the American family and its cherished values. In an era when gay men were perceived as child abusers lurking in the dark hallways of public institutions, often hand-in-hand with known communists, the bombshell obscenity trial surrounding *Howl* set in flames what had already been thawing and set a whole new literary generation into motion. Then Kerouac came along with his road trip—the dream of young folks locked into normalcy. His word wizardry led many on a long, open road of the imagination and vaulted from the norm.

Behind this literary fervor lay Allen's and Kerouac's years at Columbia: Allen as a studious, bespectacled kid from New Jersey and Kerouac on a football scholarship—but it didn't take long for them to drop out, leaving academia behind, committing themselves to the streets, creating—by that act—a genuine desire to "find the gold" in the life immediately around them. They loved the sights and sounds of the big cities and the sprawling land with its roadside diners and red pump gas stations. In this setting, they seized the opportunity to work out an inner sense of self not bound by convention. In *On the Road,* Dean Moriarty—a fictionalized Neal Cassady, as good-looking as any Hollywood star and as disdainful of conventional life—races across the bumpy roads and smooth paved highways of America to carve out a broad-shouldered myth as large as the hopes and dreams of the people who would read it.

"Gutsy" is a good word to describe the contribution the Beats added to the seething, raw, postwar America. Once home, GIs found themselves quickly locked into conformity. Rebellious minds had no chance to move. Many of these men feared their own longing for male love. Yet the nation remained largely stunned and languishing. Ginsberg would write of "the heterosexual dollar" in *Howl*, denoting the power of jobs and of family in binding the citizenry. Traditional morality would not be shaken. From church pulpits everywhere, people were warned to marry, procreate, hold a good job, and—above all else —protect the children.

But Ginsberg began his poem with a startling line:

I saw the best minds of my generation destroyed by
madness, starving hysterical naked,
dragging themselves through the negro streets at dawn

It seemed so wretched to many readers. Here were images of a society turned upside-down (in stark contrast to the prevailing propaganda), shorn of pretense, as if the poet had walked up to a church filled with parishioners and told them their houses were burning. But other lines triggered the Howl Obscenity Trial:

who let themselves be fucked in the ass by saintly
motorcyclists, and screamed with joy,
who blew and were blown by those human seraphim

This was too much. Officers from the Juvenile Division of the San Francisco Police Department, warned of Ginsberg's "dirty book," entered the store, bought a book, and the rest is history. In 1957 the trial rocked the nation, reported in *Life* magazine and on television. It made world headlines. Scores of academics and literary "experts" testified to the poem's importance and hailed it as a significant contribution to American literature. The prosecution offered a weak case, most likely knowing that they were on the losing side. Judge Clayton Horn ruled that *Howl* was not obscene, as it conformed to prevailing social standards. When the results were in, a new day for culture dawned. Soon, Elvis Presley would be gyrating his hips as rock and roll blossomed. *Howl* and *On the Road* flew off the shelves, along with a lot of other "dirty" writing.

Kerouac had been busy for years, experimenting with prose. The genesis of *On the Road* comes from road trips with Cassady, whom he loved and desired. The restless wanderer appealed to Jack's visionary view of an America that was, in the old parlance, "footloose and fancy free." Neal fit the bill. He was an outsider's outsider and his good looks fascinated Kerouac. Neal behind the wheel of an old jalopy became Dean Moriarty at the controls of a new America. And, as Kerouac rolled out his experimental prose, the heroic figure of his friend took on mythic dimension. In his novel, Kerouac, represented as Sal Paradise, writes of Cassady (Moriarty):

He was a con man, he was only conning because he wanted so much to live and to get involved with people.... Somewhere along the line I knew there'd be girls, visions, everything; somewhere along the line the pearl would be handed to me.

This is stunning and revelatory: a moment where Jack breaks through and declares his love and devotion for another man. It is one of the keys to a new sense of what it means to "be together" as men. For Kerouac, everyone was a storehouse of untapped knowledge; every man had potential to be beaten down and distorted. He saw in the land the springboard for a sense of big-heartedness that included sexuality without boundaries.

It took a special courage to recognize, and act on, the fact that people were being robbed of their true selves. In Kerouac's worldview, there was no room for condemnation—there was only room for love and the capacity for generosity of spirit.

The so-called "scroll" manuscript of Kerouac's book, where real life names are used, shows that the novel is actually a spiritual autobiography: highly personal, deeply American, and unsparingly honest—honesty being the whole point. "With the coming of Neal," he writes, "there really began for me that part of my life that you could call my life on the road." He goes on to say, "My impression of Neal was of a young Gene Autry—trim, thin-hipped, blue eyes, with a real Oklahoma accent." He is so taken with him that the entire direction of his life changes as he delves into an abiding freedom, loosed from all bonds. He celebrates Neal's masculinity and tenderness at the same time.

Ginsberg was also smitten with Cassady from the time they met until Cassady's death in the 60s. The fact that Cassady was married and would have children only heightened Ginsberg's interest. Cassady was Ginsberg's "Adonis of Denver." In "On Neal's Ashes," written in 1968, Ginsberg penned the following:

Delicate eyes that blinked blue Rockies all ash
Nipples, Ribs I touched w/my thumb are ash
mouth my tongue touched once or twice all ash

On the Road was an instant classic when published in 1957. Its clear prose matches the clarity of Kerouac's visionary style. He sought to make manifest the real adventure of living, to see the grain of the land with clear and open eyes, and bring down the obstructions that blind people to themselves. That is why he pushed himself beyond the ordinary, even as his work was a celebration of it. Yet there was pain, and suffering. In a country so moralistic, it took enormous fortitude and integrity to break through. Kerouac's vision would be a prototype for writers, musicians, and artists to come. With walls collapsing, new vistas opened up. Bob Dylan and Johnny Cash are just two who learned from Kerouac and the Beat rebellion.

Howl turns personal. As Ginsberg reaches out in a bardic yelp, he also goes inward with his transformation. This becomes a central issue, even as young men look into mirrors and wonder if they can be like James Dean or Montgomery Clift, or as young women try to imitate Monroe. Ginsberg and Kerouac led readers back into their own minds, while at the same time offering them a road out of complacency. The hunger in a youthful body for sexual liberation was always there; it just lay dormant.

Howl came to notice as a public declamation at San Francisco's Six Gallery in 1955. The "wild ones" were out, hoping for an explosion. They were given it when Allen read those haunting, mesmerizing lines. Strangely, Jack Kerouac declined to add his voice that night. He was a bystander, cheering Allen on. The next day, when Lawrence Ferlinghetti wrote to Allen and offered to publish the poem, things began to coalesce. The "Beat" was in the air—liberation near at hand. The chokehold on the human body was about to get choked.

There had been an incident in 1944 (early in Allen and Jack's friendship) that demonstrated the stranglehold that old-fashioned moral values had on the society and that prefigured the spirit yet to be born. In this nightmare period of moral quiescence, a good-looking, brilliant Columbia student from an upper-class St. Louis family—Lucien Carr—joined the Ginsberg,

Kerouac, and Burroughs group. With him came David Kammerer, an older man who'd known Carr in St. Louis and who was obsessed with him. One evening, after what Carr claimed was another attempt made by Kammerer at sexual bullying, Carr pulled a knife on Kammerer, stabbed him to death, tied and weighted the body, and dumped it into the Hudson River. Kerouac helped to conceal the murder weapon, and Burroughs disposed of a bloody pack of cigarettes. Both were arrested as material witnesses. Burroughs was bailed out by his father and Kerouac by a girlfriend, whom he later married. Carr pleaded guilty to second-degree manslaughter. In a trial covered by the newspapers, he received positive press—he had, after all, killed a homosexual—and was sentenced to one to twenty years. In the end, he served two years in New York's Elmira Correctional Facility. In a further irony, Carr would go on to work for United Press International and remain a friend of the early Beats, later becoming a part of their legend.

The break given to Carr and the media attention he received (he was portrayed in glowing terms, not as a cold-blooded murderer) added more problems for gay people. One doesn't need much imagination to see what would have resulted if Kammerer had been the perpetrator. Yet at the same time that these young men were engaging directly with a cruelly prejudiced legal system, they incorporated the lessons of this murder into their assault on that very system and the founding of a new view. Carr—the murderer of a homosexual—remained a friend of the man who would hold up a banner for gay liberation, and Kerouac's writing and life would reveal an open-hearted expression of male bonding that helped to free heterosexuals of the future.

Today, the major works by Kerouac and Ginsberg are an accepted part of world literature. Young people study *On the Road* and *Howl* in high school. Even as new and vigorous inroads are made in the written word, the Beat touch is very much alive, serving as a landmark of consciousness.

Chapter 9

Frank Kameny:
Advocate for Freedom

by John D'Emilio

Franklin Kameny played a unique and pivotal role in the history of LGBT activism in the United States. He pioneered the use of public demonstrations to expose injustice; took on some of the biggest institutions implicated in the oppression of lesbian, gay, and bisexual Americans; relentlessly challenged the exclusionary employment policies of the federal government, as well as the authority of the medical profession to classify homosexuality as an illness; and he was one of only a minority of pre-Stonewall "homophile" activists to make a smooth transition to the gay liberation movement of the post-Stonewall era.

A generation later, near the end of his life, his activist career was still generating change. In the twenty-first century, the wrongs done to Kameny by the federal government half a century earlier provided an opportunity for a younger generation of activists to demand—and receive—apologies from the government for its treatment of him, for the Library of Congress to acknowledge the significance of his activism by accepting his papers, and for the Smithsonian National Museum of American History to display artifacts from his activist years.

Frank Kameny was born in New York City on May 21, 1925, into a middle-class Jewish family. An intellectually gifted child, he started college at the age of fifteen and, after having his education interrupted to serve in the army during World War II, went on to receive a Ph.D. in astronomy from Harvard. At the dawn of the Space Age, Kameny had every reason to believe that his skills would be in high demand when he began working for the United States Army Map Service in the summer of 1957. But this was also the decade of the harshest government persecution of anyone suspected of being gay. A 1950 Senate investigation of federal employment policies had declared, "One homosexual can pollute a Government office."[1] In 1953, one of President Eisenhower's first actions in office was to issue an executive order barring all gays, lesbians, and bisexuals from federal employment. Under these circumstances, local police had a free hand to arrest patrons of gay bars or men looking for consensual sexual partners. When government investigators discovered that Kameny had indeed been arrested on a gay-related sex charge, he was immediately dismissed from his job and barred by the Civil Service Commission from all other federal employment.

At first, Kameny assumed that the dismissal would be easily reversed upon appeal, and he did not look for other work. But he underestimated the rigidity of institutionalized homophobia. While his appeal slowly made its way through the federal bureaucracy and the courts, three years of extreme hardship ensued. He found himself unemployable and completely impoverished, and his health declined as he was forced to depend on food handouts from charitable organizations for his survival. The experience toughened his will and shaped Kameny into the fiercely determined activist that he became. As he wrote to *ONE Magazine* in 1960, "I am not a belligerent person, nor do I seek wars, but having been forced into a battle, I am determined that this thing will be fought thru to a successful conclusion.... I will not be deprived of my proper rights, freedoms, and liberties...or of my right to live my life as I choose."[2] When the Supreme Court rejected his appeal, he decided to take the plunge into collective political action. With friend Jack Nichols and a few others, Kameny formed the Mattachine Society of Washington (MSW) in November 1961. "I felt I'd gone as far as I could go acting as an individual and that the time had come to act through an organization," he reflected afterward.[3]

In 1961, the few homophile groups that existed in the United States mostly engaged in forms of education and service. Mattachine Society and Daughters of Bilitis chapters held public meetings to discuss a range of issues; they met with professionals in law, medicine, and the religious community in an effort to create dialogue and build allies; and they offered help to men and women who were in trouble. Publications like *ONE* magazine often spoke out with anger and defiance about society's mistreatment of gays and lesbians, but they did not follow through with campaigns of action to make change. Kameny's goal was to do something more. He rejected what he characterized as a "genteel, debating society approach" and urged MSW members and those of other organizations to prepare for what he described as "tooth-and-nail politics." At a time when sit-ins, freedom rides, and other direct action campaigns of the Southern civil rights movement were making national headlines, Kameny argued that the homophile movement must also pursue a "vigorous civil liberties, social action approach."[4] In taking this stand, Kameny was pushing homophile organizations in more overtly activist and militant directions.

Under Kameny's leadership, the MSW began a sustained campaign to press government officials to change discriminatory policies. In 1962, he and other members wrote letters to hundreds upon hundreds of elected officials and government bureaucrats in Washington. In some cases, they managed to arrange face-to-face meetings. Kameny and the MSW won the support of the American Civil Liberties Union's local affiliate in D.C., and it became a vocal advocate of gay and lesbian rights. After New York activist Craig Rodwell organized two impromptu public pickets at a military induction center in Manhattan and at the United Nations, Kameny and other homophile militants proposed that activists stage a coordinated series of demonstrations outside various government buildings in the nation's capital. From the spring through the fall of 1965, picket lines formed outside the White House, the Civil Service Commission building, the Pentagon, the State Department and (for Fourth of July) Independence Hall in Philadelphia. Though small in size, especially in comparison to some of that era's large demonstrations for racial equality and against the war in Southeast Asia, these protests represented a historic first.

Kameny, meanwhile, continued to press homophile organizations and their members to higher levels of cooperation and a more militant stance toward oppressive institutions and policies. Early in 1963 he and his allies succeeded in bringing together activists from several organizations to a meeting in Philadelphia, where they formed East Coast Homophile Organizations (ECHO). The networks and relationships that formed through ECHO proved crucial for the successful planning of public demonstrations two years later. In 1966, Kameny and other militants took this effort a step further when homophile organizations from coast to coast met in

San Francisco and formed the North American Conference of Homophile Organizations (NACHO). For the rest of the decade, NACHO helped coordinate days of protest against federal policies, as well as set up a national legal fund that financed court challenges to the closing of gay bars by state liquor authorities, the exclusion of immigrants from the United States based on sexual orientation, and the denial of basic rights to gay, lesbian, and bisexual military personnel.

Kameny seized opportunities to put forward strong, uncompromising views. Invited by his activist allies in the New York Mattachine Society to deliver its 100th monthly lecture in July 1964, he spoke in his characteristically forthright style. "We cannot ask for our rights from a position of inferiority, or from a position, shall I say, as less than whole human beings," he told his audience. "I take the stand that not only is homosexuality...not immoral, but that homosexual acts engaged in by consenting adults are moral, in a positive and real sense, and are right, good, and desirable, both for the individual participants and for the society in which they live."[5] In the mid-1960s, such sentiments were at the cutting edge of social change efforts. A year later, in 1965, he persuaded the Mattachine Society of Washington to take an explicit stand against the medical profession's claim that homosexuality was an illness. MSW passed a resolution that declared that, "homosexuality is not a sickness, a defect, a disturbance, a neurosis, a psychosis, nor a malfunction of any sort."[6] In 1968, when activists at a NACHO conference in Chicago adopted the slogan "Gay Is Good," the homophile movement as a whole seemed to join Kameny in his declaration of self-confident and assertive pride.

Despite Kameny's efforts, the fledgling gay movement remained small. But in its self-perception as an embattled minority, it was now marching in the paths that the protest movements of the 1960s had opened up. When a June 1969 police raid of the Stonewall Inn in New York's Greenwich Village produced several nights of rioting, the time was right for a whole new era of activism to be born. The gay liberation movement, as it was called in the early 1970s, brought a new younger generation of activists into the fight for LGBT freedom. The number of organizations multiplied very rapidly, and the tactics of activists took on the forms associated with 1960s-era radicalism.

Kameny recognized the significance of the changes that Stonewall and gay liberation brought. Stonewall was "a turning point." It accomplished "what we had been trying to do for years and years and years and had never been able to do, and what we had anguished over endlessly: that the gay movement had never been a grassroots movement; it had never fired up the general gay community. Stonewall made the movement a grassroots movement." Recognizing the power of the radical mobilizations of that era, Kameny later reflected that "Stonewall happened at the right moment, and it happened because it was the right moment."[7]

Many homophile activists were not able to make the transition to the radical tactics and approaches of this younger generation. But Kameny welcomed the changes and seized the opportunities that this new gay liberation movement provided. When gay liberationists disrupted sessions of professional meetings like those of the American Medical Association or the American Psychiatric Association, Kameny joined them. "We're not the problem. You're the problem," he shouted from the audience at a 1971 conference in Washington, DC.[8] With the help of younger activists, he became the first openly gay person to run for Congress, declaring his candidacy for the District of Columbia's non-voting member of the House of Representatives. Though he did not come close to winning, the campaign set an important precedent, and he and many of the activists who worked on the campaign afterward formed the Gay Activists Alliance of Washington, DC, which quickly replaced the Mattachine Society of Washington as a newer, more militant movement organization.

Most of the activism of gay liberation occurred through the efforts of local communities. Perhaps because he was based in Washington, DC, and, from the beginning, had tackled the discriminatory policies of the federal government, Kameny was a believer in the need for national organizations. He was an integral part of the activist networks that, in 1973, created the National Gay Task Force (later, the National Gay and Lesbian Task Force). With Kameny's strong encouragement, the Task Force's first major initiative was to provide critical backing to dissidents in the American Psychiatric Association who wanted to eliminate the classification of homosexuality as a mental illness. In December 1973, the Board of Trustees of the APA voted to do just that, and the following spring the membership of the Association confirmed the decision. It was the biggest victory yet of the gay movement, and Kameny had been intimately involved in the efforts to make it happen from the start.

Two years later came another victory in an arena in which Kameny had been a key figure. The United States Civil Service Commission eliminated its blanket ban on the employment of gays, lesbians, and bisexuals in federal jobs. Though there were still limitations on the issuance of security clearances, this was nonetheless a major advance. And, in March

1977, soon after the inauguration of Jimmy Carter as president, Kameny had what might have been the ultimate satisfaction for one who had dedicated his life to the success of the movement. He was a member of the first delegation of gays and lesbians ever to meet in the White House with a member of the president's staff. Twenty years after he had been unceremoniously removed from his federal job, those in the seats of power were consulting with *him*.

Political movements are collective efforts. They require large numbers of people working together to achieve significant goals. But they also require individual leadership and vision. Frank Kameny provided both, and his vision and his goals were taken up and implemented by the larger number of activists who succeeded him.

ENDNOTES

1   US Senate, 81st Congress, Committee on Expenditures in Executive Departments, *Employment of Homosexuals and Other Sex Perverts in Government* (Washington, DC: Government Printing Office, 1950), 5.

2   Frank Kameny to ONE, 27 August 1960, ONE Archives, Los Angeles. These, and other archival materials cited, come from research done in the 1970s. Since then, some of these archival collections may have found new homes and may have been reorganized.

3   Frank Kameny, interview by the author, November 3, 1978, Washington, DC.

4   Frank Kameny, "Message to the Members of the Mattachine Society of Washington from the President of the Society on the State of the Society" (speech given at the New York Mattachine Society in April, 1964), Mattachine Society of Washington File, Kinsey Institute for Research in Sex, Gender, and Reproduction, Indiana University, Bloomington, Indiana.

5   Frank Kameny (speech given at the New York Mattachine Society in July, 1964).

6   "Policy of the Mattachine Society of Washington," adopted March 4, 1965, Mattachine Society of Washington File.

7   Kameny interview by author.

8   Jonathan Capehart, "Frank Kameny: American Hero," *Washington Post* website, October 12, 2011, accessed January 27, 2014, http://www.washingtonpost.com/blogs/post-partisan/post/frank-kameny-american-hero/2011/03/04/gIQAH2DRfL_blog.html.

Chapter 10

Josephine Baker's Dream without Fire or War: An Interview with Jean-Claude Baker

by Adrian Brooks

Josephine Baker (1906-1975)—an illegitimate African-American enter-tainer born into terrible poverty in St. Louis—moved to Paris in 1925. Once there, she became the first international black sex star and symbol of the Jazz Age, the most famous woman in the world—legendary for dancing naked, and the first black woman to star in a major motion picture. Celebrated by Pablo Picasso and Henri Matisse, she was a spy for the Allies and put her life at risk during WWII. After the war, she was a highly visible spokesperson and activist for civil rights who refused to appear in segregated clubs and was one of only two women to speak at the 1963 March on Washington. Baker also championed cross-cultural consciousness; adopting twelve children of different races and back-grounds, she raised each according to his/her own heritage. Among them was Jean-Claude Baker, a French-born singer/entrepreneur. He appeared with her for seven years—up to her sensational triumph in Paris four days before her death—and became the official spokesperson for her "Rainbow Tribe." Having become a U.S. citizen, Jean-Claude created Chez Josephine, a celebrated restaurant in Manhattan, over which he presided until his death in January 2015. AB

AB: How did Josephine go from being poor, black, and obscure to being the most famous woman in the world at only nineteen?

JCB: She went to Paris. And from then on, she became immensely popular all over the world—Madonna, Beyoncé, and Lady Gaga put together.

AB: Is it true she entered the stage upside down riding on the back of a naked black man and her entire costume was one flamingo feather?

JCB: Yes. That was a number called "The Dance of the Savage," meaning a savage from Africa. And in that number, everything went on but penetration. Half of the theater left screaming that black Americans and Jazz would destroy the white civilization. Meanwhile, Jean Cocteau and the rest of the people stood up and crowned Josephine Baker the first black sex symbol. It was October 2, 1925.

AB: It's said she was the first woman who made it all right for white men to look at black women on an equal basis—not as objects, that she made her overt sexuality fun and something to enjoy without shame a generation before Marilyn Monroe.

JCB: The French and European men had sexual dreams of the black girl, and the Asian girl. And in Paris, she became the symbol of those dreams. And do not forget Josephine was the only person who performed almost in the nude. There is no recipe for it. There was no choreography. She took it and there she was.

AB: You say she witnessed black people running away from the race riots in East St. Louis to St. Louis proper when she was 11 years old.

JCB: The young Josephine in 1917 would hear firsthand the horror of the riot in East St. Louis and be traumatized by that. She was not a witness of it. Also, that year—nobody forced her—but Josephine (on her own) did some business deals on Market Street in the colored section of St. Louis near the railroad station, and she would give herself to anyone who would pay one dollar. But with that money she would buy food and clothes for two sisters and a little brother.

AB: How important was her race to her when she was young?

JCB: What we should not forget and what some people don't like to hear—especially African-Americans—is that there was very ugly racism in America between black and white people or white people and people of color, but there was a second, very painful discrimination among black people themselves. And Josephine Baker—born from a white German father to a very dark-skinned mother—would be "too light" for her own mother, her half brother, and two half sisters, who were much, much darker. When she was fifteen, she left St. Louis and started performing and joined "Shuffle Along" as a chorus girl; and there she was the darkest among the high-yellers. So in the nineteen years that she was in America, Josephine was never comfortable with her skin, because for colored people she was either too dark or too light, and, of course, for white people she was the "n" word. When she arrived in Paris, the French fell in love with Josephine. And indeed, she was the one who made "café au lait" such a label. Which is why French women went out in the sun. Until then, people—the elite—would always have very white skin. So Josephine can be credited to being the very first woman to make color from the sun a sensation for European women.

AB: You told me a story; I'm not sure if it's been told before: She had an affair with Picasso.

JCB: Yes, when I was living in Berlin, she told me, "I remember when I was with Picasso at 'The One-Two-Two.' One-Two-Two was a famous whorehouse." And she told me, "On the ground floor you could have drink; you could socialize, and it was nice. The second floor you could have sex, and the third floor was an opium den, and my dear friend 'Jeano,' [Jean Cocteau], was smoking opium. Promise me, my darling, that you will never do drugs." And I was very shocked because I remember thinking: what was Josephine doing with Picasso in a whorehouse? That was in 1926, 1927. She did not go only once; she went many times there.

AB: Having a liaison with Picasso?

JCB: Yes, but you know at that time Josephine was having sex with many men and women. And the next year she was at the Folies-Bergère dancing in the nude with a belt of bananas. And that was scandalous and made her even more famous. She was served in the hotel and in her room; the bed was on a platform and you had to go up two steps to visit the queen and share her body, or whatever she was willing to share...for some money. It was nothing for free.

AB: In World War II, why did she not seek safety in the U.S. or U.K.? So many other people got the hell out, but she stayed; she fought.

JCB: When France started the war, Josephine was a French citizen, because she had married her third husband, Jean Lion, who was a French Jew. Hitler said no Jews, no blacks on the Paris stage, so certainly Josephine Baker was twice guilty in the eyes of Hitler. She loved France very much. When Jacques Abney from the Deuxième Bureau went to see her, Josephine said, "French people welcomed me with open hearts; I'm willing to give my life for them." And that's how she began working for the French government, not for the Allies. Since she was famous, she would be invited to the Italian embassy and would listen when they were talking about the war. She loved it. Sometimes she would come back and have written on her arms some of the things that she thought were very important and Jacques said to her, "Are you crazy?" and Josephine would say, "Nobody would think I'm a spy."

AB: Is it true she crossed international frontiers during World War II with invisible ink messages, military secrets written in her sheet music?

JCB: Yes, it's true. None of those German officials would think of searching Josephine Baker. If they had searched her, she was carrying in her dress secret codes, secret documents, and the sheet music was full of invisible ink with documents, which is unbelievable. I don't want to know what they would have done with her. But she did that out of the cover of her fame, out of the cover of Josephine Baker.

AB: They would have shot her if they had found out.

JCB: Who knows!

AB: During the war in North Africa she was terribly ill—some thought she was dying—yet she got out of the hospital, and she went to entertain black troops. She said that her experience made her suddenly realize her own blackness and embrace the issue of racial justice.

JCB: We cannot blame Josephine Baker. In 1930, she was performing at the Casino de Paris and was singing "If I was White." She had been embraced by the white world; she became a white woman. She never complained about the French colonies in Africa. She was a queen, and she was a star; she forgot she was a woman of color. The only time she came back to America was in 1935, to perform in *Ziegfield Follies*; she was badly received, and it reminded her that she was a person of color. Of course, America had changed since 1925; it had gone far, but you were still a second-class citizen. In November of 1942, that's when American troops came to Morocco. At the time, the army was still segregated. And you had the terrible thing: the soldiers, black and white, who were willing to fight and die, but the whites were terrible to the black troops. So Major Donald Wyatt, an African-American, went to Josephine, who had been very sick for eighteen months at the clinic of Docteur Comte. He asked her to perform at the opening of a club for only colored or African-American soldiers. And Josephine performed, and suddenly she was confronted again with Black America. And she said (and very dramatically), "My people, my people, I have abandoned my people." Of course, she was very guilty; the year was 1943: she had left America in 1925, and she discovered that people of color were still humiliated. And that's the first time that Josephine was confronted and willing to do something for her people...

AB: In 1944, I heard that a million Parisians came out to welcome her when she returned home.

JCB: We cannot put a number—because in those days we are not like today, where you could have estimated the count—but a large, large crowd came and Josephine Baker was reborn; she was not anymore the little girl who danced with bananas. The war had changed not only Josephine Baker, but the French people and the rest of the world. And suddenly she had become one of them; she fought on the side of the right people. So many French people embraced Hitler and the German occupation in France. There were also a lot of French people who hated that and were fighting, and Josephine Baker and all of them were fighting on the right side for a free France.

AB: Is that when she decided that she wanted to leave a legacy, like Lincoln or Gandhi?

JCB: I wouldn't say like Lincoln or Gandhi, but there is one person that she admired above everybody: Charles de Gaulle. She performed for him in Algiers during the war, and there is a rumor that the two of them had a little affair. So yes, she liked de Gaulle and had great admiration for him. She wrote about him, without telling about their affair; she said, "I like tall men where you have to raise your head to look at the head."

AB: When she returned to the U.S. in 1945, she confronted American racism in a major way.

JCB: When she came back from the war she was married to Jo Bouillon, who was a homosexual. She was bisexual, too; don't forget that. She came to America, not just the United States. She went to Argentina, to Mexico; she came back to the U.S., and of course there was still racism, so she plotted that she would be "Mrs. Brown," and she would cross the border between New York and Washington, where you had the color barrier.... You know what I mean? And then, when she would be put in jail, they would take photographs (while she was in jail); since she was a French citizen with a French passport, she thought that the President of America would have to apologize to the President of France for the way a French citizen had been mistreated. But American Civil Rights leaders said, "That's very nice, Josephine, but we—black American, Negro—we do not have a French passport; so your intention is very good, but we can do nothing." And that's the way it ended.

AB: Why did she remain physically removed from the civil rights struggle in the United States until the March on Washington?

JCB: In France, she had the 600-acre chateau, which she had to rebuild, because it was an old place. She had 12 children of different races, colors, and religions. In 1963, when Martin Luther King was preparing the March, she knew nothing about it. She was away; she was struggling. But she still had great admirers in America, who had followed her stardom in France. She was a legend. And those people loved her, and I'm very happy to share with you that a gay school teacher in Harlem said, "Josephine has to be there for the march on Washington; it is something too important; we want her to be here." They gathered money for her to fly from Paris to New York. They put her at the Waldorf Astoria, in one of the most expensive suites. And the next day she took the bus and train and went to

Washington. And out of the blue, at the March, she was asked to speak. And she spoke spontaneously.

AB: My God, she didn't even know she was going to be asked to speak?

JCB: Absolutely not.

AB: Was it ever told before that it was a gay teacher that brought her to the United States?

JCB: No. I met some of them, and they were wonderful human beings. And to them, Josephine was the greatest star. She was the goddess; she was the one that could help them, and she had to be there and witness the march, and it was unknown to them that she would be speaking.

<hr />

On August 28, 1963, Josephine Baker was the only woman to address the crowd aside from activist Daisy Bates, a heroine of the 1957 integration crisis in Little Rock, Arkansas. Excerpts:

Friends and family.... This is the happiest day of my entire life. The result of seeing you all together is a sight for sore eyes. You're together as salt and pepper, just the way you should be, just as I've always wanted you to be, and people of the world have always wanted you to be. You are a united people at last. Because without unity, there cannot be any victory. Me—I'm glad—I'm glad that in my homeland...where I was born, and love, and respect, I'm glad to see this day come to pass....Because you are on the eve of a complete victory. And tomorrow, time will do the rest. I want you to know, also, how proud I am to be here today, after so many long years of struggle—fighting here and elsewhere for your rights, our rights, the rights of man. I'm glad that you have accepted me to come. I didn't ask you; I didn't have to ask. I just came because it was my duty. And I'm going to say again: you are on the eve of complete victory. Continue on. You can't go wrong. The world is behind you. And we know that "that time" is not someday. We know that time is now.

On August 31, Josephine Baker wrote Dr. King from her home in France, saying:

I was so happy to have been with all of you on our great historical day. I repeat that you are really a great, great leader and if you need me I will always be at your disposition because we have come a long way but we still have a way to go that will take (unity) so don't forget that I will be one of your sincere boosters. Your greater admirer and sister in battle.

JCB: *Martin Luther King wrote to Josephine on November 5th, 1963.*

We were all inspired by your presence at the March on Washington. I am deeply moved by the fact that you would fly such a long distance to participate in that momentous event.... You are certainly doing a most dedicated service for mankind. Your genuine good will, your deep humanitarian concern, and your unswerving devotion to the cause of freedom and human dignity will remain an inspiration to generations yet unborn.

∞∞∞∞∞∞∞∞∞∞∞∞∞∞∞∞∞∞∞∞∞∞∞∞

AB: How did you meet?

JCB: It was 1957; I was fourteen. I was a bellhop: I did some errands for customers; that was a part of my job. When I came back, she said, "Did you love your mother, my little one?" And I started to cry and told her that I had been abandoned by my father and I was alone in Paris. And she said, "You have no father; from this day on, you will have two mothers." I thought, *She is crazy. Where is my tip?*

AB: Later you reconnected?

JCB: From 1958, for eight or ten years, it was very difficult for her; she had no money—she was not famous anymore. She didn't have big engagements. By that time, I was a young and successful owner of Pimm's Club discotheque in West Berlin. I used to be a singer; I had a boutique, and I met her in terrible conditions. She was performing under a tent on Christmas Eve, and it was freezing cold. So I went to her, and she almost fell from the stage dancing the Charleston in a very pathetic way. I thought she needed help. I never knew of the famous Josephine Baker of the twenties; none of us children knew anything about her past. But deep inside, I knew that if Josephine once again would have a first-class production, it would astonish the people. The last seven or eight years of her life, I became the spokesperson of "The Rainbow Tribe": my brothers and sisters of different race, color, and religion. I performed with her all over the world, and I used to sing two songs in the show. I was her *chargé d'affaires*.

AB: What was Josephine Baker's vision of "The Rainbow Tribe"? Why did she call it that, and if she could have succeeded, what would the result have been?

JCB: She had a utopian dream. She wanted to transform the world. She had a beautiful, dignified dream, which nobody has achieved today. She had a dream of removing social discrimination among all people. The first five years of her life, Josephine was raised by her adoptive mother, Elvira, who had been a slave on a tobacco plantation in Holy Springs, Arkansas—and that would traumatize Josephine for the rest of her life. Then she became the most famous woman in the world. She had the Chateau, but she still suffered. Her own journey through life was so tragic that she thought it would all be so simple if we were all brothers and sisters and loved each other.

AB: It's a heroic position that with her haunted past—

JCB: She is a very heroic woman. When Josephine came back to America for the first time in 1935, she went to St. Louis to see her mother and grandmother, Elvira. She used to wear a fabulous evening dress from Paris; she would cover herself in all the diamonds (worth millions today), and she was sleeping with her grandmother, holding her grandmother in her arms.

AB: What do you think the force was in her? Where did the vision come from—this idealism that would cross racial and cultural barriers in a vision of universal brotherhood?

JCB: That I cannot answer. But having broken all the barriers in the world, who knows what kind of bubbles—like champagne—went through her head? When you are that famous, you think that you are invincible; nobody can stop you. Look at Napoleon: he was first Bonaparte, and then he became Napoleon the emperor. She was first poor and black and unknown, and then became the famous, the fabulous, one-in-a-million Josephine Baker.

AB: Yet even so, she was always going out of her way to help simple people, to give money to poor people, to do things invisibly—just out of kindness.

JCB: That's true. She did that many times. She used to bring the pot-au-feu to the poor people of Paris. She used to help people without looking for publicity. That, too, is Josephine Baker.

AB: Yet when she came back to the United States in 1949, she noticed that there weren't enough black employees on the train line between New York and Washington, and she went down to the train company and—

JCB: She went to complain! And she went to San Francisco, and complained that no bus driver was black people. So Josephine did all of that under the cover of being a French citizen.

AB: She was also responsible for desegregating white and black clubs—

JCB: Absolutely; when she came out of Copa City in Miami Beach, the owner was a Jew—don't forget that Jewish people have always been very good to the struggle of black in America. She said, "I will not perform if my people are not there." So he kept eleven seats in the front, the best place for people of color. And of course, people of color in America, they didn't walk into a white club; they usually were not welcome. So Josephine did what she wanted in a small way, but she was the first person who could do that.

AB: What would Josephine make (if she was alive today) of marriage equality, of gays adopting children, of the gay movement, of feminism?

JCB: Josephine come from a time that to be gay, you had to hide it. But I cannot honestly say what Josephine would have been doing in today's revolution with same sex marriage and all of that. It's not because she is a heroine and a barrier-breaker yesterday that she would have been the same heroine or barrier-breaker today. We cannot answer that.

AB: But she was seventy-five years ahead of her time in terms of race, sexuality, her ideals—

JCB: She never came out of the closet, because she never was in the closet.

AB: If she was alive today, what causes do you think she would embrace?

JCB: Once again, she may revolutionize the people and come out and tell them the details of her life. She would once again astonish you in the way that Josephine Baker astonished the world when she was alive.

AB: What do you think she would see as her legacy or her message?

JCB: She was very humble about her life and what she did. She never bragged about what she did during the war; she did not brag about many things. And I guess with that dignity she could be a grande dame—a lady with a lot of class—and I'm sure that she would say nothing. She would say, "Look at what I did, and think about that."

Chapter 11

April 4, 1968

by Adrian Brooks

I sit up in the bed at 1453 Crittenden Street—in the home of Lawonne Price—and stare at the radio. It's April 4th, 1968. For three weeks, I've been in Washington, DC, working as a volunteer for Martin Luther King's "Poor People's Campaign." He's summoned the poor from all over the country, but especially Appalachia, to build a tenement city on the Mall to illustrate their plight and to stay put until Congress passes sweeping legislation to end poverty and hunger in America forever. Eleven thousand are there, living in hastily constructed plywood A-frames and tarpaper shacks in a place that's been dubbed "Resurrection City." It's been a cold and rainy March here in the nation's capital, and they need food and blankets, medical care...everything, really.

Working twenty-four to thirty-six hours at a stretch, I feel as if I've almost ceased to exist. There is no time to think about myself. I love the other people in the office—mainly black people. We're bonded by something huge. The true spirit of America pulses through that narrow building. Race—or any sense of a color barrier—has disappeared at last, at last! I feel invisible. I feel useful. My Quaker credo isn't merely a privately held belief, it's being held up by the greatest man in the country, possibly the world: one who, like Gandhi, is forcing everyone to be aware of what they're doing; that every single choice we make is indicative of who we are. That civil rights aren't just about color issues, they're about every single aspect of our lives: what we buy, where we live, what we do with our soul, how we use our vote. Everything.

Though bone weary, I'm happy. I've redeemed myself (a bit, anyway) from running away from a 1966 peace demonstration in Iowa where hundreds of pro-war people threw rocks at ten friends and me. In the end, we fled. We had to. It was either that or stay and get seriously hurt. But it still haunts me to have buckled when the chips were down. I vow I'll never repeat that act of cowardice.

I'm also united with the other people. What we're all doing is so gallant and so clear it's beyond argument. We don't have to ask ourselves nagging questions about right or wrong; right and wrong are so revealed in Dr. King's summons to nonviolent civil disobedience; to stout opposition to war in Vietnam (which claims a disproportionate number of black victims—blacks being less able to evade the draft than whites); to a fundamental reappraisal of how the United States uses its power and resources (there's no need to doubt—no room for it). How could we debate when Black Panthers call for armed insurrection and violent revolution?

The nation is falling apart, and we're glad. President Johnson hardly dares to leave the White House, but, even in the oval office, he can hear the daily chants: "Hey, hey, LBJ, how many kids have you killed today?" He's paralyzed by fears of ending the war in Vietnam and looking less masculine than the Kennedys. The fear of being perceived as unmanly is ruining the country.

The perception of national ruin was pervasive. In 1967, Johnson authorized an official investigation into the race riots that tore apart American cities in 1965. The Kerner Commission released its long-anticipated report on February 28th, 1968. It was an instant best seller: two million sold.

At that time, I was a student at what may have been the most radical school on the planet, at least in the 60s: the Friends World Institute, a soon-to-be accredited Quaker college with centers all around the world. It couldn't offer draft deferments, however, and every student who joined immediately got his or her very own FBI

file, since the avowed intention of the school was to create revolu-
tionaries: nonviolent "agents of social change." As a peace activist
inspired by the school and the Kerner report, I left FWI to go to
Washington and join Dr. King's crusade right after the Commis-
sion released its findings, which included a warning: "Our nation is
moving towards two societies, one black, one white—separate and
unequal." It went on to blame white racism for the black riots, which
came from black frustration at racial inequality and lack of oppor-
tunity. It also lambasted federal and state governments, as well as
the mainstream media. "The press has too long basked in a white
world looking out of it, if at all, with white men's eyes and white
perspective."

But while the Commission recommended urgent action, all
the money was going to fight that undeclared war in Vietnam, not
to rebuilding cities or providing for what LBJ called "The Great
Society"—an expansion/completion of FDR's "New Deal." Even
worse, LBJ rejected the report. And so the situation on the ground
in March 1968 was that the NAACP represented the "old school"
approach of gradual social progress through playing by the rules;
the SNCC advocated armed struggle—violent, if necessary—to
overthrow the oppressive white tyranny, and Dr. King's SCLC (the
Southern Christian Leadership Conference) stood alone in commit-
ment to Gandhi's nonviolent principles, coupled with an embrace of
civil disobedience, nonviolent resistance to racism and abuse, and
the rejection of hate.

In the SCLC office, we sense not only racial hope; we sense a cleansing of
the paranoia and corrosion of America that's followed WWII. This sense
of a crusade illuminates the anti-war movement, too, and the two great
causes fuse when Dr. King summons us to be the best people we can be.

I love him, just as I love Gandhi. As tired as we volunteers are, there's a
huge sense of recognition and mutual commitment. In a miracle of fusion,
I've stopped seeing color when I meet people. I just see souls. And I'm not
some privileged white kid; I'm there. With them. On the front lines.

A few office coworkers, including a gay guy named Silas, call me a
"niggah." The word gives me the willies but they don't mean it as a pejo-
rative or in a self-denigrating way; they mean it affectionately, that I am

one of them. In any case, I'm too busy to protest. There's so much to do. Malnourished new mothers whose breasts don't produce milk need infant formula, blankets have to go to a church, truck drivers need directions.

In Dr. King's three-storied headquarters at the corner of 14th and U Street, I serve as Assistant Head of the Food Committee. My boss—and one of the only other white workers—is a gravel-voiced Jewish earth mother, who really does have a heart of gold: Alice Arshak. Alice wears polka-dot dresses, chain-smokes, and is on the phone so much that we develop sign language to communicate without interrupting her calls.

The area is at the center of the nation's consciousness. Highlighting the tension, around the corner, one finds the NAACP and Stokely Carmichael's SNCC. So Dr. King's organization—SCLC—seems the last best hope to head off open racial war.

Day after day, we try to find shelter and food for thousands who've made the pilgrimage in answer to Dr. King's call. Day after day, we go to donate food in churches where the faithful huddle on tick mattresses, tired and dispirited but willing to believe in that man's promise of justice. One day, I take a truck of supplies to Resurrection City; I've been too busy at the office to see it before. It's shocking: 11,000 people in tarpaper and plywood shacks. They have haggard faces and are trying to stay warm and hopeful. But they're there because they still have faith in the country and trust Dr. King to be able to deliver on his promise to force Congress to take care of America's most needy souls. I'm not ashamed to be white— not there, not then; I'm just glad to pitch in. I feel honored. And they're not strangers to me. Nor do I feel alien. We're on the same side.

On March 31st, LBJ announces that he won't seek re-election. Hanoi declares its own willingness to attend peace talks in Vietnam. At last, the country can correct its awful series of mistakes and injustices. But on April 2nd, a demonstration in Memphis becomes a riot. Determined to stave off further violence, Dr. King has returned to lead a peaceful march. At the office, we're busy preparing for his arrival—he'll be here the next day.

After working without sleep for forty-eight hours, I drag myself home. All the way from 14th and U Street—an urban intersection of broad avenues—to leafy and residential Crittenden Street, I manage not to nod off on the bus.

Lawanne isn't home. I go upstairs and wash. The effort depletes my last strength. I look yellow against chartreuse-colored walls. I get in bed. *Music*, I think as I fuss with the dial of a plastic radio on the nightstand,

I've got to hear just a moment of pretty music and then I'll sleep, sleep for ten, twelve, fourteen hours and then go work again. Oh thank God for music...

"We repeat: Martin Luther King has been assassinated...."

I am dreaming. In the dream, the radio said Dr. King was dead. A sick comedy program; it has to be. I flip the dial.

"...seems to have acted alone. Dr. King was on a balcony when the assailant..."

My brain tries to wrap itself around this fact and, incredibly, suddenly, I am not sleepy. *I have to get back to the office,* I think. *They may need me.*

I dress. I choose my bright red sweater so no one will imagine that I'm trying to hide. It's raining. I stumble outside. It hadn't been raining before. My bus transfer is still good, the same transfer I got before I knew.... I stare at the same houses, the same streetlights, the same stores—still open—and the people...

The bus stops smack in front of the SCLC building. Wide sidewalks on both sides of the intersection are jam-packed; thousands stand silent in the rain.

All black.

There is a dead, numb, flat stillness. The building is dark. How can it be? I left an hour ago and there were people planning to stay all night. Now doors and windows are closed and shuttered, the lights are off: it looks like a tomb.

The bus takes off leaving me in the street; the sidewalks are so crowded, there's no way to get on the pavement. I'm the only white person in a sea of thousands of black faces and, of course, they spot my bright red sweater, and my face.

I realize I can't push. And I don't want to push my way through. I want them to stand back and let me pass; I want them to know that I'm here from choice, because I belong with them. But my right to pass must come from them. And so I wait quietly.

From the crowd, I heard sounds of a swell, a low growl starting to roll toward me. It's the sound of my approaching death. I must stand still and reach them from a silence at my center. But just as the noise crests, I hear a few calls from people I can't see.

"Don't hurt that boy! He okay!"

"He a soul brother. He with us!"

"I know that boy! He work for Dr. King!"

The growl subsides; the crowd hesitates, then parts—allowing me a path from the street to the door. I pass along a thin corridor of people. I knock. I knock again. Then I pound.

"*Who's there?*" A hushed, frightened voice.

"It's me. Let me in."

The door opens a crack. I see startled eyes then a hand reaches out, yanks me inside, and the door slams and locks.

"*Get down!*"

"What..?"

"*Get down you fool!*"

I obey.

"*Are you crazy? What the hell are you doing here?*"

"I had to..."

"*You almost got yourself killed, boy!*"

"But I wanted to help!"

"*You know how stupid you are?*"

"I'm sorry!"

"*Upstairs! Keep down! And don't go near no windows!*"

I scuttle across the floor and up the stairs to the top. In a front office shuttered with windows closed and Venetian blinds lowered, Dr. King's staff huddles in one lit room—waiting, just waiting.

Alice is sobbing hysterically; the others are silent. They glance at me as I enter. Silas tells me I'm an idiot.

"But I was just down there and it's calm."

"Here come Stokely..."

Black Panther Stokely Carmichael (later known as Kwame Toure) charges into the street; we can see that when we turn off the light to peer through a crack in the shutters. He jumps in front of passing autos to slow them down, followed by excited youths, then zigzags back and forth across the avenues, pounding on car hoods and shop windows, shouting that the people must close down the shops that remain open "in honor of Dr. King!"

As people begin moving fast, we hear glass breaking. It's followed by burglar alarms. Then sirens. And Washington erupts.

"*Now that King dead, we goin' over to Stokely!*"

Chaos ignited, Stokely vanishes as people charge into shops to loot TV sets. And the air is filled with bricks, flames, and smoke.

I watch the capital burn. I want it to burn. I want everything to burn and make us as homeless as the faithful thousands camped out in "Resurrection City." Who will speak for them now? Take up their cause? Yes, let the country burn to charred foundations and start over, do it better, keep faith in justice for all, equality for all.

The air is tinged with orange smoke, the wail of police sirens and fire engines. I want to die—pay with my blood—and I hate my immunity, the ease with which I could extricate myself from the crunch and sail into green and leafy lanes where white people know the right words to sound ever so concerned, but where one scarcely sees black residents.

"Liberty and justice for all...."

The riot continues all night, into the next night; 168 cities are burning. Hearing that Philadelphia is one of them, I ring my parents anxiously.

"How are you?" my father asks in a cheerful mood.

"I'm all right. The city is burning."

"Here too. It's very unfortunate.... We're having a dinner with the Lovells, and the Keenes, and the..."

I can't believe my ears. Not only are my parents conducting a dinner party, my father sounds almost ebullient.

Nero fiddled while Rome burned, I think after hanging up and returning to my perch. Startled birds fly about in the flame and smoke as looting goes on with excited people stealing TV sets from burning shops.

"It's like a party," I say to a coworker, watching the 100% discount of America.

"A sad party," she sighs.

Later on, Silas calls me a "soul brother."

"Oh..." I say sadly, thinking of where I'm from. "I'm not so sure about that."

"I am," he says quietly. "Not many white people would come down here to be with us and do what you've been doing. You're a soul brother, all right."

"I hope so, Silas. I really do."

The National Guard is called in when rioters get within two blocks of the White House. Sixteen thousand troops still can't quell the anarchy, the police have vanished; there are two hundred major fires in DC alone.

Come morning, another white boy—Peter Atwood, son of a famous columnist—and I decide we have to demonstrate solidarity. We have to expose ourselves, put ourselves on the line, be targets in a place where no other whites dare go. For me, it's a way to cope with my shame: shame at being white, shame at what white people have done.

Dead bodies lie in the street. Occasional shots. No more rioting. We walk in the middle of avenues past charred autos, I in my bright red Shetland wool sweater. I think, *Any minute now. Death. It's all right... Yes...*

let it be like this. Let me be conscious of my smallness and aware I was
only trying to do something to help.... But we walk for hours.

"Honky, you better get off the street!"

We walk anyway—our way of being able to live with ourselves as the curtains ring down on America's golden hope. Then SCLC gets a call; radicals have spared the office out of respect for Dr. King but, if the whites don't evacuate, we'll be fired on.

A curtained VW bus draws up; we're evacuated. At St. Paul's church, we stay a day. I remember sleeping on the floor with people from Alabama. Junkies get free food and sell it for their fix. And people who've lost their homes and businesses come to receive aid.

Allowed back in the office, we stay all day and sleep on the floor. But I'm alone in the building one night at three or four a.m. when awakened by an enormous roar. Pulling myself to a window, I look down to see a line of tanks. I start counting, lose interest after fifteen or sixteen roll by and, exhausted, sink down again; the roar goes on and on. The next day motorcycle wedges of police drive into demonstrators; we're tear gassed, clubbed indiscriminately, and I make a sign which is Xeroxed by the thousand and distributed throughout the city:

D.C. PARENTS: KEEP YOUR CHILDREN HOME
AND SAVE THEIR LIVES

A published author.

We hold a march on 14th Street, passing out palm fronds in front of army jeeps, tanks and soldiers with fixed bayonets. After the march and the predictable speeches about how Dr. King's dream will never die because we'll all carry on, Resurrection City is doomed. The Poor People's Campaign is finished. It's April 11th when I finally leave Washington. At the Lincoln Memorial, cherry trees are in bloom.

Chapter 12

Ground Zero

by Miss Major Griffin-Gracy

I was never a fan of Judy Garland until I heard that she'd died. But then they played some songs that she did, and they moved me to tears. I couldn't keep my nerves together so I went home, cried my heart out, then had a few drinks and decided, "I can't be in this house alone." And so I went down to Stonewall.

The girls and I called Sheridan Square "the meat rack." There you'd find the most beautiful boys in New York waiting, hoping to catch a john. Or they'd come back later, and you could scoop them up for soup and a sandwich and a warm bed. The Square was actually a long rectangle of heated anticipation for sexual activity with Christopher Street on both north and south sides. It was a sort of dog walk and meeting place.

But the Stonewall Bar was the one place we could go to relax, be ourselves, not have to explain who we were—if we still had all our parts and if they worked. Of course, there were drag queens, too, but there were more trans-oriented women because drag queens would go to gay bars and not have a problem. Transgendered people, like Marsha P. Johnson and Sylvia Rivera and Bambi Lake, would be at Stonewall so you could score whatever you needed: sex, drugs, or boys. There were two floors:

downstairs was where the bar was, and upstairs was where the activity was—cute little spaces you could stand in and prepare yourself to join the mile-high club.

At the end of 14th Street under the freeway—Henry Hudson Parkway—trucks would park, hundreds of trailers with the backs open. You could climb in and have sex from one end to the other in the pitch black. Everybody met there: the leather fags, the cowboy fags (who always seemed tiny with big hats), the muscle guys...and uptown preppies would come down. The trucks were Switzerland—a neutral zone—where everybody would meet and be okay because trans people couldn't get into some bars; we couldn't even get drinks unless we were doing shows. But the trucks were open to everyone.

Underage hustlers often hung out in the square harassing the "girls" from Stonewall; they were just being boys—acting out, protecting their little male egos. Mainly, they hassled people of color. White girls got off easy, but black girls were all too familiar with arrest procedures, paddy wagons, and holding pens. And they paid the price.

At the time, you'd be in a club dancing with someone when you'd hear that nightstick hit the door twice—always twice—*bam bam*. The moment it happened, the lights would come on; you'd step away from your partner and try to be sure you were wearing three pieces of *appropriate* clothing. And this happened regularly—not just in New York, or in Chicago, or Los Angeles, or in San Francisco. Cops would walk in slowly like they owned the place, eyeballing everyone, pushing people with nightsticks. If they put you in a paddy wagon, you'd be hauled off to the Tombs (jail). If they put you in a car, they'd take you to some alley or empty parking lot, make you suck their dick, take all your clothes, throw them in the trunk of their car, and tell you to go home naked. But at jail, a court-appointed lawyer would take your case and make you pay through the nose: get the keys to go to your apartment and take your clothes or fur coats while promising to get you out in a few days. That was another racket: attorneys received tips from cops, who then received kickbacks, but you got no bail. And if they sent you to jail three times for some misdemeanor, you could count on the fact that the fourth time you'd be sent up on a felony.

The shit had been going on for decades with severe injuries of people trying to escape bar raids. If they caught you sneaking out a window of a bathroom—there was always some cop outside waiting—he'd beat you unmercifully with that stick until you were unconscious, then haul you off to jail. Back then it was survival of the fittest.

By June 1969, everybody was fighting for someone's rights somewhere. Blacks were fighting for their rights; women were struggling to get equal rights and equal pay; everyone was trying to get that war stopped to bring people's sons home from Vietnam. New York was boiling. We'd all melted together at anti-war demonstrations, women's rights marches, and civil rights campaigns. Most of us had been busted at sit-ins, be-ins, and smoke-ins.

The night of Stonewall, two friends and I sat in Sheridan Square talking with the boys, trying to have a good time. Some were talking about Judy Garland; some were talking about a party. Sylvia Rivera was talking about a group she was trying to start—a trans group for girls who worked the street: Street Transvestite Action Revolutionaries. Finally, we went to the bar. Not long afterwards, we heard the nightsticks, and the lights came on. It was a weird feeling. Everyone just looked at each other this time. The police poked us in the back as they issued us toward the front door. Up the street, there was a paddy wagon; cops were there. Some girls were already inside. Others inside the bar were refusing to be frisked. Then there was a loud crash; some said someone threw a shoe or a beer bottle; some said it was the boys standing around—spectators—raising all kinds of commotion. Some said the cops tried to beat up one of the lesbians and she fought back, which was when all hell broke loose.

We started fighting; I could hear people screaming. I heard some guy tell the cops, "Don't hit me in my face," and thought, "I should just turn and knock him out myself." So I turned back and spit in the face of that cop, and he knocked me out, and that's all I remember. I woke up in the Tombs.

At the jail they kept us all together. I woke up when it was getting light. Everyone was talking about what had happened and that it had continued, that it hadn't stopped with us. It felt kind of good not to take that shit any more. They let us out that morning at 10:30 or 11 a.m., and that night we went back to Stonewall.

We didn't know where anyone was; we didn't know who was still in the Tombs or where our friends were. I didn't find some for days. A couple of girls who hadn't been arrested took friends home and helped them heal—gave them baths, gave them clothes. I lived uptown at 85th and Amsterdam and didn't know what was happening for a few days. Most trans girls didn't like the Village; the people down there (who were mainly white and middle class) weren't nice to us trans girls. That's why we all went to the Stonewall bar in the first place.

One of Sylvia's friends called to tell me that a new political movement was getting started. But things were still sort of splintered. Right after that, Sylvia and I went to Central Park, where she'd been asked to speak. I went with her; we thought it would be okay. Maybe it was Sheep's Meadow? There were all these beautiful white boys there, but they started booing and throwing things at her. We were in tears. We swore we weren't going to take that shit anymore after Stonewall, but rumors were flying that we did drugs and were thieves and junkies and whores. So I stepped back. Sylvia and Marsha started doing their thing—becoming trans activists...

The most amazing thing for me out of all this is that the movement had a meeting to decide whether they should put "T" into this political thing of LGB.... Why even vote on it? It should have been there from the beginning. I don't understand why the "T" shouldn't have been the first letter because of Stonewall riots, because we were the ones who were out front before they took it, stole it—like they do everything else in this country. But now we're rising again, and we aren't going anywhere; there are no closets to hide in. We burned the house down.

PART 2

There are many divergent, contrasting, and contradictory accounts of what happened at Stonewall. No other event in LGBT history has been so disputed. This may be unavoidable considering the symbolic importance of such a flashpoint. But here are other contemporaneous voices from that night. AB

"The police [had] pushed open the front door of...Stonewall and marched in.... It was one-twenty a.m. Sylvia [Sylvia Rivera] tried to take it in stride... but...[w]hen one of the cops...asked with a smirk if she was a boy or a girl, she almost swung at him.... The cop gave her a shove."[1] Still, according to Officer Seymour Pine, "[the] transvestites resisting...made the raid take on a broader scope."[2] That view is nixed by another participant: "The pigs decided to start playing games...because when did you ever see a fag fight back? Now times are a changin'. This shit has got to stop!"[3]

"[C]ampier patrons emerging...took the opportunity to strike...poses, starlet style, while the onlookers whistled and shouted.... But when a paddy wagon pulled up, the mood turned...somber.... [I]t turned sullen when the police started to emerge...with prisoners.... [A] few people started to boo; others pressed against the waiting van, while the cops... yelled angrily for the crowd to move back."[4]

"[T]he explosive moment came when 'a dyke dressed in men's clothing'...started to act up. Harry Beard, the Stonewall waiter, [said] one of the cops slapped her in the head with his nightstick.... The crowd... started screaming—'Pigs!' 'Faggot cops!'"[5]

"The crowd was so whipped up.... The police became targets. [Activist] Craig Rodwell...saw Marsha P. Johnson climb to the top of a lamppost and drop a bag containing a heavy object on the car's windshield, shattering it."[6]

"One queen mashed an officer with her heel, knocked him down, grabbed his handcuff keys, freed herself, and passed the keys to another queen.... By now, the crowd had swelled to a mob.... People were... throwing...coins, bottles, cans, bricks. Someone even picked up dog shit...and threw it.... Stunned and frightened[,]...the police retreated inside the bar."[7] Here, "[they] heard...windows being shattered, and... bricks pounding on the door. Molotov cocktails exploded. The fear of a fiery death, the great din of voices[,]...and the incessant reverberations from metal and rock pounding against the walls and doors were about to overwhelm the police.[8]

"With the cops holed up inside...the crowd was...in control of the street, and it bellowed in triumph...like a powerful rage bent on vendetta."[9] Then:

At two-fifty-five a.m....the fearsome Tactical Patrol Force...was... rounding the corner...[,] wearing helmets with visors, carrying... weapons, including billy clubs and tear gas.... Two dozen...in a wedge formation.... But the crowd would not be cowed.... The TPF would disperse the jeering mob only to have it reform behind them.... When the police whirled around...at one point, they found themselves face to face with their worst nightmare: a chorus line of mocking queens, their arms clasped, kicking...Rockettes-style and singing: *We are the Stonewall girls/ We wear our hair in curls/ We wear no underwear/ We show our pubic hair....* It was a deliciously witty...revelatory kind of consciousness. Sylvia...said, "Something lifted off my shoulders."[10]

"Special credit [for the riot] must be given to gay homeless youths, transgendered men, and to the lesbian who fought the police."[11] But "considerable blood had been shed. At three-thirty-five a.m....an uneasy calm settled over the area."[12]

"I was just walking past Sheridan Square," says Edmund White. "We could tell that it was a raid because there was a Black Maria [a paddy wagon] parked out front. Although I was basically a middle-class prig, afraid that everyone would go too far, I felt a strange exaltation. It was one of the first times that we didn't run away from the cops."[13]

Felice Picano recalls:

Big black police buses surrounded the area. Fire hoses made walking difficult. Scores of police in full riot gear with helmets, shields, and sticks filled the square. The big plate-glass window front of Stonewall was gone. Its door lay on the sidewalk. The doorway was being boarded up. A Volkswagen parked at the curb in front of the bar had been flipped over. It looked like a turtle on its back. A Yellow Cab appeared to have tried to mount a fire pump, knocking off its cap so water gushed twenty feet high. The cab was on fire.[14]

Rita Mae Brown recalled:

I was walking home with a friend, headed to my hole-in-the-wall apartment at Charles Street. We'd passed the Stonewall when we heard sirens and saw the police go into the bar. We figured that it was the usual "clean up" by the vice squad. Then we saw the police come flying out again, pushed out by the people inside who were fighting and screaming. That evening became like nuclear fission. Inmates at the Woman's House of Detention a block away had also rioted when they heard all the sirens, burning mattresses and pushing them out of their cells and windows while they shouted, "I want to be free! I want to be free!"[15]

ENDNOTES

1 Martin Duberman, *Stonewall* (Boston: E.P. Dutton, 1993).

2 David Carter, *Stonewall: The Riots That Sparked the Gay Revolution* (New York: St. Martin's Press, 2004).

3   Ibid.

4   Duberman.

5   Ibid.

6   Carter.

7   Duberman.

8   Carter.

9   Duberman.

10 Ibid.

11 Carter.

12 Duberman.

13 Edmund White, phone interview by Felice Picano.

14 Felice Picano, e-mail message to Adrian Brooks.

15 Rita Mae Brown, phone interview by Felice Picano.

PART II

◇◇◇◇◇

After Stonewall

Chapter 13

The Revolutionary Joy of Gary Alinder

by Paul Gabriel

Two couples rest in a shade-dappled spot, out of the California sun. The men stand in conversation, one with his hand companionably atop the shoulder of the other. Behind them on a bench, the two women sit in intimate ease, one's hand casually lying on the other's knee. Four figures of abstracted innocuous whiteness set against the sandstone and eucalyptus.

But this idyll is a refuge, and those figures are outcasts. Neither New York nor Los Angeles would suffer their presence. After much debate, Stanford University offered the pariahs sanctuary. But within a month, in the black of night, the faces and torsos of all four were battered forty times with a hammer. After a year of restoration, and within mere months of their return, the male figures were tagged with the scrawled invective: "AIDS." Eight years later, beset upon by drunken athletes, black paint was splattered across their whiteness and a bench violently rammed between a pair of them.

George Segal's sculpture was commissioned in 1979 to commemorate the Stonewall Riots of 1969, making it the first piece of public art of its kind. Controversy dogged the project from the outset. Why not a gay or lesbian artist? Why not more overtly activist content? Why such white, middle-class looking figures, drained of all visible difference?

Segal explained that he'd sought to depict normalcy: "The statement I tried to make is not political. It's rather a human one regarding our common humanity with homosexuals."

Our common humanity with homosexuals. The tensions in that phrase pointedly raise the question: What alienating "other" is there to *see* that is so radically threatening, so *queer*? If Stonewall was the moment when America was finally confronted by gay and lesbian people insisting on being themselves in public and on coming out, what was it seeing? And was the whole point to return to some kind of conformist invisibility?

Such questions resound in me. I wasn't one of Stonewall's generation of activists. Born in 1964 in a small rural town 90 miles from San Francisco, I am a child of Stonewall who grew up in a world in which homosexuality was seen with increasing frequency. Later, at Stanford, I recall being aware of the Segal statue, secretly wishing to see it but dreading being seen doing so—public identification with a dangerous identity.

The vicious battering of the statue symbolized the lessons I'd received growing up about boys found insufficiently masculine. After I came out, I lived and worked in Taiwan. As there were no public role models, no public spaces, no public means of association or identification, my partner and I improvised what being gay meant to us. Even so, on visits to my family I recall standing before Lesbian and Gay sections of bookstores in the Bay Area and wondering why the majority of the books were various versions of coming out "how to" manuals. Just what *was* this identity that was so intent on revealing itself? Was it mine...?

When my partner and I moved to San Francisco, I became deeply involved with the Gay and Lesbian Historical Society of Northern California and embarked on what became a ten-year passionate avocation of public history, gathering oral histories, and developing exhibitions and public events. Collectively, the people I met—organizers, lawyers, clergy, bar owners, bartenders, bar flies, drag queens, performers, bikers, freaks, leather men and women—were all radical activists. Each shaped me; each helped define me; each transformed me.

The origin of the word *radical* is...root, as in what turns some place deeply into a native soil and anchors it. One elder in particular taught me about how he uprooted what had been seen as abnormal and cultivated something radically different in the culture at large, and in himself. In him, and through him, a public movement for social justice and civil rights stood its ground. Homosexuality became something defiantly visible, defined resolutely and with dignity on its own terms—something that one might identify and associate oneself with, publicly rally around, and demonstrate and fight for.

Gary Alinder was born in 1944 in a rural Minnesota town of 400 residents. His Swedish Lutheran family was straitlaced. Because he didn't play sports, he felt like an outsider in the farming community where other boys called him "Mrs. Alinder" and "cocksucker." With no positive images of homosexuality, he had no frame of reference for his apparent difference. Years later, he recalled seeing two drag queens in Fellini's *8 1/2,* but that only reinforced their exotic nature as feathered creatures of far-off lands such as Europe or New York.

At the small college he first attended in 1962, his apparent femininity effectively excluded him from the campus community and was a major reason for his transfer to the University of Minnesota in 1964. There, as a major in journalism, he attended SDS meetings and had friends who had been Freedom Riders in the South. But during his sophomore year, when a friend took him to his first gay bar, he found it "dark and scary" and filled "with old queens" who struck him as "pathetic."

The 1965 March on Washington protesting the Vietnam War was the "life-changing event" that triggered a "social political awakening" in him. He attended as a reporter for the school paper, but the mass of over 50,000 people pushed him out of the role of neutral observer into that of a committed radical. As he met and mingled with a group that included whites, blacks, and communists from all over the country, he saw the Civil Rights Movement and earlier worker rights movements joining and broadening into the great social uprising of the Peace Movement.

After graduating college, he headed to New York to be part of what he saw as a revolution. Like many kindred spirits, he found subsistence work, but all of his time and energy from the fall of 1966 to the summer of 1969 went into the Peace Movement. He quite literally dropped out, turned on, and became a freak—smoking dope, dropping acid, growing his hair, and working to bring about a new world. As he remarked, "it was all civil disobedience," and "you couldn't be a long-haired hippie drug-taking freak and be a good soldier in Vietnam."

While doing mundane volunteer tasks for various peace organizations, he spent hours talking with older leftists, who mentored him with stories of past struggles. In 1967, he was part of a group that replicated the Summer of Love in New York, and in an SDS offshoot, participated in Teachers for a Democratic Society. Living in the Lower East Side, he would head down to Max's Kansas City Café at night, where he crossed paths with Andy Warhol's Factory crowd.

In early 1967, he joined over 100,000 demonstrators in the Peace March in New York. In October 1967, at the Washington, DC, Peace March, he was part of the Pentagon Sit-In. Seeing troops beat non-violent protestors with rifle butts was "radicalizing." He felt the same way about the draft, which deeply personalized political choices and glaringly high-lighted racial and socio-economic inequalities, since white college students like himself could so easily obtain deferments.

After DC, frustration at the inability to change the world through normal means led to anger; anger triggered further activism. He joined a group trying to close down the Induction Center on Whitehall Street by creating chaos in front of it. When President Johnson came to New York, Alinder was swept up off the streets with other protesters and jailed. He grew enthusiastic about the Yippie movement, since to him they were counter-cultural, politically active, "and wanted to have fun at the same time." Ultimately, he traveled with Yippies to Chicago for the protests at the 1968 Democratic Convention. But the chaotic violence that ensued gave him pause.

As did something else. Despite his intense activism, he had remained not only closeted but essentially celibate—his sexual life held in limbo. How could something so important remain so alien or be something he couldn't identify with or act on? How could he have remained so de-radicalized in this way?

Put simply, visibly gay people repelled him: "I had visions of what it looked like to be gay...[:] queens in Minneapolis...really funny muscle queens around Sheridan Square...swishy Puerto Rican guys.... I hadn't seen any image that I could identify with and say, oh, that's the way I could be gay." Alinder could not turn his radical training toward self-liberation until he could see others whom he wanted to be like. And be with. Though he'd attended peace marches with 100,000 people, he couldn't bond with gay men. Instead, for him, sexuality and gender were in a straitjacket, one that betrayed a haunting conflict between the image of American mascu-linity and queerness.

In the late sixties, Alinder lived in New York's Lower East Side, his building reflecting the motley groups seeking low rents—immigrant

Puerto Ricans and Polish/Ukranian Jews, and "long hairs" who brought with them "psychedelic shops." Upstairs was a neighbor living with her nineteen-year-old friend. When his boyfriend moved in, "a light bulb went off in my mind.... [We] became friends and it all fell into place...."

Another gay, longhaired freak who helped Alinder embrace his sexuality was the Yippie Jim Fouratt, a Gay Liberation activist. "It seemed," Alinder observed, musing on Fouratt's influence, "like the people in the [Peace Movement] weren't necessarily out to each other. Jim was radical, he was political, he was hip, he smoked dope, and he did all these things I could identify with...and he was out as being gay.... This was unusual in 1967/1968.... Even in the 60s among radical hip political people, counter-cultural people, it still wasn't hip to be gay."

Alinder was in New York when the Stonewall Riots occurred. Although he went by the next day to see the smashed storefront, it had no effect on him. He found drinking alcohol in bars "old school"; freaks smoked dope with friends and planned the revolution. And so he shrugged off the seminal scene, left New York, and moved to the Bay Area—determined to come out and fully integrate his activism with his sexuality. He saw Berkeley as the vanguard of counter-cultural leftist politics, San Francisco of alternative culture. Soon after arrival, he followed gay longhairs into a bar in San Francisco's North Beach, picked someone up, and finally had sex with a man. Ironically, a bar had launched his sexual freedom.

Alinder now turned his energies into gay activism. In October 1969, just a few months after landing in California, he co-founded the Gay Liberation Front in Berkeley. One of their earliest statements read:

> Complete sexual liberation for all people cannot come about until...
> we reject society's attempt to impose sexual roles and definitions of
> our nature.... We are going to be who we are. At the same time, we
> are creating new social forms and relations...based upon brother-
> hood, cooperation, human love and uninhibited sexuality.... [We]
> commit ourselves to one thing[:]...revolution.

Meetings often became consciousness-raising sessions; dances offered celebration; agitprop street theater and street actions, such as wearing buttons and holding hands, were staged. Unsupportive gay bars and homophobic newspaper columnists were picketed. And to commemorate the anniversary of Stonewall in June 1970, a Gay-In at Speedway Meadows in Golden Gate Park was held, with roughly 200 people gathering.

The hope for the cumulative effect of this flurry of activity is best captured in the name of a street sheet put out by a queer-freak collective Alinder co-founded—*Gay Sunshine*, referencing a particularly beloved type of LSD. Reading it was tantamount to tripping, unleashing a mind-blowing experience that would transform "closeted, self-hating gay persons into open, out, affirming, loving, wonderfully happy gay persons."

By 1971, Alinder felt burned out. "I was living on food stamps and hope and you just can't sustain that very long.... But 1966-1971 was the most intense period of my life." And there, his story of the sixties ends. Yet political activism and radical change aren't simply matters of organized protests and mass actions. Personal choices of dress, of behavior, of appearance, of how we look to others, signal who we are or what we dream. And these too are acts of civil disobedience.

Visually, the 60s were wildly kaleidoscopic. During the years of Alinder's activism, the Beatles grew their hair longer and longer, sprouted enormous manes, donned fantastical costumes, and invited the culture to join them in getting high with a little help from their friends. African-Americans wore enormous afros like halos about their heads, announcing exuberantly that black is beautiful. Women's bras burned along with draft cards. Breasts hung open. Belly buttons flashed as nudists gathered and painted themselves. In London, one month after Stonewall, Mick Jagger strutted and preened on stage in drag; one month after that, Woodstock flowered. It was a free-for-all and free to all.

Except, perhaps, for homosexuals.

In 1965, twelve homophile activists had picketed the White House. To us, they appear strangely quaint in their tailored suits, starched shirts, and prim dresses. It is easy to look with disdain on the homophile leaders of the 50s and early 60s as craven conformists, yet even the celebrated, radical founding members of the Mattachine Society all hid their identities.

Not until the mid-60s were there much more than a few dozen people who would publicly dare to identify by face and name as homosexual. Power is in numbers, and homosexuals were driven into the fearful isolation of dissemblance and double lives in much of the United States. Queer people might cavort, but were always at risk. They had no ownership over their places of assembly, which in large part explains the pent-up frustration unleashed at Stonewall. One activist, who lived in New York, remembers barely escaping a raid by climbing through a basement duct and exiting through a manhole onto the street. Mass action depends on free association, a fundamental right guaranteed by the Constitution. But free association depends on personal identification. A key early activist in San Francisco credits the hippies with inspiring gay people to become more expressive in public, since they exploded rigid codes of appropriate dress and deliberately blurred the lines between genders. Yet acting gay in public might mean being beaten up, just as living on one's own terms or challenging stereotypes (of gay men as inverted women and lesbians as inverted men) often created panic.

As Alinder trenchantly noted, "obvious gays" were often visibly unwelcome in a broad-based social justice and civil rights movement, ostensibly since they didn't fit the cause's public image. Or they made other activists personally uncomfortable. Liberation depends on individuals feeling good about themselves. And since the power of numbers is predicated on pride, there is something revolutionary about joy. Being gay is about the joy of physical proximity and touching. Alinder described the radical act of walking the streets of Berkeley while holding hands. Another kind of joyful gathering, one that is so emblematic of the sixties, is a dance; and as anarchist Emma Goldman is reported to have said, "If I can't dance, I don't want to be part of your revolution."

In June 1964, the year that Alinder had made his trip to the "dark and scary" gay bar in Minneapolis, an activist arranged for the first major gay dance held by a gay rights organization. Five hundred attended, and when the band struck up, they rushed to the center of the floor in a great roar of exuberant release and freedom. That joy is what activists were fighting for—the right to feel good, to be free, and to be together to share that wonderful elixir of liberation. It resonated in the histories and lives I had witnessed: a fully open visibility. If hippies had Woodstock, gay men and women also had their tribal gatherings of life-altering celebration.

San Francisco's activism definitely changed after January 1, 1965: a New Year's dance, the third large event of its kind. The occasion was public; the authorities were notified as to its time and location, and that the dance would be a fundraiser for gay and lesbian organizations. Arriving with klieg lights, still cameras, movie cameras, and paddy wagons, the police meant to shine a bright, shaming light on the attendees and all night sought a pretext to shut it down. Yet once they had forced entry with four arrests—despite all the men in extravagant drag, despite the dancing of same sex couples, despite there being hundreds of queers in attendance—only one further arrest occurred. The offense: that two men, dressed as men, rested their hands on each other's shoulders to steady themselves as they stood on chairs to get a better view of the festive crowd.

In a world in which LGBT people come in all shapes and sizes, the whiteness of Segal's figures gestures towards the presence of all colors in equal measure. All things being equal that way, when all else visible is stripped away, what is left is the simple act of same-sex touch in public. How can anything so small and innocent loom so large and threatening?

At the 1968 Olympics in Mexico, two American black athletes stood on the podium, medals hanging down from their necks as their clenched fists rose up in a defiant salute to Black Power. They had made that brave choice, but still had no choice as to their race.

LGBT people can choose to hide, to cover, to deny, and to play straight. But coming out radically personalizes a larger social and political decision, and makes the public and private fully intermingled. It is a decision to step into visibility, to take it to the streets, to demonstrate by being demonstrative. There can be no denying its meaning once performed for all to see. It is radical. It is quintessentially queer. It is a revolutionary joy.

Chapter 14

Lesbian Nation: Jill Johnston and the Revolution of Women

by Victoria A. Brownworth

Jill Johnston was the face of in-yer-face radical lesbianism, who taught us all how to be lesbians in the decade after Stonewall. We read the *Village Voice* in our bedrooms, our parents downstairs none-the-wiser that we were learning how to be radical lesbians from a weekly column printed all in lowercase letters from a lanky, long-haired lesbian who was nothing like what "lesbian" meant to their generation. When we started writing without caps, they thought we were emulating the poet e. e. cummings, and found it sweetly adolescent. But we were really emulating Johnston. And she wasn't sweet. She was revolutionary. She was our role model and our parents' worst nightmare.

From her we would learn the most important lesson of our young lives: "All women can be lesbians." It was the kind of permission slip we would never get from any other teacher. But we got it from her, and we ran with it into the arms of the lesbian movement.

People come out every day, now. Actresses and sports figures, well-known musicians and low-level politicians. It's commonplace, yet it's still news—because being lesbian or gay is still shocking, still a surprise, still makes people say, "I didn't know *he* was gay" or "She doesn't *look* like a lesbian."

But in 1971, when Jill Johnston came out in her *Village Voice* column it wasn't merely newsworthy, it was incendiary. Johnston was the first to state, unequivocally, without any bisexual fallback position, that she was a lesbian on the pages of a nationally known publication. *Lesbian, lesbian, lesbian.* She was the walking evocation of Pandora's box: once she pried the lid off the sexual orientation that dare not speak its name, she was off and running—stream of consciousness lesbianism, quirky linguistic tropes, encoded revolution: these were her stock in trade as every week she flooded her column inches with words and images no one had seen in print before, except in *those* kind of books.

She was Second Wave feminism's rowdy Gertrude Stein; for her, Rose was a rose was a lesbian was a legs-spread-wide sexual convert to Sapphism. Johnston would keep saying it until we got it. (She even sounded like Stein, with passages like "it is all a change. writing is changing. the writing is changing. changing is such good writing.")

Johnston had begun writing for the *Village Voice* in 1959 as a dance critic. The paper founded by Dan Wolf, Ed Fancher, and Norman Mailer (the man with whom she would later tangle in a very public battle of the sexes) was then only four years old. Johnston was a thirty-year-old devotee of the dance genre. She had danced briefly, but then had worked in the New York Public Library's Dance Collection and had been writing dance criticism for various journals.

At the *Voice,* Johnston became entrenched and entranced; her work began to evolve, melding her reporting and criticism with personal inter-polations. She became both critic and performance artist. Her columns, written in all lowercase letters and with only sporadic punctuation, had the look, feel, and sound of something urgent, something brewing, some-thing about to erupt.

She would write of that time:

As the combustible sixties progressed, writing itself, such as collage-like assemblages of 'found' sentences, increasingly devoured the space allotted to me for the review of works by artists and chore-ographers. The *Voice* was collusive in this subversion, ultimately altering my status to that of columnist. Now I was a chronicler of my own life, by sixties standards perhaps not too egregiously adventurous and experimental, but in a newspaper in full public view, in the most fractured Dada style of work I had admired as a critic–a rather wild spectacle in those woolly times.

She went on to say:

As more time passed, and my subjects expanded to include the feminist politics and activism of the late sixties/early seventies, this extreme style of writing, by then a signature, became a problem. An art of high amusement and contempt for authority often seemed unserviceable for serious political rhetoric. But a deeper conflict of interests was at work.

Awakened to my life in the mid-sixties, I was seized by a new ambition—more powerful in its way than my first. Not, as it may seem, to write about my life, i.e., in any diarist or memoirist sense, but rather to address my story. The life I had awakened to was my story, my origins, which in my case were fairly unusual, now seemingly impossible to ignore.

Johnston was on the verge of coming out on the pages of the newspaper. Something for which there was no template. Something which demanded a new rubric—and yet there was none.

So she created it.

It was a brief run, but a powerful one. She left the *Voice* in 1981, before AIDS, before the mainstreaming of lesbians. But in the 1970s, people who could not name a single other lesbian in America could name Johnston, although Gloria Steinem was the face of mainstream feminism.

In the 1970s, when she was the lesbian voice of the *Village Voice,* hers was a voice like no other. Unlike those voices from women-only spaces that abjured anyone but lesbians to buy their music or books, Johnston was a lesbian separatist with a mainstream newspaper platform promoting subversion to all and sundry. Her columns read like poetic yet urgent reports from the front lines in the battle against patriarchy. Weekly she was fomenting something that should have been perceived as dangerous, with her statement that "until all women are lesbians, there will be no true political revolution."

And yet, there was something about Johnston that allowed her to keep writing those subversive, revolutionary missives without being stopped or silenced or stymied. In 1973 Johnston published *Lesbian Nation,* a collection of essays culled in part from her *Village Voice* column. Yet here's what the *New York Review of Books* wrote of this iconoclastic collection: "Nobody could be more American than Jill Johnston in her very original book *Lesbian Nation.* Johnston comes on like a flood, vivacious, mile-a-minute, with an uncontrollable eloquence. No, not uncontrollable. The writing has liquidity, but also energy, and wit. Johnston is a genuine writer."

Had they even understood what they had read? Did they note the title? It was just four years after Stonewall—it's not as if out lesbianism was being embraced nationwide or even in New York City. But the book's title quickly became part of a popular lexicon of hip metaphor and gay subtext. Its essays included "Slouching Toward Consciousness," "The Making of a Lesbian Chauvinist," "Lois Lane was a Lesbian," "There Wasn't a Dyke in the Land," and "Amazons and Archdykes."

Dyke.

Johnston used that word in her columns and in the book. It was 1970s lesbian separatist radical argot, and *Lesbian Nation* was a pivotal text. Kate Millet said *Lesbian Nation* was "the most important book to come out of the women's movement."

"Intersectionality" has shunted lesbian separatism aside. But at the time it was written, *Lesbian Nation* was an essentialist primer, with its unavoidable title. In the early 1970s, when feminism was splintering into straight and lesbian, *Lesbian Nation: The Feminist Solution* seemed a clear-cut answer to a nagging question.

In *Lesbian Nation*, Johnston elucidates her vision of what that means, deconstructing radical lesbian feminism for the neophyte and doyenne alike. She makes her case over and over for lesbian separatism, explaining why women needed to make a complete break from men and the male-dominated capitalist system that was 20th-century patriarchy.

She riled up mainstream feminists, who were already purging lesbians from the ranks of NOW (National Organization for Women) and other feminist groups, because straight feminists feared the lesbian taint. They didn't want feminism to be associated with "man-hating," and lesbianism was already synonymous with that.

Johnston couldn't have cared less what mainstream feminism wanted or thought. She threw gasoline right on that sparking fire, writing that female heterosexuality was a form of collaboration with patriarchy. Which meant straight feminists were in bed with the oppressor. And not just that: Johnston was making out with women in public at literary forums before performance art was even an idea. She kissed a girl, and she liked it, and she was going to show everyone that lesbians didn't have to hide. Those days were over, she explained. Johnston had presaged groups like ACT-UP and Queer Nation by more than a decade.

Yet all over America, closet doors were still firmly shut in the vast space between Greenwich Village and Haight-Ashbury in San Francisco, the loci of out lesbians and gays.

How to create that *Lesbian Nation*, that revolution of women? Johnston urged women to become lesbians, to leave men behind to fend for themselves. Johnston made history by stating that women did not have to be with men sexually, nor marry them; in fact, Johnston wrote, to do so would be complicit, to be a collaborationist who engaged with the enemy: the same patriarchy that promoted and supported the oppression of all women. Johnston was adamant: all women were inherently lesbian and just needed to access their lesbian selves by divesting themselves of men.

Johnston was saying to women what Malcolm X had said to blacks.

Johnston had left her husband in 1958—still a shocking event at that time, especially as she had two children. In the sometimes restrictive era of Second Wave feminism, Johnston's declarations stirred passions: anger and resentment, adoration and fealty. In the burgeoning Second Wave of feminism, to state unequivocally that men were the enemy was considered tactically inappropriate, particularly among feminists who were trying to re-create feminism as a mainstream movement, ostensibly for straight women—lesbians need not apply.

Johnston's often outrageous statements made those in the feminist hierarchy, like Betty Friedan (Friedan called Johnston "the biggest enemy of the movement") and Gloria Steinem (who had written of *Lesbian Nation:* "Jill Johnston's book is honest, outrageous, stylistically unique, brave, vulnerable, and full of love. If you read it, you will never be sure of anything.") either acutely uncomfortable or secretly thrilled by her in-yer-face politics.

Confusing matters was the fact that *Lesbian Nation* hadn't been published by an alternative women's press, like Daughters or Persephone, two main lesbian presses of that period. It was published by one of the Big Six: Simon & Schuster. Mainstream New York hardcover publishing. The significance of that simple fact can't be overstated. Johnston left people in awe. How was she doing it? They didn't know what to make of her, this Ché of radical lesbian feminism. They gave her a wide berth, tried to size her up, but she defied description. No one else was spouting the rhetoric of lesbian separatism on a weekly basis anywhere except perhaps in their own living rooms or on women-only land in Oregon.

Johnston gave up lesbian separatist politics and altered the style of her writing before the end of the 1980s. As she explained in 2007, "Once I understood the feminist doctrines, a lesbian-separatist position seemed the commonsensical position, especially since, conveniently, I was an L-person. Women wanted to remove their support from men, the 'enemy' in a movement for reform, power, and self-determination."

In the few years between Stonewall and when Johnston came out, lesbian separatism had become a burgeoning movement, and Johnston was its most visible purveyor and loudest voice. Gay liberation had largely excluded lesbians; it would be a few more years before L joined G to form the lesbian and gay movement, and longer still before it would become the LGBT movement. But separatists like Johnston wanted that "lesbian nation" she envisioned, and Johnston saw it as not only necessary, but inevitable.

She wrote:

A small but significant number of angry and historically minded women comprehend the women's revolution in the visionary sense of an end to the catastrophic brotherhood and a return to the former glory and wise equanimity of the matriarchies. We don't know how this will take place exactly, nor the resultant nature of the new social forms, [but] we know that it *will* take place, and in fact that the process of its development is now irreversibly underway. Of supreme importance in this process is the recovery by modern woman of her mythology as models for theory, consciousness, and action....

The glory of the matriarchies.

This language—and Johnston's own description of herself as "east west flower child beat hip psychedelic paradise now love peace do your own thing approach to the revolution" was part of what separated her from heterosexual feminists, despite her insistence that all women could and should be lesbians.

Johnston's outrageousness was never more keenly on display than during the (now-notorious) literary panel disrupted by Johnston at New York's Town Hall, as she challenged—in person—everything she had previously challenged in print: patriarchy, mainstream feminism, collaboration with the enemy.

One of the most scandalous events of the feminist movement, the "Dialogue on Women's Liberation," was held at New York's Town Hall on April 30th, 1971, and later detailed in the documentary *Town Bloody*

Hall, directed by Chris Hegedus and D.A. Pennebaker. A group of staid feminist lions—the critic Diana Trilling, NY NOW president Jacqueline Ceballos, feminist writer Germaine Greer, and then the wild Johnston—took on Norman Mailer and his recently released anti-feminist treatise, "The Prisoner of Sex," in which Mailer addressed the role of feminism on male-female relationships.

Like the tennis match between Billie Jean King and Bobby Riggs that would happen in 1973, Mailer was utterly outmatched.

The debate would ultimately be between Mailer and Greer, but that was because Johnston so disrupted the proceedings that Mailer was in a state while Trilling and Ceballos were simply stunned.

This wasn't some intimate meeting—the event had been widely publicized, and many literary and feminist heavyweights were in attendance, like Susan Sontag and Johnston's nemesis, Betty Friedan.

Johnston had already angered straight feminists by jumping into a pool, topless, at a fundraising event. The Town Hall event started out tame and then became a free-for-all, thanks to Johnston, who used the event to bring her guerilla feminism to a larger audience.

Johnston's first statement set the stage, literally, when she declared: "All women are lesbians except those who don't know it yet." Then Johnston had one of her female lovers jump onto the stage and began kissing her. A third woman joined them, and Johnston mimicked sex on the floor of the stage with the two women—clothed, but explicit—flummoxing Mailer and prompting him to plead, "Come on, Jill, be a lady!"

But Johnston, true to her revolutionary spirit, was proving that women no longer had to seek male approval or be "ladies" in public or private. Mailer was trounced by Johnston's activist approach. Johnston later wrote about the event, and Mailer's own biographer noted that the Town Hall evening was "one of the most singular intellectual events of the time, and a landmark in the emergence of feminism."

That was two years before *Lesbian Nation* was published. Mainstream feminism was already tired of Johnston, and her controversial theories and behavior before that book never saw print.

It's difficult to explain to a post-feminist, post-Stonewall audience how dramatically iconic Johnston's writing was at the time, and what a trailblazer she was. As Betty Friedan had broken the silence about women's unhappiness in the middle-class home in *The Feminine Mystique*, in *Lesbian Nation*, Johnston had broken a different code—the one in which women, even closeted lesbians, were bound irrevocably to men. As she wrote: "Many feminists are now stranded between their personal needs and their political persuasions. The lesbian is the woman who unites the personal and political in the struggle to free ourselves from the oppressive institution [of marriage].... By this definition lesbians are in the vanguard of the resistance."

It was heady stuff in those days, when marriage to a man was the goal for women, and to not be married was somehow to be less of a woman (and thus a perennially incomplete person). Johnston's words were so influential—and unsettling—that her approach to lesbian feminism caused a schism within the lesbian and feminist communities. Some lesbians insisted on referring to themselves as "gay" to differentiate themselves from the women who followed Johnston, while straight feminists distanced themselves from her and her anti-male rhetoric.

Johnston spent her later years writing about art, dance, literature, politics, and her own life. She published more books after *Lesbian Nation* and was a book critic for the *New York Times* and an art critic for *Art in America*. She, who had been so bawdy and written about her sexual exploits in *Lesbian Nation,* married her partner of thirty years, Ingrid Nyeboe.

For a full generation, Johnston's manifesto was the foundation for feminist theory. She redefined how lesbians looked at their lives—not in relation to men, but in relation to themselves and each other. She reinterpreted our gaze to reflect only women. She made us understand why we had to put women first, last, always—whether we were separatists or not.

The memory of *Lesbian Nation* may have faded. But what Johnston did was tear that closet door off its hinges and toss it right in the face of patriarchy. She spoke openly and passionately about her lesbian sexuality at a time when no one had done so. She recounted days of lovemaking with more than one woman, and in writing about these experiences for a newspaper—a newspaper—she obliterated all mystique of hidden lesbian sexuality.

What we gleaned from her was a way of being: She gave girls (and women) a crash course in lesbianism. She waved men off like flies. She put Mailer in his sexist place in a way no one has before or since. Compelling, provocative, prescient. Jill Johnston was indeed an iconoclast. And she breathed life into an idea/ideal: lesbian nation. That is her legacy and our history.

Chapter 15

The Angels of Light: Paris Sites Under the Bourgeois Sea

by Adrian Brooks

Backstage, footlights spread a blue wash on a scrim behind enormous velvet curtains. It was 8 p.m. I could hear our audience roar. Whooping and hollering were commonplace at Angels of Light performances, but this was virtual pandemonium. Still, I was preoccupied.

Behind me stood a cardboard palace. In the show, my character presided over it. The glittery white and silver residence faced slums on the far side of the set. The visual contrast couldn't have been more explicit. Off in the wings, I saw props and masks: a carriage with prancing horses, plague monsters resembling fanged crabs, giant rats, icebergs...

I was alone. The rest of the cast was getting into costume or smoking grass outside. So for a moment, I had the stage to myself.

An aquamarine-colored haze resembling fountain mist rose from a prompter's box to the proscenium forty feet above. I held a white ostrich feather in sapphire blue glittering talons; the billowing plume wafted across my field of vision.

I looked at my costume and laughed.

My ball gown was pale blue lace and pink satin spangled with silver stars and violet velvet bow. Birdcage-like contraptions at my waist thrust the skirt out three feet on each side. My neck was sheathed in rhinestones, a virtual pillar of "diamonds." Amethyst-colored drops dangled from the bodice. But that was just the beginning.

As the show's Big Meanie—Countess Flushette, a shuddering, vicious totem of bile—I sported a life-sized toilet on my head. It crowned a grey-powdered wig festooned with tiny pink roses. From its bowl, a massive forearm thrust triumphantly upwards, its fist clasping a pink ostrich feather. I stand six-foot-two. Factoring in the headgear and huge hoops sticking out from my waist, from my shoes to the tip of my nodding plume, I was six feet wide and ten feet tall. I'd become something *else*, transformed into a creature no longer bound by the Ordinary.

Someone gestured urgently from the wings. *"Have you seen the audience?"* he cried. *"Look!"* Following his cue without crashing my headdress into the wall, I peeked out from a backstage peephole. For an instant, I couldn't believe my eyes. Startled, I drew back before leaning forward again.

Something has gone horribly awry, I thought. *This is way more than we bargained for!* I tried to appear confident but my knees felt weak.

Herbst Auditorium was a neo-classical theater. Crystal chandeliers were suspended from a ceiling painted with cherubs and angels. Tapestries and murals adorned the walls. The upholstery was maroon velvet. And from the orchestra pit to the top of the last row of balcony, the eleven hundred seats were packed. Packed. Despite the throng, hundreds crammed the aisles, trying to find a place to sit before the house lights blinked and dimmed. By unanimous opinion—then and later—no one had ever seen anything like it.

Naturally, the adoring gay community was out in force. But all manner of other folk were also present, people who'd never—ever—crossed the boundary from "normal, social daylight" into the subterranean zone of the sexual underground.

Further complicating the surreal situation was that no one group clearly outnumbered any others. This meant that none of the contending delegations could stake a believable claim to being an indignant majority.

Mavens in black dresses and pearls sat beside bearded drag queens in black dresses and pearls. A virtually naked bald man draped in a bright-green sari sat next to a Marine colonel in full uniform, family in tow. Glittering cross-dressers sized up representatives from the Lions Club. Masons and Elks stared as black men in sequined dresses paraded in. Suburban station-wagon families scanned dykes in plaid shirts. Stoned-out hippies offered joints to veterans of World War I, some tottering in on canes, sporting medals won at the Marne. Studs in black-leather caps and straps, their bare buns hanging out of chaps, gazed quizzically at white-haired ladies in flowery summer dresses and sneakers. They crocheted as cowboys strutted past Korean War vets and hairy gay "bears." Pom-poms on a Mexican sombrero bounced ever so gaily as a man giggled beside a tweedy pipe-smoking type whose wife wore sensible shoes and tortoise-shell barrettes; they huddled over the program to be sure they were in the right place as Latino queens and Chinese businessmen maneuvered for a spare seat next to stodgy museum-going types and blond androgens in satin slips (their hair braided with flowers and ribbons), beefy truck drivers, and grande dames in fur stoles, diamond brooches, and chic hats with delicate veils. Wheeled in by nurses, the aged clutched lap blankets, grinning in toothless delight, eyes bugging out of their heads. Every imaginable contingent in the Bay Area was out in full force and, by contrast, now found that *they were in drag, no matter how they were actually dressed.* Meanwhile, hanging overhead like a pungent shroud, there was a thick haze of marijuana smoke.

What we didn't know—what no one had ever told us—was that Herbst Theater, which was under the auspices of the San Francisco Museum of Art, was also shared and claimed by the United States military, who called it Veteran's Auditorium. Anything sponsored by the museum would also be publicized on mailings distributed to veterans of the Armed Services. In short, every local soldier of every war, going back to the Spanish-American War of 1898, had been duly notified that the Angels of Light were staging a free multi-media spectacular—"a pièce de résistance"— in a forum they considered theirs! Moreover, it was playing to a packed house, with police vans and fire engines parked outside, ready to rush in and rescue the crowd because the inside screams triggered rumors that a riot was about to break out. Hearing that the police were about to make a mass arrest, television channels dispatched news teams. Helicopters with cameras whirred overhead, but even when people explained, "it's just an Angels of Light show," neither the Fire Marshal nor the Chief of Police dared try to invade or interrupt for fear of triggering a panic in which people could be trampled and killed.

At our best, the Angels created shows that seemed almost conjured into existence, as if arising from Aladdin's magical lamp. And yet it was more— much, much more. But every single component—onstage and off—could be mysterious and alluring. It was like a world of Chinese boxes; the further in one went, the more spellbinding it could all become. What the people out front would see was only the dazzling and outrageous surface.

Part of the living poetry evoked existed full-blown backstage, in the wings. Between there and the audience were other layers of reality and theater magic—in a revolutionary underground subculture inside San Francisco's radical gay liberation vanguard. These were psychic choices, too. They permitted each of us to shuck off past selves and leap full-blown into existence in an odyssey of self-discovery and self-manifestation.

Costumed dancers wandered by. Off to the side, there were giant puppets. Backstage, people were doing stretches or practicing tumbling. A few children were also there, children raised in the theater commune. To them, all this was normal, their way of life. And a few were even in the show.

Was this my life? Yes. But I hadn't stumbled upon this by accident. Most Angels had managed to extricate ourselves from dysfunctional families to go searching for something magical, even if we hadn't known what it was until we found others as intoxicated by dress-up and the delirious refuge of "let's pretend." And so we'd created a safe zone well beyond the reach of controlling elders, where we could choose magic over reality.

This was our secret society, then: a free political movement and new theatrical art. It fused Gilbert and Sullivan to the Mummer's Parade, or Cirque du Soleil to Brecht with a dose of Antonin Artaud thrown in for good measure. In this world, "more was more." But it was no mere avant-garde; avant-garde implies social connectedness, or possible future integration. We were Underground—part of a wholly different tribe. Yet this Beggar's Opera had become the thrilling cultural figurehead of gay liberation culture, so far past the point of being past the point that, even in San Francisco, we set the wild pace. Andy Warhol had asked me to be his front person in 1970, but San Francisco was so much more interesting. Here, Harvey Milk worked for political change inside the system, but the Angels, who decorated our truck for his rallies and who were his artistic counterparts and friends, were co-equivalent: the electric, provocative radicals out on the cutting edge. The whole point was a gift of love to community, as well as self-expression mirrored by like-minded souls.

"We were exploding the myth of success," said Martin Worman, a writer, playwright, actor, director, and, later, a teacher at New York University. "Of course, it was political, but no one among us verbalized it. We had no need of rhetoric. We were madcap chefs cooking up a storm. The ingredients were magic and tribal anarchy."

* * *

Act 1 Scene 1: the curtains part on *Paris Sites Under the Bourgeois Sea*—
say it out loud and fast—to reveal a street scene in which starving people
curse their poverty and lament a plague decimating the populace. As the
ragged peasants struggle to survive, a cardboard carriage suddenly shoots
out from the wings, running over and killing a small child.

The coach's curtains part. Countess Burst-Wyth-Pee sticks her head
out, her rubbery jowls hanging down to her shoulders, her wig capped
with a urinating little man who shoots pee from his penis.

Countess: What was that bump? Why have we stopped?

Poor man: A child is dead under the wheels of your carriage!

Countess: Well you should have thought of that before overpopu-
lating. But you people have absolutely no sense of social responsibility. (*to
her coachman*) Drive on.

The countess swirls away, leaving the poor to vow revenge. They gather
to sing their anthem of defiance: "We're tired of being hungry and poor.
Soon, you aristocrats will know how we feel."

A mime sequence follows. Poirot enacts "The Spirit of Victory Comes
to Paris" as noted in the program: a tribute to a slain Black Panther militant. Windows in the palace open, and, in a lovely pas de deux, the beautiful girl Nostalgia Flushette throws a red rose to her revolutionary lover.

Nostalgia emerges into the street, but her mother follows: in a mother-
daughter confrontation, the villainous Countess Flushette tries to manipu-
late her rebellious child's concern for the plight of the downtrodden poor.
She sings a song titled "Let Them Eat Shit":

Let them eat shit—mangez gateau
Especially baked at our country chateau.
Their clothes are so shabby and their hair, a mess
Their cuts are quite scabby, and I couldn't care less.

Refusing to listen to Nostalgia's outrage, the Countess bulldozes her
daughter inside.

Scene 2 takes place in a boudoir. Here, three countesses, each of whom
measure ten feet tall and six feet wide (thanks to enormous *panniers*),
sit on thrones twenty feet tall. They squawk like demented chickens
while being attended by a servant girl, who helps them prepare for the
surprise betrothal of Nostalgia to wealthy Prince Mince. While "Countless" Tricks *oohs* and *aahs*, Countess Burst-Wyth-Pee's little man urinates

into Countess Flushette's toilet, prompting an orgasm of aristocratic glee. In an aside, Countess Flushette reveals that, in the event of revolt, she'd take flight into her secret submarine, now concealed in the garden. Never suspecting that everything they said would be passed on to their enemies by the servant girl/spy, the three Countesses gush and primp in solipsistic and depraved decadence.

Scene 3 is set in the grand gallery of the palace: a Hall-of-Mirrors-like perspective with pilasters capped with bleeding dragons. Here, two Counts—gay as tunes—simper over their flings with slaves, their "chocolate bon-bons." Joined by the three countesses—the still-unsuspecting and resentful Nostalgia in tow—the Flushettes suddenly reveal the true purpose of the gathering: to introduce the girl to her future husband.

Accompanied onstage by baskets of his money, Prince Mince wafts in: an anemic fifty-year-old in violet satin, scarcely able to stand. None of that matters, however, as the giddy aristocrats stick their noses in the cash before turning to gorge on a banquet.

Countess Burst-Wyth-Pee: Oh! I love money! The older and smellier the better!

Nostalgia: I won't do it! He's disgusting!

Countess Flushette: But everything is all arranged!

Nostalgia: I don't care. You can take your plans and stuff them!

A guard: The poor people are storming the palace!

Countess Flushette: Quick! Let's eat while there's still time!

The aristocrats stuff their faces as the poor and insane and plague-stricken invade, accompanied by giant rats. Sword fights ensue.

Countess Flushette: Get out! Get out! You're not on the list and you weren't invited!

An insane man (*legs up, his ass to the audience*): Fuck me! Fuck me!

The nobles are toppled, but the Countess escapes.

Scene 4 takes place in the secret submarine. Though Countess Flushette bursts in, ordering the crew south to her Villa Caprice, they mutiny when a heroic clairvoyant urges them to go to the North Pole to find a cure for the plague ravaging Paris. The Countess kicks her to death, but is imprisoned as the crew sets off on their quest.

Act 2 begins at the North Pole. Here, penguins do a tap dance among glittery icebergs of the minimal, lunar landscape. A Kabuki-dancing blizzard freezes the Countess Flushette to death. As she dies, the servant girl spy and her lover—Harlequin—rush in, but fall through the ice to their doom.

Scene 2 unfolds at the bottom of the Bourgeois Sea, with a life-sized whale lowered onto coral reefs populated by mermaids and a starfish. The blissful underwater idyll of Harlequin and the servant girl is interrupted by a bathyscope lowered from the submarine. Divers emerge, having found a mystic rose—the cure for the Plague—and return to the vessel to sail back to Paris.

Scene 3—a wild finale: the poor celebrate their victory over the Forces of Oppression. Their triumphal dance includes hoisting colorful banners and waving North Vietnamese flags right in front of U.S. Veterans of Foreign Wars, who love it and applaud, cheering along with the rest of the audience in a flash or bolt of San Francisco joy.

It was a moment of pure art and pure anarchy: radicals slipping in under the radar to take over a major American cultural institution. This was revolution we could believe in! *Paris Sites* was only the second free event the Museum ever sponsored. In content, and as agitprop, nothing could have been more political.

The mime piece brought the issue of prison violence to the stage. The inclusion of first-generation gay lib poets like Tede Matthews and myself infused the theater with another artistic voice in the social and political vanguard. Beyond text, however, the creative melding or overlapping was a form of solidarity.

As Harvey Milk hoped for election, *Paris Sites* was a public manifesto. This was our avowed intention. The radical gay culture of San Francisco fused with rising social, personal, and political community aspirations. *Paris Sites Under the Bourgeois Sea* represented a crystallization. And in that one instant, the Angels spoke for all gay people.

As the show's villainess, I thrilled in my off-the-wall parody of the *ancien régime,* rendered in plummeting yet defiant fall. Countess Flushette was on a bad, bad trip—spitting evil, hissing with greed and spite, a shuddering tower of loathsome venom, jewels, pastel plumes, and bows—even worse than horrible (and *very* funny). There was nothing feminine about her. It takes a man to be a woman that bad, and I was surely a monument to odium and stinking bile. The audience loved that blow-it-out-your-ass über-symbol of Awful symbolizing the rising tide of gay outrage, gay love, and gay revolution after ten years of government malfeasance, all crowned by a fisted toilet.

Yet even as I performed I thought: *Don't try to hold on to this. This is too big. It's something to adore in the split-second, but let it go; you only represent it or incarnate it in this brief flash. It's Truth using you as its figurehead. So love it, revel in being the lightning rod and electric weathervane, but don't cling... because it's unmanageable.*

With *Paris Sites*, the Glitter Age—an offspring of the hippie movement all dolled up in spangles—and one part of the radical underground gay culture crested, so soon replaced by Punk Rock and then by an unimaginable plague, which the show surrealistically forecast.

Chapter 16

Anita Bryant's Anti-Gay Crusade

by Jeanne Córdova

Anita Bryant ruined my softball career. At thirty, my playdates ended in 1978 as the Gay Liberation Movement was compelled to morph from a radical sub-culture into a national civil rights struggle.

Born in 1948, and growing up with eleven siblings in Southern California, I'd left the sisterhood of a Catholic convent by twenty-five and joined the sisterhood of lesbian nation—becoming the president of Los Angeles's Daughters of Bilitis. Young, angry, and butch, I was the dyke a sexist didn't want to meet at night: a veteran who had organized two national lesbian conferences and a national newsmagazine, *The Lesbian Tide*.

By 1977, gays and lesbians were confident. In seven years, we'd won the repeal of sex laws and gay protections in jobs and housing in 19 states and 40 cities. Our latest victory was in Florida, where Dade County Commissioners passed a gay rights ordinance. But Anita Bryant—a Sarah Palin-like 1950s singer, now promoting Florida oranges on TV—led a local protest pledging to overturn Dade's "evil decision." The evangelist seemed laughable when she first spoke about "men wearing dresses" teaching in public schools and "the devastation of the moral fiber of the youth of America."

But six months later the parody turned serious.

Bryant gathered the necessary signatures to put a referendum on Dade's June 7th, 1977 ballot—one that would repeal the city's new gay ordinance. Voters sided with her. They repealed our employment and housing rights.

Five days later, gays and lesbians from fifteen cities across America took to the streets. Ten thousand marched in Los Angeles. Five thousand angry San Franciscans protested. Activist Harvey Milk, a newly elected city councilman, was the main rally speaker. Lesbians in Los Angeles marched under a banner proclaiming, "Hitler. McCarthy. Anita." Speaking to the crowd, I announced Bryant's new alliance with Phyllis Schlafly, America's top anti-feminist and an arch-foe of the embattled ERA—equal rights for women.

But Dade County sideswiped our fledgling movement. As Anita moved from Florida to Minneapolis-St. Paul, then to Wichita, Kansas, and then onto Eugene, Oregon, she championed the values of Jerry Falwell's Moral Majority, and her own new nonprofit, Save Our Children, Inc. As she did, gay and lesbian Californians began to realize: she had national plans.

Watching Minneapolis fall was especially depressing. It was a university town, a liberal city. How could they have lost? Worse yet, Bryant convinced her followers to call gay rights "special rights." Within months, she'd become a national anti-gay spokesperson: an advocate who railed against a woman's right to choose (abortion) and called the peace movement to end the Vietnam War, "a war between atheism and God." What we didn't realize at first was that John Briggs, an ambitious state senator from Orange County (Southern California's Bible belt), had rushed to Florida to support her. Briggs aspired to higher office. So when Anita came west and joined him, our community went on alert. But where would she attack? Rumors abounded that they'd target San Francisco's year-old gay rights ordinance or Governor Jerry Brown's recent decriminalization of sodomy.

Two days after Dade, Morris Knight, L.A.'s grassroots leader, had summoned gay leaders to his house to talk about its implications. The mood was anxious, but angry, as sixty hardcore activists—gay men and lesbians—formed the Coalition for Human Rights, one of the first groups to organize. The next evening, I was at the Westside Women's Center, where 130 lesbians formed the Ad Hoc Committee for Lesbian Rights to bring straight feminists into the fight against Bryant. Months later, gay Leftists would form the Action Coalition and target people of color like voters in Watts, with the door-to-door message, "Discrimination: Who's Next?"

But Bryant and Briggs hit us where we were weakest. Victories made them ready to go statewide in California. And they did so, by launching a ballot measure dubbed Proposition 6. Instead of a city-based attack on gay employment or housing, the Briggs Initiative played to the fear of heterosexuals that we wanted to "recruit" their children. It mandated that all "teachers, counselors, aides or administrators" who "advocate, solicit, impose, encourage, or promote private or public homosexual activity" could be dismissed, *as could any heterosexual who supported gay rights.* Reading it, the first thing that came to my mind was Senator McCarthy's vicious anti-communist smear campaign of the 1950s.

Activists were shocked and panicked. How the hell were we going to convince a statewide majority of straight people that gay teachers posed no threat to their children? Most of us, estimated to be 25% to 30% of all teachers, were still in the closet. Losing would decimate the school system.

We had good reason to worry. According to the Harris poll, only 27% of the country believed that "homosexuals" should be allowed to work as "counselors in a camp for young people."

Panic turned to rage as Oklahoma and Arkansas banned gay teachers. Yet Bryant created a surge. Thousands of gays and lesbians came out across the country. Galvanized rank and file, as well as leaders, seemed to say, *"We've slaved for a half decade and sworn to destroy our closets. We will not give up."*

In the spring of 1978, as San Francisco, Los Angeles, and San Diego mobilized, I flew north with our "No on 6" statewide campaign to find the Bay Area more organized and yet more fractious than Southern California. Still, we realized for the first time we had to fight on television as a united people. And TV ads meant money. Not thousands, but millions.

In the meeting hall, I saw the northern community divided along political lines. Their assimilationist wing wanted to persuade straights that, "We [gays] are just like you and deserve our rights." Harvey Milk's centrist populists coined and embraced the phrase, "the suits versus the streets." Even so, they agreed to jointly strategize with David Goodstein's conservative Concerned Voters of California. The socialists—the Bay Area Committee Against the Briggs Initiative—would fly separately, but they brought in labor unions and the POC (people of color) community. Goodstein, publisher of *The Advocate*, had publicly predicted, "We will lose." But we agreed that there would be no more public airings of our personal doubts.

Returning to Los Angeles, I became part of my city's largest gay rights "get-out-the-vote" campaign. But first we had to bring disparate organizations into a united front.

The Westside of Los Angeles, adjacent to Beverly Hills, quickly organized into New AGE, the New Alliance for Gay Equality. This campaign was formed by the country's first and only gay political action committee MECLA—the Municipal Elections Committee of L.A.—created one year earlier.

I joined the centrist Coalition for Human Rights and the lesbian rights group, but recognized that the grassroots would be heavily dependent on our community's moneyed conservative wing. California had had the seven years since Stonewall to develop activist organizations for every kind of Democrat. Would the just-born gay Republicans, the Log Cabin Club, come along? Could these usually bickering wings actually work together?

There are dozens of unusual connections in our history, but my personal bond with MECLA lesbian leaders did aid and abet an alliance between the conservative and centrist wings in Los Angeles.

My friendship with MECLA co-chairs Diane Abbitt and Roberta Bennett (a lesbian couple—both lawyers) was forged in the National Organization of Women's early trench warfare in '72 over acceptance of lesbianism as a feminist issue. Now they asked me to persuade the Human Rights Coalition's leadership to come to what amounted to a summit meeting with MECLA's leadership to see if we could cooperate.

The organizations didn't respect or like each other, but we'd all heard about Dade County's gay leadership fracturing during Bryant's campaign. Right before the summit meeting, Diane told me, "You know, Jeanne, you'd be a great asset if you'd join MECLA." I asked jokingly, "What would I have to do to do that?" Diane smiled. "The first thing you have to do is change the way you dress—starting with those gold chains around the heels of your boots." I laughed, realizing that she objected to my too-butch dress style. "Never gonna happen," I quipped. And we got down to business.

Ivy Bottini, Morris Knight's co-chair in the Human Rights Coalition, predicted that New AGE would be assimilationist male-dominated, and would ignore lesbians. Yet after hours of haggling, we agreed to combine our grassroots organizing and street power with MECLA's fundraising ability. We also devised a plan to hire the gay political consultant team of David Mixner and Peter Scott: the first time the infant movement had hired outside campaign experts. Later, Mixner wisely appointed Bottini to be Deputy Director of Southern California's "No on 6" campaign.

Finally, the cooperation I'd dreamed about: socialists, centrists, lesbians, and gay men.

The bleak summer of '78 flew by. No one enjoyed the beach. No one had "free" time. We worked frenetically, on television with ads made possible by donated money, and on the streets marching, chanting that gays weren't pedophiles or recruiting children. All summer, we looked for opportunities to reach out to straight folk urging them to "Vote No on 6." Finally, the labor unions joined our coalition saying Prop. 6 "endangered teachers' right to work." By now, the ACLU and National Organization for Women were on board; the feminist movement had our back. Our statewide organization, "No on 6" went on a massive educational campaign: "We Are Everywhere." We urged gays to come out, since polls showed that 60% of those who knew someone gay opposed Briggs. As my spouse, the secretary of New AGE, came home each night, we'd ponder: how could we get more Californians to allow gay and gay-friendly teachers to keep their jobs?

As much as we tried to argue that the Briggs Initiative was about civil liberties and not a morality issue, a summer NBC television program, "Is School Out for Gay Teachers?" tried to show how dangerous Prop. 6 was for the constitutional rights of all Americans. Yet it ended by quoting a housewife and mother insisting, "Our children come before any civil rights."

I realized that publicly arguing the obvious—that heterosexual families created "homosexuals"—would never fly. I remembered hearing my sisters, aged nine and ten, ask, "Can we catch being gay from Jeanne?"

Since a surprising late poll indicated that average Californians didn't believe gay or homophobic spokespeople anymore, New AGE produced a concert starring Joan Baez and Harry Chapin. Backed significantly by the Jewish community, Hollywood's pro-gay but closeted industry recognized the parallels between Prop. 6 and the gradual—but fatal—loss of civil liberties in Hitler's Germany. Paying $100 a plate—a hefty price tag in '78—stars like Burt Lancaster, Lily Tomlin, John Travolta, Brenda Vaccaro, Jane Fonda, Paul Newman, Joanne Woodward, Woody Allen, Carol Burnett, Rock Hudson, and Diane Keaton came out against Briggs, as did Angela Davis, Tom Hayden, former President Gerald Ford, and then-President Jimmy Carter. The concert raised $150,000.

Thankfully, the usually conservative *L.A. Times* advised a "no" on Prop. 6 vote. Their editorial read: "Calculated to appeal to parents' concerns and camouflaged as an education issue, Proposition 6 is actually part of a vicious nationwide campaign against homosexuals. Teachers have become the latest pawn. They deserve public backing..."

It still wasn't enough. We still trailed by five percent. But Mixner/Scott hatched a plan to go after the biggest straight fish in California: Ronald Reagan, the former governor and presidential hopeful.

Mixner manufactured a pitch designed to appeal to Republicans by defining the issue as one of privacy. To Reagan, he would argue that the Briggs Initiative was a question of government meddling in private life, and then he would proceed to label the initiative as one that would "create chaos in the public school system," allow students to blackmail teachers who gave them low grades, "destroy student discipline," and, in the endless litigation it inspired, "waste taxpayer money."

It was a perfect conservative strategy, but how could he get an audience?

The answer was surprisingly simple—*we were everywhere*! Because of his prior movie career and public statements, people knew that Reagan wasn't *personally* anti-gay. And his and his wife Nancy's social circles overlapped with the movie industry. Mixner found a Reagan aide who knew someone, who knew someone, who knew someone.... Mixner/Scott's sit-down with Reagan lasted for more than an hour. No promises were made, but on August 20th, and seemingly out of nowhere, the "Citizens for Reagan" presidential campaign issued a statement: "The measure [Prop 6] has the potential of infringing on the basic rights of privacy.... It has the potential for causing undue harm to people."

Reagan's endorsement headlined the news for a week. Polls began to shift. A broad coalition of Democrats, Jews, blacks, those with "no religious preference," gays, voters under thirty, and other liberals began to form. A September *L.A. Times* poll revealed that 52% would vote with gays in November. Our scrambling intensified. Suddenly, it looked like we could actually win! What would voters do?

November 7th saw three thousand jubilant lesbians, gays, and allies celebrate as the anti-Briggs tally came in 58% to 42%—the margin a little over one million pro-gay votes. As Diane Abbitt later noted, "Every attack, even those we lost initially, ended with our community becoming stronger, better organized, and more visible."

California was the first time our movement had faced a statewide threat. Before 1977, we'd organized city by city or by counties. By forcing us to face a ballot measure, Briggs and Bryant deflected our early radical underpinnings and accidentally gave birth to what would become a national gay civil rights struggle.

Chapter 17

"The Mayor of Castro Street"

by Adrian Brooks

People gathered quietly at 18th and Castro streets at 7:30 p.m. on November 27th, 1978. Darkness had already fallen. No one had summoned us; we came because we had to. Someone blew a conch shell. Its doleful sound rolled forth as volunteers passed out candles and jars. Slowly, the street became a trickle of darting flame as we walked to Market Street and headed east towards City Hall—thousands, tens of thousands, some say forty thousand—moving in still silence, holding white candles to honor two men who'd been murdered that day. One was San Francisco Mayor George Moscone. A handsome, liberal, and charming family man, he was everything voters might want to represent our feisty white-haired boy of a hometown.

The other dead man was a city supervisor—one of eight representing the city districts. "Our supervisor" was the second openly gay person elected to high public office in the United States and an advocate for our Cause. Now he was dead—slaughtered—and, on that night, at that moment, something that had only just been considered "decided"—our place in society, our seat at the table—was cast into doubt. And so we'd met to walk in tribute and sorrow and, perhaps, unconsciously, seeking some sign or reason to believe that our seat at the table might still exist. But we weren't sure of that. At least, not when we came together....

Harvey Milk was an unlikely leader, hero, or martyr. But whatever his foibles, he was the lightning rod at the political epicenter of 70s San Francisco. And now, through a tragic death, he'd become the Movement's most potent human symbol.

Born in 1930, Harvey was raised on Long Island in a Jewish family. As a child, he became a class clown—possibly, in part, as a defense, since he realized he was gay early on. After college, he joined the Navy, serving during the Korean War until 1955. In 1962, Harvey was in love with someone, but he disapproved of this person's involvement with the Mattachine Society. By 1964, he worked on Wall Street supporting Barry Goldwater, a conservative Republican considered an extremist. Five years later, he hit San Francisco, just then at the cusp of gay liberation. He grew his hair long, but, when told to cut it by his employer (an investment firm), he refused and was fired.

Milk was more comfortable with "out" gays and flamboyant types by now. After bouncing around again, he moved to San Francisco's Castro District in 1973. Here, he and his partner Scott Smith opened a small camera shop with their last $1000.

Infuriated by what he saw in the Watergate hearings, Milk grew more engaged in politics. Snubbed by the local Democratic Party hierarchy, he campaigned for the Board of Supervisors—endorsing legal marijuana and opposing government interference in private sexual matters. While his bid was unsuccessful, he'd found his vocation.

More savvy and committed now, Milk organized a boycott of Coors Beer for their discrimination against unions, and he founded the Castro Village Association to boost small businesses. In 1975, he made a second run for supervisor, in the process cutting his hair (an image appealing to more voters), swearing off marijuana, dubbing himself "the Mayor of Castro Street," and vowing never again to visit a bathhouse. By now, he didn't have to. He was attracting good, hardworking people such as Anne Kronenberg. But runaways appeared, inevitably, and street people, as well as hangers-on and craven opportunists, who made lifelong careers by riding on his coattails.

In private, critics said Harvey could be temperamental and manic. Still, charming, witty, and media-wise, he was everywhere. We first met in 1976, when we were on the same bill at "the Hula Palace," a seasonal event run by activist Lee Mentley, who featured painters, poets, theater artists, and speakers. Later, we had coffee two times at the Café Flore, a pleasant outdoor café, which functioned as the Castro's village green. We occupied parallel universes. By the mid-1970s, he was the lightning rod of the burgeoning political gay community; the angels were its cultural totems, appearing at his rallies to support him. And he told me that he'd loved *Paris Sites Under the Bourgeois Sea.* According to his friend and roommate, Denton Smith, "Harvey felt that the inspiration he got from the Angels of Light was central to his reason for being in San Francisco and for doing what he did."[1]

In 1977, Harvey ran again for a seat on the Board of Supervisors. This time—his third try—he won. Opposing a moderate, he argued: "We don't want sympathetic liberals. We want gays to represent gays. We have to make up for hundreds of years of persecution."

His swearing-in made national news. After walking to City Hall from the Castro, he said, "You can stand around and throw bricks at Silly Hall or you can take it over. Well, here we are."

That election signified change. Previously marginalized LGBT folk now realized that we could work within the system. Victory also signaled visibility and growing acceptability. And since the world takes its cue from the United States, and new trends in the nation almost always begin in California, and California so often takes its cue from San Francisco (which runs a few years ahead of changing times)—*the future had arrived.*

In short order, Harvey took on developers to limit ruinous urban expansion. He was the impetus behind landmark legislation protecting LGBT folk at work. But even as he made crucial gains, an ugly storm was brewing in the form of Anita's crusade.

No one had foreseen such an assault. But on the night Dade County, Florida, rejected its pro-gay legislation, Harvey led a demonstration of 3,000 people chanting, "Out of the closets and into the streets!"

Still, Bryant had us in her crosshairs: Proposition 6 was on the November ballot. A mania was rising fast.

On June 21st, 1977, a gay man—Robert Hillsborough—was stabbed 15 times while his assailants chanted "Faggot!" and, "This one's for you, Anita!" The Gay Parade shortly afterwards was militant, furious. Now, Harvey went to every rally Briggs organized in order to confront him. And when Briggs claimed that homosexuals were out to "recruit children," Milk's reply was devastating: "If that were true, you'd have a helluva lot more nuns running around."

Milk went forward throughout the year (and into the summer of 1978) taking Briggs on and confronting homophobia, urging voters: "Come out, come out, wherever you are."

One day, we met at the Flore with Tony Vaughan: a (heterosexual) visionary poet/musician and part of a coalition of artists who wanted to paint Castro Street lavender to protest Prop 6. Harvey loved the anarchy of it, and, laughing, urged us to go ahead with the sassy project. Heartened by his encouragement, I wrote a poem, which got plastered and staple-gunned to telephone poles, community billboards, and street posts. As Denton Smith remembers, "Without the rabble and street people and runaways and quirky idealists, the work would never have gotten done."

Let's paint Castro Street so San Francisco
Seen from the skies will dazzle the birds.
Let's paint the street so this city will sigh
Not sink in cement strips smothering her earth.
Let's color her, streak her mud face with berries.
Let's apply her cosmetics so the rain will wash
Ultra-violet pastels down her iron pipes and drains
Taking water-washable ribbons out to open sea.
Let's paint our street, re-consecrate the ground
Straight men chose to own/divide/keep bleak.
Before they set stone to stone, this was country—
Undulating valley pocked with blueberry, lupin,
Jack rabbit and deer. Poor street, cut into shares,
Street of tea and bourbon, street of cruisey trade.
Let's paint our village street so when it finally rains
Colors will kiss her beaches and gray ocean waves
And birds will see more than beasts here.

In June, Harvey was grand marshal of the 1978 Gay Freedom Day Parade. But as the day neared, he was dogged by threats of assassination. "You get the first bullet the minute you stand at the microphone," read one typed message on a postcard.

Still, he led the parade in an open car as a crowd, estimated at 240,000—the largest held to date—roared its love and approval of him. And standing on a podium below City Hall on the anniversary of Stonewall, he said, "I ask my gay brothers and sisters to make the commitment to fight. For themselves, for their freedom, and for this country. We will not win our rights by staying in the closets. We are coming out to fight the lies, the myths, the distortions. We are coming out to tell the truth about gays, for I am tired of the conspiracy of silence."

Across the esplanade, on "the poet's stage," I was in a lineup to read to the crowd. But that day was the last time I ever saw or spoke to Harvey.

Polls began to shift. Then, on election night—November 7th—Prop 6 lost. *Bigtime.*

The triumph solidified Milk's status as the champion who'd carried the flag. Also, it sent a signal to the nation: "The Gay" was here to stay. Yet a freakish confluence followed.

The spat first seemed minor. Dan White—a boyishly handsome ex-cop on the San Francisco Board of Supervisors—abruptly resigned his seat, giving Mayor Moscone the right to appoint a successor. It was a chance to secure one more vote on the Board for the liberal policies Milk and he endorsed. White was their foe, a conservative darling of the large reactionary and resentful voting bloc in San Francisco.

Meanwhile, in Guyana, self-declared refugees from San Francisco—mainly African-Americans—were in a cult around a paranoid megalomaniac preacher, Jim Jones. Upon being visited by a concerned California Congressman, Jones ordered his henchmen to kill him. Then the sociopathic guru told his followers to commit suicide. Most obeyed. Those who refused or who tried to escape were murdered. Nine hundred died.

When he heard that news on November 18th, Harvey Milk taped his will. By now, the White issue was complicated; the erstwhile "supe" wanted to retract his resignation. Moscone remained noncommittal.

On November 27th, Moscone planned to announce his appointment of White's successor. But shortly before the press conference, White gained entry to City Hall through a basement window (to avoid metal detectors). He went to George Moscone's office, shot him, found Harvey in a hall, asked to speak with him, and murdered him. Harvey was 48.

An hour later, White surrendered. Police saw the 32-year-old as one of their own, but shockwaves reverberated across the country. "A City in Agony" headlined *The San Francisco Examiner.*

That night, the crowd marched in silence from the Castro to City Hall, a flickering river of flame.

Since he'd smuggled his weapon into City Hall, White was held without bail and charged with two counts of premeditated murder. He was eligible for the death penalty, since his victims were public officials. But the prosecution pulled its punches. It failed, for example, to see that gays or ethnic minorities were put on the jury, or even to call George Moscone's widow to testify. And the judge was clearly sympathetic to White. The city was riven between liberals and its police, which raised $100,000 for White's defense fund. But one undersheriff observed that "the more I observed what went on in the jail, the more I began to stop seeing what Dan White did as the act of an individual man and more as a political act in a political movement." White showed no remorse, and, ultimately, argued for "diminished capacity" based upon his binging on pastries. On May 21st, 1979, he got seven years for involuntary manslaughter—the lightest possible conviction. As Supervisor Carol Ruth Silver said, "Dan White got away with murder."

Three thousand of us marched to City Hall. The protest quickly became a riot. Bricks and rocks flew as the furious mob tried to smash in the doors of the building. Above our heads, the night sky was maroon with the glow of a line of burning police cars, sirens shrieking. The cops broke up the fray. Later, several officers—defying orders issued directly by the chief of police to stay out of the Castro—concealed their badges and embarked on a retaliatory raid. They burst into a bar at 18th and Castro streets, clubbing patrons and bystanders indiscriminately. Over one hundred individuals had to seek medical treatment in hospital emergency rooms.

The city and the nation were in shock. The message, which the jury had sent, appalled everyone. Put simply, the verdict translated as a blunt statement of values: *It's okay to kill a fag and a fag-lover, because you'll get away with it.*

In January 1984, after serving five years, White was released from prison. After a year on parole, he came back to the city. Later, he told a homicide inspector that he'd intended to kill Moscone, Milk, Carol Ruth Silver, and State Assemblyman Willie Brown: "I was on a mission. I wanted four of them." Captain Frank Falzon admitted, "I felt like I had been hit by a sledge-hammer... I found out it was premeditated murder." Two years later, personally disgraced, his marriage in shambles, and his career over, White committed suicide. "Perhaps the most hated man in San Francisco's history," one paper suggested.

By contrast, as we carried the candles down Market Street, there was a quiet sense of a will: that we would endure and survive and keep moving forward until there was equality for all. Harvey became an emblem of the crusade for LGBTQI human rights. And in the end, understanding that clearly when he taped his will, he finished with prophetic words:

"This tape should only be played in the event of my death by assassination.... I fully realize that a person who stands for what I stand

for—a gay activist—becomes a target for a person who is inse-
cure, terrified, afraid, or very disturbed themselves.... If a bullet
should enter my brain, let that bullet destroy every closet door in
the country."

According to Denton Smith—who lived with Harvey "for only one
decade" and shared his life—the myth of "St. Harvey" and historical
revisionism are inaccurate. Denton wants Harvey to be remembered as
a human being. As he recalled on March 14th, 2014, "Everything was
more immediate than imagining where it was all going or what Harvey
wanted for the future. Every moment, especially his getting up and going,
was purposed by the situation, by the demands made on him. He wasn't
becoming anything. What he was *was* who he was; that was it. He didn't
consider more than who he *already was*."

ENDNOTES

1   Right after the November murders the Angels of Light reconvened, united by the double
tragedy. In May, we staged *Holy Cow!*. I was honored to write it. Dedicated to George
Moscone and Harvey Milk, with a theme of reincarnation, the show was a smash hit and
a balm for community healing. An epic triumph, like *Paris Sites* in 1980, *Holy Cow!* was
revived by popular demand as the group went public after eight years of defiant underground
status; we garnered rave reviews, national acclaim, and won four Bay Area Theater Critics
Circle awards, including Best New Show of the Year. But our May 1979 offering was the last
free show that the Angels ever did. Time had sobered us—the flower children and Glitter Age
were long since gone—and the 80s were upon us.

Chapter 18

Interview with Charlotte Bunch: Human Rights and Gender Equality

By Anahi Russo Garrido

ARG: How did you begin your career?

CB: My activism was formed in the 1960s, when I was a student partici-pating in the black civil rights movement in the South. The energy, passion, and vision of changing the world propelled me.

My view of racism began with a sense that it was not fair to discriminate on the basis of color. Gradually, it expanded to a larger understanding— that racism wasn't just unfair, but an entire social and economic system had been constructed around it. I was inspired by how the movement was seeking to change society and started to learn the complexities of working for change.

Of course, many of the leaders understood this and had wider goals, but for me, it was an important learning experience that taught me that progress is possible, but complex. And it also propelled me to see other issues of inequality and how they connected to each other. My political beginning was a typical 1960s trajectory: civil rights to issues of poverty and the anti-Vietnam war movement and an understanding of US imperi-alism, to feminism and eventually coming to LGBT issues.

ARG: At a talk, a woman was talking about her experiences in college in the 1950s. She said she had curfews. Were there similar rules for women on campus? How did that impact activism?

CB: I went to Duke University Women's College in North Carolina in 1962 as a freshman, and we had to be back in the dorms by 11 o'clock during the week and midnight on weekends. If you were late several times, you could be expelled. Male undergraduates certainly didn't have as many restraints. In the 1950s, women had to wear gloves to Sunday dinner on campus. Colleges were really seen as being substitute parents for us. The questioning of that came later as students learned from the civil rights and anti-war movements to challenge authorities.

By the late 1960s, student activism emerged all over the country over issues of what was happening on campus—often connected to the draft and university complicity with racism and imperialism.

ARG: In which ways did your work begin being connected to sexual rights and, more particularly, LGBTQ rights?

CB: I came to those issues through the feminist movement. Feminism challenged us to examine social construction—sexuality was a part of that. You couldn't look at your life as a woman and not see how much of what society said was connected to controlling your sexuality. Reproductive rights are about controlling women's sexuality. Questions of violence against women are about control.

In 1968, I helped start the first women's liberation consciousness-raising group in Washington, DC, where women began to spend a lot of time together and to talk about our lives in both intimate and political ways. I was married and saw myself as heterosexual, but I was going to meetings with other women nonstop. Many of us began to question the male centeredness of our own lives, as well as of the world. We had strong friendships and emotional ties in the process of creating a new movement, and questions of sexuality emerged very naturally. Some of us realized that we loved the women we were working with and began to reconsider our preferences. Not only did many of us become lesbians, but we also began to analyze the social construction of sexuality and sexual choices and talk about heterosexism, or what is now called "heteronormativity." We wanted to show how those assumptions operated and led to the oppression of lesbians and gay men.

Of course, many of these feminists were lesbians already; for them, it was about "coming out" of the closet. Though I wasn't already a lesbian, I might have been if I'd even imagined that option. It was outside of my frame of reference growing up in a sexually repressed family in a small town in New Mexico in the 1950s.

ARG: What were the women spaces?

CB: From the late 1960s on, women created many spaces that enabled feminism to thrive. In Washington, DC, we began by renting an apartment for meetings, and soon there were women's centers—buildings in San Francisco, Boston, Chicago, Los Angeles—where women had offices for newly emerging organizations and all sorts of meetings, courses, dances, and other activities. Feminists created many alternative spaces like bookstores and printing houses, where women's culture emerged more explicitly with women's music, art, and publications in almost every major city.

ARG: What connected your activism to sexual rights/LGBT rights?

CB: The critical moment for me was when we proposed that lesbianism was a political—not just a personal—choice, and demanded that it be an explicit part of the feminist agenda. We soon experienced the homophobia and fears of many in the movement.

For example, there was an alternative left-feminist community daycare center, where one woman in our lesbian feminist group sent her children. After she left her marriage, she sent her female lover to pick up her children. Some of the parents were really upset about her partner—a more butch lesbian—being around their children. I remember the sense that women we'd worked with so closely in creating women's liberation were terrified of having us be openly identified as lesbians.

Part of it was fear of having feminist groups further marginalized as "lesbians," and part of it was fear of the unknown. Difficult divisions amongst feminists over this issue arose and led some of us to declare ourselves "lesbian separatists." I was trying to figure out what it meant to be lesbian in a feminist context, and our discussion group on this became The Furies Collective in 1971-72.[1]

The collective sponsored a number of projects aimed at raising consciousness (such as film discussions in gay bars), but the primary focus was publishing a newspaper that expounded on lesbian feminist analysis.

The Furies Collective lasted for about one year and published ten issues. I came to see that separatism was not a viable long-term strategy. I wanted to make lesbian issues visible, but didn't want to work in an isolated space.

After The Furies, I worked with other groups in DC. In 1974, we founded a journal of political analysis coming from movement activism called *Quest: A Feminist Quarterly*. *Quest* was published out of my office at the Institute for Policy Studies in DC, and I was the primary editor, as well as a writer for it, for five years. We wrote about different theoretical strands of feminism—radical, liberal, socialist, lesbian, cultural—and how they applied to concrete issues and their implications for movement strategies, as well as what could be learned from different experiences. We looked at race, class, sexuality, and other differences among women and [asked what] could be done to connect our issues better—what is now called intersectionality. I wrote and spoke about lesbian feminism to show why lesbian rights was not just a minority rights issue but also a key part of all women's oppression. In response to questions like, "How can you talk about lesbianism when women are poor and beaten?" I wanted to explain how the suppression of sexuality is connected to women's economic status and vulnerability to violence—that it is part of how women are subordinated: through fear and control. When we are afraid to discuss these issues, we give into and reinforce those fears and that control.

I joined the Board of Directors of the National Gay (and Lesbian) Task Force (NG[L]TF) in 1974. Women on the Board organized a caucus and initiated "lesbian visibility projects" related to both the gay and women's movements. I participated in the first White House meeting with LGBT groups in 1977, organized by NG(L)TF, where I spoke about the immigration problems faced by LGBT couples from different countries. Little did I know that I would soon face this problem personally when I entered into a long-term relationship with a Peruvian.

One of the most important projects we organized was a lesbian caucus for the National Women's Conference in Houston in 1977. Houston was the national event for the UN International Women's Year—the only one ever sponsored by the US Government. Statewide meetings open to the public elected delegates to the national conference and passed resolutions about what they wanted included in its platform. We coordinated a national network of lesbians, who attended their state events and sought to be elected as delegates to Houston, as well as to get lesbian rights on the agenda. We built political alliances with feminist organizations like NOW and worked with mainstream groups like the YWCA and the AAUW, as well as collaborated with women of color who wanted to address racism and multiple discriminations faced by minority women.

This broad feminist coalition was successful in getting agreement on a 26-point platform that included planks on sexual preference, reproductive rights, poverty, minority women, etc. It was a turning point for me in seeing that the future of sexual rights lay in building coalitions. However, it was also sobering as a massive showdown, with right-wing forces from conservative states that scapegoated issues of abortion and gay rights in their efforts to defeat feminism and the Equal Rights Amendment (ERA). It foretold many battles ahead.

Feminism in the 70s had been moving rapidly forward with legal and structural, as well as attitudinal, changes. The Supreme Court affirmed the right to abortion with *Roe vs. Wade*, anti-discrimination laws like Title IX regarding women in sports were adopted, and feminists brought changes in domestic violence and rape laws, as well as developed shelters and crisis centers for victims. But the right wing was getting better organized and saw the feminist movement and its growing alliances with other movements as a real threat.

1977 was a high point for US feminism, but within four years, we would lose the battle for ratification of the ERA by a small margin. And then Ronald Reagan was elected president. The 80s backlash brought a sense of demoralization and confusion. I felt a need to see from some other perspective, so I moved to New York City to explore possibilities for global feminism and entry points for cross-cultural organizing, including through the United Nations and, particularly, its world conferences on women.

I helped organize networking events around the 1980 Second UN Conference on Women in Copenhagen, where I began to see the importance of violence against women as an issue that enabled women to work across North-South divisions. There was not much open conversation about lesbianism at these events, but there were some workshops and informal side conversations where networking began.

In 1983, I began a relationship and political collaboration with Roxanna Carrillo from Peru.[2] Over the next two decades, we led workshops on feminist theory for activists in Latin America, which we took to the Third UN World Conference on Women in Nairobi in 1985, and later to South Asia.

When I became a professor at Rutgers University in New Jersey, I founded the Center for Women's Global Leadership (CWGL) in 1989-90. For over a decade, CWGL helped feminist activists get training in international human rights and made feminist strategies to advance women's issues together. Initially, we focused primarily on violence against women, as it illustrates concretely what are gender specific human rights violations and problems everywhere; at the same time, we could explore differences among women, as violence is usually shaped by the particularities of each culture.

We also created both the 16 Days of Activism Against Gender-Based Violence Campaign[3] (which still happens every year in over 125 countries) and the Global Campaign for Women's Human Rights to organize women—around the world—to lobby for recognition that "women's rights are human rights," and to put violence against women on the agenda of the UN World Conference on Human Rights in Vienna in 1993. The campaign influenced the agenda in Vienna, where the UN acknowledged the universality of women's rights as human rights and began to address violence against women in this framework.

CWGL and its partners around the world continued the campaign and organized tribunals at the International Conference on Population and Development in Cairo (1994), where women's health rights as human rights were addressed, and at the Copenhagen UN Social Summit (1995), to show a gendered approach to economic and social rights. In Beijing, at the Fourth UN World Conference on Women in 1995, global feminism had its greatest success, including when Hillary Clinton gave governmental legitimacy to our claim that "women's rights are human rights."

ARG: Do you remember a particular campaign or event at the global level, in which you worked on sexual rights?

CB: My approach was to integrate lesbian rights and issues of sexuality into all my work on human rights; I connected it to women's struggles against violence and subordination in the family and saw it as part of women's right to non-discrimination and control over our bodies. In Vienna, we included testimony from a Peruvian lesbian about how discrimination against lesbians violated various human rights principles. It was also addressed in another testimony on how women were treated as political prisoners in anti-apartheid South Africa, where the accusation of being a lesbian was used against them, whatever their sexual orientation.

At the 2001 UN World Conference Against Racism in Durban, South

Africa, we included testimony from a Roma lesbian from Serbia, who talked about linkages between her oppression as a lesbian, a woman, and part of an ethnic minority. This event focused on the intersectionality of gender with race, ethnicity, class, national origin, ability, sexual orientation, etc., with a focus on the ways that women specifically experience racism, xenophobia, and poverty. It also emphasized human rights protections, to which all women are entitled—their civil and political, economic and social rights—and how violations might be redressed and prevented in the future.

Lesbian rights have also been included in any list of demands when we lobbied at the UN for recognition of women's diversity and the right to non-discrimination. Sexual orientation usually fails to get included, but the struggle for it has kept the issue visible. In Beijing, the debate over inclusion of "sexual orientation" was heated. While it failed, it opened the eyes of many government delegates. Growing numbers of governments support this issue, but progress on it in discussions of women's issues at the UN has stalled.

During the 2000s, more support for LGBTQ, or SOGI (Sexual Orientation and Gender Identity), rights has been made through the UN Human Rights system. As director of CWGL, I often played a role in these debates through my work with Cynthia Rothschild[4] on naming lesbian-baiting in women's organizing,[5] organizing around the linkages between HIV-AIDS and violence against women, and ensuring that this was a key issue in the creation of an International Coalition on Women Human Rights Defenders.

ARG: Today, in the women's rights and LGBTQ worlds, what do you see as key challenges?

CB: While life has improved for a lot of women and LGBT people, there are too many others who have been left behind. In particular, we must challenge the growth in economic inequality over the past two decades. In much of the world, less than half of the population is employed. If we ignore the fact that unemployment and economic inequality shape the environment, we cannot effectively end sexual discrimination. If there are not enough jobs for over 50% of the population, there will be an awful lot of women and LGBT people out of work. We have to figure out how to challenge the economic system that has created this situation.

Economic inequality is also linked to the rise of fundamentalist power, as those groups often provide services for the poor when the state fails to do so. Those left behind are targets for fundamentalists; women are already being mobilized against feminists and LGBT activists. If we don't deal with economic issues, we are allowing the opposition space to mobilize against us. It is a big challenge, but the feminist and LGBT movements must focus more on economic disparities and empowerment if we are to continue to advance and to link our struggles to larger numbers of people.

ARG: What do you feel has supported you remaining active and not giving up?

CB: There is an easy answer. I have worked and played with a global community of feminist activists that inspire me. I don't focus primarily on what's wrong. I spend my time looking at and working with people who are doing things to make it different, in little or big ways. I get excited by the young feminist activists fighting for reproductive rights in Texas, or the men seriously addressing violence against women. What keeps me going are the activists and my global community of friends.

ARG: What final thoughts do you want to share about the future of our movements?

CB: We need to build more coalitions and to have a greater generosity of spirit. We can have strong positions on issues and still respect and listen to others. The movement needs to be as diverse and as inclusive as possible, within the frame of seeking progressive human rights and change.

I see a tendency—when we get specialized on one issue—to start closing out the rest of the picture. I think this leads to burnout. We need to open up to hearing things that aren't usually in our universe. Of course, one focuses on the specifics of your work, but we have to keep listening and including other issues and perspectives, or we narrow our lives and the political potential of the work.

ENDNOTES

1   The Furies were a group of twelve women who lived in three communal houses in Washington, DC. They embodied communal values by sharing their salaries and all their private property. They disseminated their vision through a newspaper, *The Furies: Lesbian/Feminist Monthly*, which published ten issues in 1971-1972.

2   Roxanna Carrillo is a Peruvian feminist who pioneered the United Nations Development Fund
     for Women (UNIFEM)'s work on human rights and violence against women, retired from
     the UN in 2011. She was a co-founder of *Centro de la Mujer Peruana Flora Tristan*, one of
     the first non-governmental feminist organizations in Peru (http://www.alainet.org/publica/
     femlead/en/presenters.html). She has been Charlotte's life partner for over thirty years.

3   The "16 Days of Activism Against Gender Violence" campaign was born in 1991 out of the
     first Women's Global Leadership Institute at CWGL. The activities of the campaign begin
     each year on November 25, International Day Against Violence Against Women, and conclude
     on December 10, International Human Rights Day, which marks the anniversary of the adop-
     tion of the International Declaration of Human Rights Day, which marks the anniversary
     of the adoption of the International Declaration of Human Rights by the UN in 1948. Since
     1991, more than 3,500 organizations in approximately 164 countries have participated in the
     campaign. The campaign literature is translated into at least 25–30 languages each year.

4   Cynthia Rothschild has been a human rights and sexual rights activist for over twenty years.
     She is a former member of Amnesty International USA's Board of Directors, and a member
     of the Board of the Astraea Lesbian Foundation for Justice, the Advisory Board of Human
     Rights Watch's LGBT Rights Program, and the Board of the International Center for Sexual
     and Reproductive Rights in Nigeria.

5   See Cynthia Rothschild, *Written Out: How Sexuality Is Used to Attack Women's Organizing*
     (New York: GM Printing, for International Gay and Lesbian Human Rights Commission and
     Center for Women's Global Leadership, 2005).

Chapter 19

The Enemy Is Me: Becoming a Man inside a Feminist World

By Max Wolf Valerio

My parents are gone and I'm in the bathroom peering into the mirror. I comb my hair back and to the side, male hairstyles. It doesn't look right, I know, but I can almost see it, if I look long and hard enough. An instant, a flash where I look like a boy or the grown man I feel I should become. It frustrates me that I can't make it more real.[1]

The possibility of life as a man eluded me until I was 31 years old. I had never once seriously considered such a transformation in my teen years, or even in my chaotic and experimental twenties. The possibility was not simply a closed door; it was a door that did not exist—even in remote dreaming. I was a dedicated bohemian and a poet, with an outsider's edge and an omnivorous rage. I was incandescent with rage—toward patriarchy, capitalism, and what I considered to be the American lie. I lingered at the margins of many radical movements, and reveled in the chaos and fury of the San Francisco punk scene. Though I remained mostly buoyant—even ebullient—in my exile from rote femininity and "society," I nonetheless developed a thin carapace of hardened angst. Not once did it occur to me with any clarity that another life was just around the next edge, that I was just about to topple off a worn surface and into a new and perilous place.

On Sunday, I have to wear a white dress to go to church, as well as little white anklets, Mary Janes, and, to top it off, a lace doily on my head! One Sunday morning I'm so upset by this charade that I'm in tears, and refuse to go out to the car in that dress. I feel absurd, embarrassed, like a weird French poodle wearing this outfit. What if one of my little buddies, one of "the other boys" in the neighborhood that I hang out with, battle and explore with, sees me? It'll ruin my reputation for sure. But I have to wear this weird dress, and I run to the car, shaking with tears and humiliation.[2]

Certainly, I was an ardent feminist, having been properly schooled during my coming out in 1975 in the anti-patriarchal rigor of lesbian feminism. In those days in Boulder, at the University of Colorado, I hung out in a small room—the office of the Women's Liberation Coalition—where the iconic fist in a Venus sign was painted boldly in red on the window. Overcome with a shy anticipation of revolution and triumphant lesbian bonding, I immersed myself in the atmosphere of woman-positive culture. Although the uproars of the sixties had passed, and the seventies were midway through, those were still heady times of tumultuous social change. Arriving at university at age eighteen, excited to come out, eager to date women, I encountered a bewildering yet mesmerizing labyrinth of political ideas. I was to discover, in short order, that coming out as a lesbian was about way more than simply being a woman attracted to women; it had become an escalation of primal femaleness, a radical epiphany of women enunciating themselves into existence beyond male definitions. Women becoming "womyn", extracting "men" from "women," and taking on power. Lesbianism became a prime mover in a new liberatory vision of female possibility, offering a new grammar to situate femaleness as primary, as powerful. Lesbianism enabled feminists to reconstruct femaleness without need for masculine definition or complement.

The momentum toward this radical realignment of lesbianism with feminism began a bit before my own coming of age. The moment was one lit with ferocity and discovery at the Second Congress to Unite Women in New York City in May 1970. A group called the Radicalesbians took over the event by surprise, performing a political action called a "zap" that included cutting the lights, commandeering the stage, and taking over the microphones to announce their anger at having lesbian speakers excluded. These brave women changed feminism forever with a mimeographed manifesto passed out to the bewildered yet enthralled audience, inviting them to participate in this new subversion.

Radicalesbians began their manifesto, "The Woman-Identified Woman," with this opening salvo: "What is a lesbian? A lesbian is the rage of all women condensed to the point of explosion."[3] This manifesto was a call to authenticity, to freedom, to a life larger than defined by traditional sex roles. But this was more than a clarion call to women's liberation.... This freedom, the manifesto declared, "was aligned with being a lesbian". The manifesto continued, speaking of lesbians: "She is the woman who, often beginning at an extremely early age, acts in accordance with her inner compulsion to be a more complete and freer human being than her society—perhaps then, but certainly later—cares to allow her."[4] "Lesbian" was no longer a simple sexual preference or—as it would have been seen by psychiatry and the mainstream in 1970—a maladapted perversion. The manifesto announced a sea change.... To be a lesbian was instead to be free; it was an announcement of authentic female being in liberation from patriarchy. A lesbian was the pinnacle of authentic femaleness; she was the "Woman-Identified Woman," who was defined not by her relationship to a man—be he husband, boyfriend, or father—but by her relationship to her own core womanness. If she wore a "man's" suit coat, that suit coat was now a "woman's" suit coat. If she wore masculine wingtips or a tie and had her hair cropped in a crew-cut, all these styles were now women's styles. Never again would a woman with an unconventional gender expression be stung to her core with the dismissive taunt, "she just wants to be a man!"

From this mimeographed manifesto, written years before my own coming out, I learned that I had been a woman oppressed by the patriarchy all along, and I surmised that most lesbians felt as I did when they were young. Any girl would have hated the doily on her head, the anklets, and the frilly dress! I also believed I had taken the cure. This new form of feminism, aligned with lesbianism, would recreate me finally as the genuine, real woman my mother had always wanted me to be—albeit without a bra, without makeup, and in jeans, and, naturally, wearing my father's well worn army boots!

Lesbianism, then, was less about the individual expression of a particular love interest or an enduring sexual preference for women and more about being a vanguard of the collective liberation of women. This alliance of lesbianism with utopian, liberatory feminism became the lesbian feminism that I found when I came out in 1975, searching for myself in the faces of the lesbians I saw, and understanding very shortly that I needed to become fluent in a sexual politics (that would prove to be as suffocating for me as they had initially appeared liberating).

When I came out...in 1975, we all sat in a circle and introduced ourselves one by one at the meeting of the Lesbian Caucus of the Women's Liberation Front on campus.... Women didn't just state their names. They always had lengthy rejoinders, subtle anthems.... "Hi, I'm Sally and I am a socialist feminist, not a separatist." "Hi I'm Naomi and I am a socialist feminist who is against imperialism in all its forms..." "Hi, I'm Nadine. I am a lesbian separatist and a member of the Isis Women's Community Orchestra.... We are trying to demystify the process of music making and clarify our struggles with class and women's oppression." When it came to me—eighteen years old, green, just arrived on campus, looking at the first really out lesbians I had seen in my entire life—I was scared to death.... What to say? An impish impulse in me thought, What if I say I am a Republican and I like girls? No, that wouldn't do, that much was clear.[5]

The second wave of lesbian feminism didn't sit well with me for long. Once I hit San Francisco in the late 70s, I was doing all the things you weren't supposed to do: dyeing my hair black or bleaching it; wearing black leather and chains; listening to aggressive male punk bands; dating women who liked to wear dresses, heels, and makeup; hanging out with people who were not always politically fluent, but were artistically in the crevices and edges. I had many straight male friends, and because of my predilection for arcane outsider art and avant-garde poetry, I was soon giving poetry readings to audiences of edgy literati and neo-beats instead of reading exclusively in feminist bookstores or cafes. In no time flat, I found myself preferring Black Flag, Joy Division, and X over Holly Near, Alix Dobkin, or Chris Williamson. Possibly, before I even considered medical transition in 1988, I had already left.

Without question, second-wave lesbian feminists were very brave and changed the world in many ways for the better; they expanded the roles and lives of women and of men in concrete, tangible ways. Let there be no mistake: the world before second-wave feminism was a world where men and women had separate "help wanted" columns in the daily newspaper, where women often could not get a credit card without a husband's signature, where women and girls were not encouraged to participate in sports, and where battered women were not protected by shelters—where marital rape was legal. I want to make it clear that while there were excesses from the second wave, there were also necessary triumphs.

Some of the excesses of the second wave were issues built into having the worldview of a collective identity locked in struggle with another group: a Marxist paradigm of struggle between competing classes—in this case, women against men and, further, essential femaleness against essential masculinity and maleness. Then, because they believed it was counterfeit—existing only in contrast to an oppressive masculinity—the second wave also rebelled against culturally received definitions of femininity and femaleness. Certainly, taking a wider view of gender expression and abolishing the obligation of each individual always to follow sacrosanct sex roles are positive developments. However, I knew that in order for me to leap into the life of a man through medical transition, I had to look more closely.

Ironically, just as my own mother had been critical of my masculinity, the world of feminism had also. In my search for liberation from restrictive norms, I had simply traded one disapproving mother figure for another. At some point, I had to ask: what was this maleness, this masculinity, and was it really as bad as what I had been told? I knew my mother's interdictions against maleness were an attempt to mold me into sex-role conformity, and certainly I had shaken off that conformity with relief. Articulated in the eighties and into the nineties, lesbian feminism (and even the latter third-wave feminism) was more embracing of diversity and even of some contradiction—still, they cast men primarily as paragons of oppression and suspicion. I had to ask myself...were all men oppressors and violent agents of the patriarchy?

Taking on biological maleness, masculinity, and the increasingly embattled mantle of manhood, has not been an entirely easy transformation. Like a high-class finishing school for women, being a lesbian in the age of feminism had certain rules, taboos: things you said and did not say, and certainly one of them was that men and women were capable of the same things, but, of course, men were oppressors. I had been told that my feelings of being male were bad and wrong my entire life, first by the entire society around me, and then by the world I had escaped to for solace, the world of lesbianism cloaked by feminism. And, certainly, as the Radicalesbians knew well, the epithet, "She just wants to be a man!" had been the ultimate shaming insult hurled at independent women, at women who dared to color outside the lines and strictures of their gender roles, as well as women who dared to love other women. *But what if…it were true! What if I did want to be a man? And worse, what if…I discovered that somehow, in spite of all visible physical evidence to the contrary, I actually was one?*

I know. At that moment I know, with the sun streaming in and the air bright with some kind of hope, some shining clarity…. No wonder I've always wanted to relate to women as a man. No wonder I have always had that ineffable feeling in the background of my life…a feeling of maleness, that somehow I was male…inside my core, my center…

I thought I was a lesbian. I begin to smile. All those years I thought I was a lesbian. Fourteen years of believing I was a dyke, and here I was a straight man all along![6]

I cannot say exactly when it came to me that I had been wrong about men and masculinity. When it occurred to me that really there was an entire world, multiple worlds, that I had misunderstood and vilified. Walking down the street that first week after taking my first shot of testosterone, the world opening up in an energetic array of forms, a new joy overtaking me as I discovered myself feeling in sync with the other men on the street, even though I had only just begun my journey…. Feeling a tangible and ecstatic closeness to them, a deep recognition, that *"I was these men that I saw, walking down the street as I walked, and they were me, I was—a man! This is what being like a man felt like…"* This sounds a bit mystical, and maybe it was. This feeling, a kind of epiphany, was not entirely to be explained even by the testosterone, since at that point, I had not really changed at all physically. Certainly, I was alone in my perception of myself as being an actual man at that moment, on that teeming street. I did not yet look or sound like a man. Although—I was starting to feel that expansive yet strongly *rooted* androgen energy often experienced in the beginning. Even so, this recognition of masculinity and of my own in tandem—that soaring perception that we were walking in sync and in similarity as *men*—was overwhelming.

I'm beginning to understand certain things in sharp relief. The adolescent boys who whip past me on skateboards—shouting, grinning, turning wild tricks, jumping curbs, weaving in and out of traffic oblivious to skinned knees and passing cars. Men in groups—loud, boisterous, joking with *maniacal enthusiasm. Gay men in Castro bars—sweating, stripped to the waist, dancing to throbbing, relentless music. It's **that** energy—sizzling, pounding, surging, thrusting, a little loud or tight-eyed, paranoid around the edges, territorial, tense, on guard, expansive, cranked up.*[7]

With some trepidation and a growing determination, I began to question what I thought I knew: the ideas about women, the concepts about men—the entire gamut of sexual politics. I also grew to enjoy and celebrate my own complexity and unique journey as a trans person—supple, yet entirely ordinary in my masculinity as time progressed. The feminism that I had learned from both the second and third waves of feminism would continue to inform my life. However, as years passed I came to question more feminist verities and to find myself often on the other side from my former peers in discussions or debates. I came to see that there actually *is* another side: in fact, many perspectives, many ways to create meaning from the ragged experience of a life.

I was the enemy I had been warned about all along. I laughed out loud and still laugh at that moment of discovery! I looked into the mirror and saw, finally, that man my eyes had searched for with such yearning and secret stardust as a child. *One man*—singular in a world of collective and competing identities—*one individual. A person.* In time, I would come to understand that no man was really always the cartoon male oppressor. All men, like all women, were finally free moral agents in a world of shifting gender roles. Individuals who grappled with choice and uncertainty, who felt joy and obdurate longing, and who pursued dreams.

As I enter my new life, I realize with awakening joy that the ground underneath me has shifted, and finally I am free—to dream and love and to become.

ENDNOTES

1   Max Wolf Valerio, *The Testosterone Files* (New York: Seal Press, 2006), 90.

2   Ibid., 41-42.

3   Radicalesbians, *The Woman Identified Woman* (Pittsburgh: Know, Inc., 1970), 1.

4   Ibid.

5   Valerio., 196.

6   Ibid., 106.

7   Ibid., 19.

Chapter 20

My Battle with the University of California

by Merle Woo

In my fourth year in Asian American Studies (AAS), UC passed a new four-year limit on visiting lecturers. This meant that after teaching for four years, no matter what, visiting lecturers were let go. It was this revolving door of a four-year rule that AAS used to fire me. During this period, some full-time lecturers were still getting the equivalent of tenure, called *Security of Employment*. Between 1981 and 1982 Ron Takaki, Chair of Ethnic Studies, demoted me without telling me from full-time lecturer to visiting lecturer, so I could never qualify for Security of Employment and could now be fired under this four-year rule. Moreover, I was the only lecturer at UC (including all nine campuses) ever fired under this rule. But to understand who I am and what this meant to me, I have to start at the beginning.

I was born in San Francisco's Chinatown in 1941 to an orphaned Korean mother and a Chinese immigrant father. I earned my BA from San Francisco State University (SFSU) in 1965, and then, while married with two children, got an MA in English Literature in 1969. While pursuing the latter degree, I witnessed the 1968-1969 student strikes at SFSU. That radicalized me. The student movement had caught fire across the country, and by 1968-69 and 1969-70, over five hundred institutions experienced disruptive protests each year.

I had attended Catholic schools, and I respected authority as most Asian-American kids were taught and never questioned the nuns assigned to teach the curriculum foisted upon us. And the striking students (a majority youth of color, including Asian Americans!) were making demands that were shockingly bold:

1. They demanded student participation in decision-making, whether in hiring or curriculum—they would actually take responsibility for their own education!
2. They demanded that professors or lecturers be not only academics but also activists.
3. They demanded that there would be a guarantee that, eventually, there would be established an autonomous Third World College, which could grant its own degrees.

Since I was the only woman of color at that time getting an MA in English at SFSU, I was offered a teaching position in the fall of 1969 as coordinator of the Educational Opportunity Program (EOP) in English. In essence, I was a beneficiary of the Third World Student Strikes, the liberation/anti-colonial struggles in the Third World, the anti-Vietnam War, and the black liberation movements in the U.S. I never forgot this in my 31 years of teaching at UC, SFSU, San Jose State University, and all the community colleges in the Bay Area as a migrant, visiting lecturer with no job security.

As soon as I started teaching—and by then, I was a single mother—I was determined to teach my students of color that standard English was simply a skill and had nothing to do with intelligence. We would never apply adjectives like "mutilated" or "broken" to our way of speaking Spanglish or Cantonese English. I fought for and taught a Third-World Literature course in the English Department, and developed and taught Third-World Women in the new Women Studies Program in 1977.

The years I spent as a lecturer were one long class struggle marked by fierce and ugly competition: the fight for basic worker's rights (such as job security and health benefits, raises and promotions) and the betrayals of selling workers out and firing them for a piece of the managerial pie.

Most students wanted a degree so they could get a decent paying job. At the same time, they wanted tools to survive in order to give back to their communities. These were the students I would fight for: students oppressed by poverty, racism, sexism, and homophobia. One of my major goals has been to help students discover the truth that the debased and inferior status of people of color, women, and queers in American society is used to justify exploitation for profits. I wanted my students to grow into empowered individuals who, by working collaboratively and together, could educate themselves to reach their potential.

This education would confront the fundamentals of patriarchal capitalist education: submissiveness to authority, unquestioning work habits, passivity, obedience, competitiveness with coworkers.

In 1968-1969 Third World Strikes, students, faculty, community, and radical activists led the way. Despite police brutality and attacks by campus administrators, the rebels were tenacious, united, and they won ethnic studies, affirmative action, student democracy, the hiring of activist, and academic faculty, and the implementation of community-related courses. *Self-determination* and *relevance* were key concepts. These studies were about changing society.

SFSU's take-backs began in the spring of '69. They got underway with a few lecturers being terminated. At the end of each semester, I had to go in to the dean's office to make sure that my courses would remain on the schedule. Fighting to keep my courses became part of my job. If I didn't, my ideas (and I) would be out on the street. Still, these were heady times. Asian Americans and women of color were becoming visible as militant protestors against our invisibility and second-class status.

In the spring of 1978, I accepted a full-time lecturer position in Asian American Studies (AAS), UC Berkeley. I felt like I had come home as my true self. I had evolved into a proud Asian American feminist, a lesbian... and whole. I could be a leader in movements for radical social change.

It took only one year to realize that all was not well. I was teaching the humanities courses, but also coordinating the Reading and Composition series, which placed me above the other long-time lecturers who were there before me, and I realized I was being used to punish them for talking back. They leveled their animosity at me.

In my second year, students asked me to write a support letter protesting the ladder-rank faculty's elimination of the community-language courses Cantonese and Tagalog. My letter turned the tenure-track faculty against me. Suddenly, I was the enemy of the powers that be.

In 1980-1981, AAS faculty were coming up for tenure. To get it, they had to play ball with the administration, which was pressuring them to shift to the right, to become more academic, more respectable. Were we going to remain true to the communities who put us on campus or become extensions of bourgeois academia? The opportunistic armchair Leftists went for the latter. These were the very same faculty who were leaders of the strikes only eleven years prior! AAS was becoming more academic; the community-related courses were eliminated, and by 1981, the longtime lecturers were fired. But not before we had a spirited teach-in and boycott of AAS.

My bosses couldn't fault the quality of my teaching, so it was my lesbianism and my membership in Radical Women (the trailblazing left wing of the woman's movement) and the Freedom Socialist Party that they spread rumors about: using things that I was proud of as weapons to ruin my reputation as a teacher and activist. I provided them with even more ammunition by addressing the 1981 San Francisco Lesbian and Gay Pride rally and march. That fall, Ron Takaki suddenly demoted me.

I had become active in the American Federation of Teachers (AFT). AFT had come to realize that tenured faculty and lecturers were in competition for teaching jobs and so, while tenured faculty and lecturers had been in the same grouping, lecturers were granted their own unit. As a result, when I was fired, AFT stepped in for me and the lecturers, filing an unfair labor practice with the Public Employment Relations Board against UC for implementing the four-year rule on lecturers. The Administrative Law Judge (who happened to have been an ally of Cesar Chavez, the union organizer and co-founder of the United Farmworker's Association) declared the four-year rule an unfair labor practice. UC was ordered to rehire me in 1983. UC refused.

When it became clear that I was being fired, Radical Women (RW) and the Freedom Socialist Party (FSP) immediately encouraged me to form a Merle Woo Defense Committee (MWDC). I was taught, advised, and supported by these two advocates for female empowerment and working class self-emancipation. RW and FSP had fought legal cases of members who were fired from their jobs, and it had a solid history of fighting union battles.

Two coordinators of the MWDC, Karen Brodine and Nancy Reiko Kato, kept the overview of the legal and public angles of the fight. With their support, I was never isolated. They taught me to politically characterize exactly what UC was doing to me and why. The powers that be want us to fight on their terms and with their rules. But instead of saying that I was being let go because of some arbitrary four-year rule, I put my case in context: that I was being fired because I supported student democracy and protested the rightward shift in Ethnic Studies. When we filed suits in federal and state courts, we charged the university of violation of my free speech rights and discrimination based on race, sex, sexuality, and political ideology.

It was a lopsided battle from the start: a single woman—and a *lesbian*—taking on a monolith. The University of California is the largest public employer in the state. In that constellation, ultimate power resides with the Board of Regents. They play a very conservatizing role. But students, unionists, lecturers, and community activists supported my case. Still, backing wasn't universal. One Asian-American male ex-student replied when approached, "Why don't you go get help from those white feminists [read: lesbians] of yours." Some Asians, women, and gays hated my Trotskyist feminism and its multi-issueism. And here we were, fighting for the equality of Asians, women, and queers! Some feminists were racists; some unionists were labor bureaucrats; they wouldn't assist.

But about 20 staunch members of the MWDC did research, organized support, and wrote press releases. Hundreds of well-known activists, academics, writers, even mainstream Democrats endorsed the case. And we in RW and FSP came up with strategy and political policy, and our radical lawyers wrote the legal briefs.

Socialism on Trial is a book containing James P. Cannon's testimony at one of the most important political trials in U.S. history. He was among 18 leaders of the Socialist Worker's Party and the Minneapolis Teamsters Union who were found guilty of "conspiring to advocate the overthrow of the U.S. government." Their defense strategy in the trial was to use the courtroom as a platform for educating the public about socialism.

We were going to do just that—my complaint would be an education about my socialist feminist politics and what I saw as a real democratic education. We also included in the complaint the fact that, at Berkeley, Ethnic Studies faculty were paid less than faculty in other departments and that within Ethnic Studies women were paid less than men! Meanwhile, in a classic case of brutal income inequality, administrators and deans were making annual salaries in the hundreds of thousands of dollars.

Our many work parties were lively and spirited. We fundraised by organizing forums on *free speech on the job*, featuring professors, lecturers, and librarians who had won cases and been reinstated. We got the support of the alternative presses and even got articles in the mainstream press.

In the spring of 1982, my lawyer in the case and I met with UC Counsel.

We had come to negotiate, because one of the AAS longstanding lecturers had agreed to testify for me. This ex-lecturer was willing to say that Ling-chi Wang, Coordinator of Asian American Studies, had said, "It is inappropriate for a lesbian to represent Asian American Studies."

I was reinstated in 1984 and received back pay for the two years that I was fighting the case. But AAS wouldn't take me back. For the next two years, I taught in the Graduate School of Education. Students who were teaching in Peace and Conflict Studies asked me to be their faculty supervisor in "Organizing Across the Color Line" and "Multicultural Lesbian and Gay Studies." I became a member of Lesbians and Gays Against Apartheid.

The anti-apartheid movement was exploding on campus, and Faculty for Full Divestment was demanding that the university divest its millions in South Africa. AFT asked me to play a visible role by simply sitting in on negotiations regarding maintaining academic freedom.

In the spring of 1986, I was fired again—this time under the ruse that I was being paid from a special fund from the Office of the Vice-Chancellor, Roderick Park. Of course, this violated the "equal treatment" for employment rule, i.e., that I was not being treated the same as other lecturers in the UC system. The MWDC regrouped, and we filed a union grievance. The AFT lawyer Bill Carder and my union rep Roz Spafford were my advocates. It took three years—until 1989—to get to arbitration, when it was only supposed to take 90 days! Still, UC tried more delaying tactics: saying that their labor representative was sick and had to postpone arbitration.

UC had tried to sabotage us because we had organized nearly 60 people to attend the hearing. So, instead, we started marching around the building, chanting, "Take two aspirin and come to arbitration!" Unionists from SFSU's California Faculty Association and lecturers crossed the Bay to support me. Although union arbitrators are supposed to be neutral, the union arbitrator was a law professor at Hastings (a UC school). He ruled that I had been treated unfairly and was to be immediately reinstated, but he wrote that my firing was not deliberate and refused to state that it was because of retaliation and continuing discrimination, which we had claimed and given ample evidence to support.

From 1989 to 1991, I tried to get reinstated. To do so, I had to interview in the Rhetoric Department. The chair singled me out during an orientation meeting and said, "The Reading and Composition Committee has decided that we will no longer teach *ideas* in our reading and composition courses. We will only teach the different types of essay forms. And that means you, Ms. Woo. We don't want you."

I interviewed with Asian American Studies. The entire faculty was there. They said, "If we have to hire you, we will have to terminate all the other lecturers who've been teaching here because of budgetary limitations. Do you want that?"

UC hired a San Francisco law firm to fight my reinstatement. They tried to drag me in for a psychiatric examination. But we couldn't find a lawyer! Our previous lawyers had been good, but they hated that the Defense Committee insisted on playing an active and equal role in determining legal policy.

My Defense Committee (which had stayed together) hit the law books and did our own research. We took UC's demand for a psychiatric examination to Alameda Court and won. The judge even said that if UC played any more nasty acts of intimidation, she'd personally throw economic sanctions at them.

By 1991, I had just had a double mastectomy, and I just didn't want to be in litigation until I died. The Defense Committee agreed with me, and we chose to stop fighting for my reinstatement.

Although never reinstated, I received back pay for all the years we had fought UC. UC also gave me a $75,000 check in 1991 just to go away. But I refused to sign a gag order. And, most importantly, we had won three legal cases against them.

From 1987 to 1997, I taught in Women Studies at SFSU. I had taught there off and on since 1977. Women Studies had begun as a collective of lecturers, with students participating. But as the program developed, there was the drive to grant a Master's in Women Studies, which meant tenure for ladder rank faculty. One was a post-modernist who believed that lesbianism was a Western construct and did not exist outside of the United States. The other was a cultural nationalist who refused to trust anyone not African American. They also got rid of student and lecturer involvement in decision-making and dropped even once-a-semester general department meetings. Lesbian-centered courses were eliminated and so were the lecturers who taught them, including myself. But students and lecturers fought back; a few of us kept our jobs and maintained a student democracy until 1997...a great victory in and of itself.

From 2000-2003, I taught in Women Studies at San Jose State University—the first time I was hired with everyone knowing exactly who I was.

I retired for health reasons in December 2003. Faculty and staff were all collegial—a great way to end my teaching career.

In January 2014, there is a national trend to dismantle public education. Public schools and colleges are cut to the bone, so that more students must attend privately run charter schools and for-profit colleges, where they rack up enormous debt. The goal of privatization is to impose the corporate model. An integral part of this trend is the threat of San Francisco's City College losing its accreditation, which might happen as soon as the summer of 2014.

The first community college to be put on the chopping block—to be headed toward privatization—is CCSF. With its 85,000 students, with campuses throughout the city, with its LGBT Studies. I have been inspired by these young student leaders, from the Women's Resource Center, from the Save CCSF coalition, from the unions. They are resolute.

Every student activist who has taken responsibility to get a decent, democratic education will have been forever changed by exerting individual power in solidarity with others. For once, they have been subjects in their own destiny rather than passive objects acted upon by others.

In a time when government funding for education is being cut back, when heroic teachers are voluntarily paying for school supplies out of their own pockets, and when the most needy are being marginalized, the possibilities for positive change are not difficult to imagine when we envision what education might be in a democracy where every child has access to free quality public education, where students are taught to think critically and to speak out. And where young individuals can choose something they would love to do and can do it—from each according to their ability, to each according to their need.

Chapter 21

The Quilt

by Julie Rhoad

"Every experience deeply felt in life needs to be passed along—whether it be through words and music, chiseled in stone, painted with a brush, or sewn with a needle. It is a way of reaching immortality."

—Thomas Jefferson

When I was old enough to begin to comprehend the impact that my brother's death had on my family (on my parents, in particular), my mother shared the story of her beautiful eight-year-old son Paul and the events surrounding the accident that took his life in an instant one fateful August day in 1958.

My parents adopted me two years later, when their healing process was well underway—or so it appeared. The truth was, though, that the pain remained too intense for either of them to unearth outside of the privacy of their relationship. So, in our household, the subject of Paul was—and to some degree, remains—taboo; his memory was for many years a carefully guarded secret held only by my parents. Throughout my childhood, I naively thought that ours was a family devoid of emotion (other than overprotection and worry), and I didn't know why. Once the story was revealed in intimate detail, it became apparent that, in their silence, my parents *were parenting*—trying to shelter their living children from some of life's harshest realities—tucking their grief away in order to give us the gift of precious childhoods unburdened by knowing profound grief and loss.

In telling Paul's story nearly 25 years after his death, my mother offered me a glimpse into her journey filled with agonizing pain, sorrow, and, ultimately, survival. In her re-telling of the story of that horrible Saturday in August, she included what I thought at the time was a side note to the main story.

Not long after Paul's death, my mother and her dear friend, Frances— herself a mother of four—sat next to one another at a small dinner gathering. They spoke of Paul, and, at one point, Frances uttered that well-worn phrase used by those who attempt to console those who grieve, saying: "I simply could not have borne it." My mother couldn't remember how she responded at the time (something unfailingly polite, I'm certain), but she did remember what she was thinking: "My dear, being human, you will one day be faced with the sheer necessity of bearing the unbearable. The question is not *if* you will bear it—for no detour around disaster is possible. The only question is *how* you will bear it."

To this day, I wonder if my mother was deliberate in her timing. Did she sense—even without my revealing the truth of my life—what was happening? Did she know that I was already feeling the impact of AIDS in my community? That my friends and I were being asked to bear the unbearable?

It was 1983, I was working in the professional theatre, and many of the people I cherished, people I loved, were getting sick. They were young, beautiful, talented men—in the prime of their creative lives—and they were dying rapid, hard, inexplicable deaths and we—the survivors—were going to have to determine *how we would bear it.*

Early responses to the epidemic (that would eventually be called AIDS) varied: public health officials, scientists, and medical professionals searched for answers but were making little headway against the disease; friends and loved ones marshaled their individual and collective resources: creating care circles and taking shifts at the bedsides of the sick and dying, forming teams to care for pets, to deliver meals, to raise awareness, to advocate for action, and so much more.

In my world and in those early years, the professional artistic community experienced a cataclysmic loss of life—we literally lost a generation of artists. We did not bear this loss quietly, but we bore it nonetheless. Friends and colleagues across America responded using the most powerful weapon in our arsenal—our art. Professional artists gave freely of their talent, unleashing their artistic imagination in order to raise funding, awareness and support for service and advocacy efforts in desperate need.

The numbers were *staggering*. In just four years, 15,527 cases of AIDS had been reported, resulting in 12,529 deaths in America. And still, in the face of this tragedy—in the face of overwhelming evidence that this was rapidly becoming an epidemic of global proportion—many in power elected to turn their backs on the suffering simply because the sick and dying appeared to be predominantly homosexual men.

To some, these individuals were merely statistics, and their loss appeared to be of little consequence. This level of indifference at the highest levels of government added a heavy burden to everyone experiencing the very worst that this disease had to offer: the burden of diminished hope. We were suffering great loss, experiencing grief, bearing witness to unspeakable suffering, and, at the very same time, being denied the value of our existence.

Then in 1985, Cleve Jones had an idea. The AIDS Memorial Quilt didn't begin with yards of fabric but with a few hundred soggy handwritten poster boards carried by marchers in the annual candlelight march to mark the assassinations of San Francisco Supervisor Harvey Milk and Mayor George Moscone. Earlier in the day, Cleve had handed out poster boards asking marchers to carry signs containing the names of their friends and loved ones who had died. When they reached the old Federal Building at end of that march, they crawled up three stories and covered the face of the building with this poster-board memorial. There, standing in the rain, watching as the boards absorbed the rain and fluttered to the pavement, Cleve thought, "it looks like a quilt".

Two years later, a group of then strangers gathered with Cleve in a San Francisco storefront to remember the names and lives of loved ones they feared history would forget. They were angry, scared, frustrated, heartbroken, and determined to create a memorial that would make it impossible for the world to dismiss or deny AIDS—impossible to ignore the value of each life claimed by AIDS. With this seemingly simple act of love and defiance, The NAMES Project was founded and the first 40 panels of The AIDS Memorial Quilt created.

With the advent of The Quilt—arguably one of the most democratic memorials of our time—statistics became souls; AIDS became "our problem" instead of "their problem," and a new era of advocacy and support for the AIDS cause was ushered in. In that same year, those first memorials began to travel the nation, and in October of 1987, they— along with 1,900 other panels—traveled to Washington, D.C., where they made their first appearance on the National Mall.

I remember learning about The Quilt while I was doing a site survey for the 1988 Democratic National Convention in Atlanta, Georgia. The Quilt was touring the nation following the first display in Washington, D.C., and Atlanta was one of the cities hoping to host a display. Sadly, the news of this powerful memorial came along with news that included more loss: three company members from the Brunswick Music Theatre, where I had been a stage manager during the summers of 1978–1981. This company—the actors, designers, directors, choreographers, musicians, stage managers and stage hands, interns, and apprentices—was *theatre family*. We lived, worked (from dawn until late into the night six days a week), and played together in beautiful Brunswick, Maine, for twelve intense weeks each year. We watched out for one another (during the season and in the off-season as well), we celebrated each other's successes, comforted each other during times of loss, and, in losing Martin, Bill, and Gregg, we were forever changed. Standing on the concrete floor of the Georgia World Congress Center that winter day, flooded with fond memories of these wonderful men, I knew that one day their names would be found in stitches on The AIDS Memorial Quilt.

The Quilt came to Atlanta. There, standing in the midst of this extraordinary memorial, my friends and I agreed that this was actually *sacred space*. Excerpts from Abraham Lincoln's Gettysburg Address began to echo in my head, including:

We can not dedicate—we can not consecrate—we can not hallow— this ground.... It is for us the living, rather, to be dedicated here to the unfinished work.... It is rather for us to be here dedicated to the great task remaining before us—that from these honored dead we take increased devotion to that cause for which they gave the last full measure of devotion—that we here highly resolve that these dead shall not have died in vain...

* * *

Several of us began panels immediately following the display, and many of us began to pin some of our collective hope on The Quilt, heartened by our shared belief that this most democratic memorial—made literally *by the people for the people*—would be able to transform the national dialog about AIDS from one of contempt, blame, and disregard for one community to one of compassion, action, and justice for all. We pinned our hopes on the potential we saw and the feelings we felt, believing that the lessons found in the stitches of The AIDS Memorial Quilt would reveal to all what we thought and what science and medicine already knew—that AIDS didn't discriminate.

Time marched on, science and medicine advanced; activists continued to apply pressure, but the epidemic continued to outpace efforts to stem the tide of new infections and death.

The Quilt continued to grow.

Throughout the late 1980s and early 1990s, The Quilt served as a weapon as evidence and testimony deployed to fend off intolerance and ignorance. The Quilt offered proof: proof that life mattered. Proof that this disease—originally burdened with the name "Gay-Related Immune Deficiency" (GRID)—had and was continuing to claim the lives of individuals from nearly every sector of society.

The Quilt continued to grow, and so did its purpose and its power.

By the end of 1995, AIDS was the leading cause of death among all Americans ages 25-44, according to the *New York Times*. The number of cases reported in the United States totaled 581,429—the number of deaths 362,004. New drug combination therapies were on the horizon, and, in 1996—when the panels numbered nearly 40,000—The AIDS Memorial Quilt returned once again to Washington, D.C., where it filled the grounds of the National Mall one weekend in October.

Standing among the panels, this time in our nation's capital, I was once again reminded of the power of The Quilt—its ability to educate and advocate effectively not with facts and figures, but with emotion embedded in powerful personal expression—once again, overwhelmed with emotion connected to my history and the history of others. Once again, moved to participate. Images from that display filled the airwaves throughout the nation and the world and moved people everywhere to respond: to act with compassion and resolve.

What began with that simple act of defiance—containing in a single 3-foot-by-6-foot piece of cloth and a single name—now records the lives of more than 94,000 individuals, weighs 54 tons, and is recognized (under the Save America's Treasures Act) as an *American Treasure*. In the years since that group of strangers first set the sewing machines in motion in that tiny San Francisco storefront, The Quilt has grown from 40 panels to 48,000, the number of names contained in its stitches from 2,000 to 94,000. It has been displayed in its entirety in our nation's capital six times and is considered the preeminent record of the human response to HIV and AIDS. Throughout its history, The Quilt has been used to fight prejudice, raise awareness and funding, link hands with the global community in the fight against AIDS, provide grief therapy and healing, and educate and prevent HIV and AIDS.

By the time I was asked to lead The NAMES Project Foundation in 2001, it was no longer a fledgling agency led by charismatic activists giving voice to the suffering of one community; it was an agency that was charged with the care and use of a remarkable (and huge) multicultural record—a primary source—that was (and is, to this day) at once a memorial, a teaching tool, a scholarly resource, and a unique documentation of life connected to the age of AIDS. The NAMES Project Foundation was an agency that was grappling with its role in society, with the current realities of HIV and AIDS, and with the impact that those realities were having on The NAMES Project and The AIDS Memorial Quilt.

The NAMES Project had achieved so very much. The AIDS Memorial Quilt had become both a catalyst and conduit: epic in scope and intimate in personal detail. Displays of The Quilt were continuing to foster important conversations in civic and private settings alike. What began as a weapon (somewhat paradoxically, as it was made of fabric and ephemeral material)— with an original intent to remember—to safeguard the memory of individuals in order to advance a movement—had become a vast accumulation of sentiment: a 54-ton handmade, aging treasure with a very different set of duties and needs. Both would require a different type of stewardship.

By then, those first friends lost to AIDS, Marty and Bill and Gregg— along with Ronnie, Michael, Ron, and my dear friend, Adam—all had a place on The Quilt. I had achieved a level of success in my career and was ready to make a shift and work in the non-profit arena. I had volunteered for The NAMES Project and wanted to make sure that, even in the face of seemingly insurmountable challenges, The Quilt would continue to be accessible to the widest possible audience. I cared for the memory of my friends and colleagues, for the memory of the movement, and for the memory of tens of thousands of individuals impacted by HIV and AIDS, and I wanted to help make sure that The Quilt would be able to impart meaning and teach for generations to come.

I have been the CEO of The NAMES Project for more than a decade. AIDS is now in its fourth decade. Science, medicine, and society have progressed to the point where it is once again possible to imagine the end of AIDS. It is possible to believe that the trajectory of HIV and AIDS has changed—that today we are experiencing the beginning of the end of AIDS. AIDS is far from over, but it is at a critical juncture with the promise of a turning point for the better.

After years of struggle, transition, and change, some of the questions that drew me to The Quilt remain. How will the experiences of one of the greatest challenges the world has ever seen be remembered? How will the lessons learned—contemporary and historical—be shared for generations to come? What can I do to ensure that the memory of loved ones will be available to teach future generations? These are all questions of stewardship. We were founded to remember their names, and in doing so, advance a movement, and today the need also includes one of safeguarding the memory of the movement as well. The work continues. Perhaps the answers lie in stitches, the very intangibility of which will ensure that they will last forever. For the panels of The AIDS Memorial Quilt—panels that once served as weapons in the fight against homophobia, stigma, and intolerance—have become ambassadors. In fact, they are some of the world's most powerful ambassadors and envoys that the cause of human rights has ever known. They will always educate and advocate effectively, not with facts and figures, but with emotion embedded in powerful personal expression. They are our guides, our navigators, our teachers—and they stand ready to remind us that we are connected one to another, that we are responsible for one another. They challenge us all to pinpoint what really matters. They are here for me, and they are here on behalf of people from all walks of life, all around the globe. They will stand the test of time and they will help us make sense of—and bear—this seemingly unbearable human tragedy.

Chapter 22

The Red Camaro

by Matt Ebert

In 1981, I was a junior in high school, and very close to dropping out. Public high school was too crowded, and focus on studies was lost to the party and my deep desire for freedom. I struggled internally with same sex attraction. At the same time, I was sexually active not only with my schoolmates, but with older men too. At sixteen, I hustled New York City on weekends with a gay upperclassman. He had a boyfriend there, a wealthy older man, who helped us acclimate to gay nightlife. Back then, it was easy to erase your birthday off those printed New York state drivers licenses and make yourself of legal age. I remember Denny and I changed my birth year from 1965 to 1962 so we could get into all the gay bars. We laughed, and we toasted to our health in the back seat of my parents' copper-colored Oldsmobile Cutlass Supreme.

My first gay bar was Julius on 10th Street, but it wasn't long before I was a regular at Uncle Charlie's, The Ninth Circle, and that hallowed gay nightclub—The Saint. Uptown and down, we took the city's pulse, and being young and inexperienced, I often went home drunk and accompanied. After some clumsy sex my partners would stay or go, and I would wake up the next morning and wonder aloud, "What was that?" Sometimes I remembered nothing—a sexual blackout with no beginning, middle, or end. That was my youth in the early 1980s.

This new world seemed so alluring. Walking the city streets I would get a hard-on, aroused by the smell of this erotic and forbidden concrete and glass metropolis. It was the proximity of people. It was the quantity, and the crush of New York City. It was one long, beautiful love story. I took my bite, and I romanced everything. A big kid, I was broad shouldered and made my way, never felt stranded or alone, no fear for my physical safety. I walked nights in the Village (east and west), Chelsea, and uptown determined to map every sign, every bent corner, every dead-end block—even the hydrants knew my name. I learned the subway system, knew where cheap food and drink could be found. The currency of cool lay in knowing where to locate diamonds in the rubble above the rock.

I started college, film school, in 1983. I wanted to be a director so bad it hurt. I felt I had, now at eighteen, a lifetime of stories to tell. I had no idea things to come would offer me two lifetimes of stories. Though I would never make a feature film—I would live one instead. Between 1984 and 1987, lives in the West Village and all over New York changed rapidly. I lost friends at a murderous rate to a horrible illness no one seemed to understand. All we knew was it appeared, made you sick, and you bounced back or you didn't. The kids I ran with from eighteen to twenty-one—the hustlers, musicians, artists, lovers, and friends, the audience for all the movies I would never make—most of them were gone by twenty-five. I knew lives we lived together could no longer be shared. I was the only keeper of night.

As it turned out, Denny's lover was the first to go. That toast to our health went unanswered when Denny stopped taking my calls. All of a sudden, I was the lone repository for all our hopes and dreams. Our memories were mine, and mine alone when he died in early spring. That was a horrible frost—I missed him, and I was shell-shocked very early by his disappearance. Would it be inevitable that one day I would be in a wooden box, or stuffed inside a plastic garbage bag? Would an urn on the mantle hold my ashes too? This was my daily dread.

I had a bright, wildly intelligent girl friend in film school. She was a documentary major and a cinematographer. She had decided in 1986 to make a documentary about a gay man with AIDS. I believed, and later she confirmed, she had thought of me when she chose her subject. We had become very close, and I knew she was right—death would come for me before age twenty-five. It now seemed inevitable; I would get AIDS and die. There are no words to reach this depth; the pit in my stomach was an unsealed well. I was thrown in like the last son.

The documentary process was strenuous. I was assigned sound, and I stalked the village with a boom microphone and a tape deck, recorded interviews and tracked our subject. I listened to his diminished pulse. My microphone became a stethoscope to his heart, and it picked up the sluggish beat of a community on the way down. It boosted the deafening silence of a sick world in free-fall. I can tell you by 1986, the West Village was a powder keg ready to explode. The anger, fear, and guilt we felt as our beloved died, it pulsated in the avenues and alleyways—especially on Christopher Street.

Christopher Street was the epicenter of my gay universe. It was for my teenager years liberation row. Now it was paralyzed, catatonic with fear—it was dying. Where once men ran with lust and longing, blood in the streets clotted and clustered like pools of rot. In fall, when the trees turned their backs, our crew went to a rally in Sheridan Square, right in the heart of the village. It was near Halloween, and the speaker at the podium was Vito Russo. Vito was the town crier. He stood there, microphone in hand, and screamed at the world around him. His words still resonate:

There are more people making dresses for the Halloween Parade than standing out here on the streets. They are teaching the children of this world to hate you. We are going to die, we are all going to die!

I was in shock. I had never heard gay rage articulated. His voice was a powerful mix of compassion, horror, fear, and frustration at this inevitable end of the road. I looked downward—he drew the needle on my tape deck into the red. I dialed down while he blew the metal from the marker.

ACT UP, the AIDS Coalition To Unleash Power, hadn't staged its first action (Wall Street—March 1987), but activists bloomed like algae in a springtime pond. I knew the teamster picket lines my father organized. I grew up in a democratic, union-strong family, so the scab was not an unfamiliar sight. Union placards, bumper stickers, and worker's rights came naturally. But this—AIDS—how could I morph what I knew about direct action into an epidemic?

When the movement finally coalesced, I went to my first meeting and officially became ACT UP. I drove the distance from my small studio apartment in Port Chester, New York to the LGBT community center on 13th Street every Monday night. I radicalized my fear and shook paralysis from my brain. There were young men and women in this group, they were politically motivated, and that was sexy. In fact, this was a very sexy coalition. Once there, people could be honest about their status, and it was appropriate to love them without divisive plus versus minus stigma we see today. We were young, we sung in unison. My first lover in ACT UP was a sweet young fellow—he was blond, a Canadian with a great sense of humor and a sturdy, muscular body. His HIV status was not important to me, and it didn't stop me from loving him. Sex was trans-formative—but eventually, within the year, we both moved on to other lovers. He moved to San Francisco as he always wanted, and that is where he died. It crippled me, and when it finally tapped my ears I collapsed in a ball and begged for mercy.

ACT UP taught me to use condoms; it was my sex education. As lovers, we learned to protect ourselves. That's an important distinction: ACT UP was sexy because it was an LGBT group not devoted to drink and drug, there was no shame here. We were political and hungry to learn. I had never met such radicals, let alone joined a group of them. My refusal to live in a closet aside, I was naive and inexperienced with gay politics and true love.

I had other lovers in ACT UP. One stands out because he picked me up in a red Chevy Camaro and drove me to meetings. We spent four years in an embrace that may have lasted a lifetime. I was so in love, and for the first time in my life I had met a guy who loved me just as much. It was short lived—his health declined rapidly. But I was determined to stay with him, follow my heart, and navigate our now crippled sex life. He was that beautiful, a Mexican and Italian-American mix with a face divine, a flawless body white as marble, chiseled as Michelangelo's David. He was a fighter flushed out of a desperate corner, strained with no gloves or head gear and, like me, he had grown up wild and free, only to watch his world crumble like a sawdust dumpling.

He died on October 16, 1992. I will never forget that day. Sometimes you hear people talk about where they were when JFK died, or 9/11. I would easily forget those dates before I would forget the day my true love died. That day a meteorite struck my heart, and the crater made a carbon footprint for life. I drank so hard I died again. Now the blackouts came like mighty waves with no warning.

I like to bookend my time with ACT UP from the moment I met Canada to the moment a Camaro died. That would be mid-1987 to late 1992. I was a quiet member at first. Then I realized I had power—sexual power. My job? I was an ACT UP marine. I could use sex to bring young men to the room. I could walk into a bar, pick up a guy, steal his underwear, and tell him to meet at the center next Monday night if he wanted them back. They came in droves, with or without underwear. I used to say: "Give me a brick and tell me where to throw it." The seasoned activists would laugh at me, but they loved me when the world did not. My new ACT UP comrades and I formed a youth movement because we shared the same goal—end the plague before it ends us.

Every Monday night, a list of our dead would be read aloud, and the tears would hydrate dirty flowers of discontent and damnation. I participated in actions against the FDA, CDC, Wall Street, and the Catholic Church. The Days of Desperation, the Waldorf Astoria, Trump Tower, Grand Central Station—these endless weekly battles were fought and sometimes won. I wheatpasted Gran Fury posters all over town. In the middle of the night, we'd smoke a joint, mix our paste, then hit the streets to share the message. I even wheatpasted an AIDSGATE poster onto the back of my truck. Those glorious, upturned pink triangle "Silence = Death" stickers—we blasted them up and down the coast. A woman's voice whispered: "Give a kid a sticker, tell him where to put it, then watch an activist grow." We were political and medical science, LGBT history manifest—up in arms like Stonewall before us. Dare I say we were more? Not only did we confront our sexuality, we saved it.

These women and men turned me from a lazy party boy to an AIDS activist. And at every demonstration they'd foist my rugged mug front and center like candy on a stick. I didn't mind at all. I would have auctioned my body, burned or sold everything I owned if it would make ACT UP richer or bring back the dead. I was so tired of death, and I knew like everyone else without direct action we were going nowhere in this pandemic. And then I walked home, and I grieved. You watched, helpless, as more people died. Some you knew, some you didn't. Now this was war.

I was arrested and released from jail many times. By 1992, I had to drift away. I needed work, because I was broken. I started using drugs— heroin was easy to score and I needed to triage the pain. Dope became my panacea and my sex life. I snorted glycine bags of white powder to anesthetize my grief. I would steal and swallow AZT, then shoot China White as a bitter chaser. Heroin and AZT—my clinical trial. It was commonplace among my closest allies. Sudden as a thunderstorm in June, dope infiltrated the East Village, and a hard rain fell on every corner.

The team broke up fully loaded—these gone boys. The march ceased, our feet iced out by the bruising winter of '92, blackened from exposure to the elements—we were all worn thin by an early frost.

I left New York. This town had by now become a ghost town for me. Brownstones and apartment buildings emptied of souls—they were decrepit mausoleums now. My mind was ill—heated by fever and detoxing from services rendered. To the child that was, the teenager who waltzed in dark alleys, the young man of no political conscience—ACT UP was my lifesaver. There were days when ACT UP was disorganized and fraught like teased hair, but they are still some of the best years of my life—a strange thing when you consider all the death that occurred.

When my father, a World War II vet, lay dying, we talked often about his years in service. We discussed post-traumatic stress, but I never relayed my belief—ACT UP was my World War. There was a tacit understanding, a steel bridge built on complementary struggle, on combat and early death. I loved my father. He passed away in 2011, and I was at his bedside. He was a Merchant Marine and he loved to sail, so I whispered into his ear a dream. I placed him gently on a sloop, rocked him from island to island, until he found a perfect beach to rest his weary bones. I was lucky to have him, and I credit him for that tiny spark that allowed me to become part of a flame that blew up the powder keg. And when my time comes, I'm not sure it will be a sailboat. Instead, what brings me to paradise may very well be a red Camaro.

Chapter 23

Between the Sexes

by Tiger Howard Devore

Intersex children are born somewhere between male and female. Genetically, humans are female first. Maleness is actually a mutation. What matters are the hormones. As it develops, the fetus moves, basically, from female to male in many steps, and its sex organs literally change how they look and function. If there is an interruption in that masculinization, then that child appears at birth as being between the sexes.

When those children are born, they aren't always identified, because sometimes doctors just don't notice and think the baby is female or male. Sometimes, those kids are raised for the first year or two in whatever sex they were assumed to be when they were born and, later on, the birth difference becomes apparent. At that point, the doctors and the experts are called in.

If a child is identified at birth, surgery typically happens within the first year. The parents are told what the guessed-at sex is going to be, girl or boy, and then the child is set on a course of surgery and treatment to make that child as much of a boy, or as much of a girl, as possible. Sometimes it doesn't work out so well. If the sex of assignment doesn't match the sex of identity, the individual may need more surgery to change sex or may simply commit suicide.

Many intersex advocates are working to get the medical establishment to wait—to let intersex children determine their sex of identity—so that when they are three, four, or five, they can make that decision themselves. Some kids will identify as being neither male nor female, and that is difficult for parents. They may want their child to grow up like they did: to have children, a family, and to have that kind of life. But that doesn't always fit for an intersex person.

For parents, it is a great psychological challenge to raise your children understanding that they may reveal to you that their identity doesn't match with the sex they have been assigned. Or to be told by doctors that, in order to preserve genital functioning and sensation, the treatment will be no surgery, no hormones, and that, until the child can decide for themselves, nothing that could irreversibly change this kid will be done until the child can make that decision.

This is called "informed consent"—the right to determine what medical procedures your body will endure instead of having some other authority decide that without your knowledge or permission. With children we don't do informed consent, in particular when it concerns their sex organs being different.

Very few parents are willing to raise a baby as "gender neutral." Most want to have a provisional assignment of sex so the child can avoid being stigmatized and teased. In general society, everybody is going to ask: are you a boy, or are you a girl? That kid doesn't want to answer that question, because they don't have an answer until they know themselves.

Medical providers must support the family by providing the potential results of what their choices might look like as their child matures and faces development of sexual identity. Parents are promised one or two surgeries, but, in fact, it can involve more than twenty surgeries over time. This situation has improved, but we are still cutting into flesh and stitching it up with something, so as much as the techniques have improved, we are still cutting into healthy flesh—and that means scarring. No one can tell how skin is going to heal, but we know that scarred skin is not as flexible as healthy skin. We know that a scar does not have a blood supply or nervous feeling, so this needs to be considered when doctors tell parents that they are just going to cut the skin up "a little bit," and the child will be fine. No doctor can promise that.

Doctors assure parents that children will not remember early childhood surgery. If surgery is done in the first year, children typically don't remember, but many kids have terrible traumatic memories of what it was like to be in the hospital; they often report this in therapy. Parents are not prepared to talk about early childhood surgery. They often have no support in dealing with their children's memories of being abandoned in a place where they were hurt by strangers. And that is the way kids often remember it.

How intersex infants are treated differs from culture to culture. When we look at war-like societies that have to raise warriors and breeding females (such as Spartan and Apache societies), the kid is thrown off a cliff or left on a hillside to die—destroyed right after birth. In agrarian cultures there tends to be a spiritual element, like the Zunis and more ancient East Indian societies. They have a whole set of traditions, according to which they raise intersex individuals to be shamans, healers, and spiritual teachers. They are given a special place, because they are special looking and different from the men and women who have assigned roles. In other cultures, intersex individuals are given the chance to be basically high-status females. They are identified as something between male and female and are given a more female role, but are in charge of all the females in their family group. This is true in the South Pacific and in other Pacific Islands.

The most common association—a mythical hermaphrodite—is impossible. No baby is ever born half-male and half-female. Babies develop into male or female, or something in between. There are very rare individuals that have a breast on one side, a flat chest on the other side—where they do look split in the middle—but they don't have a penis on one side and a vagina on the other. Those rare individuals that you will see in sideshows, circuses, and other such attractions are the evidence for that ancient mythology.

In our society, at least until now, an essential choice has been made: to make a predetermined assignment of gender, as if the nature of that human being has nothing to do with the natural state at birth. We deny the right to self-determination.

Regarding the kids that we force changes on: the surgery is always cosmetic. Not one doctor will say that it is medically necessary, except out of concern for the discomfort of parents over how their kid is going to be accepted. The idea is to fix the child quickly so they look "right"...so that everybody else is comfortable. But hundreds of thousands of adults confront their treating physicians to say: "It didn't work; you should stop doing this.... It is a big mistake." Because these medical professionals thought these kids were fixed and their job was done, they never checked on these patients as adults. When they do (or try to), the doctors can't find these intersex children because they have committed suicide or they are murderously angry. Some intersex people want to hide out and not be known as having ever been intersex. But a very large vocal group is saying: "We were cut, we were scarred, we were molded into something that doesn't fit for who we are. It was unfair to do that to us, and you shouldn't do that to kids."

While parents do the best they can to make this issue disappear, the child that must live with these decisions has the chance to find out how to be accepted, to discover societies that allow for different genders (aside from the established binary), and to locate where the laws favor intersex people and make genital surgeries on infants illegal.

When the United States Congress realized that female circumcision was being practiced by Muslim clerics, Congress condemned the act, but when we activists pointed out to them that this happens every day to American-born kids (who don't really need it), the Congress didn't want to see the direct association.

When we wait for kids to grow up enough to be able to make their own choices, they make the choice to dress as male, female, or mixed. They find places where this is acceptable. They discover their way on the basis of all the Internet-based international support organizations. For families, there are many psychologists and therapists who can help make this adjustment easier on the kid and the family. They can teach how you don't have to reject your own child as they make the choice not to be something that everybody thinks is normal.

The medical establishment refers to us as troublemakers and activists—people who do more harm than good by making it harder to do "good work" and get kids access to the treatment they say is needed. We encourage people to find support groups first: Accord Alliance, Androgen Insensitivity groups, or any of the groups around the world that have organized to offer support to one another. There are also trans family associations and trans family unity groups, offering services to kids who identify differently from the sex they were born.

In 2006, the American Academy of Pediatrics released a consensus statement about how physicians should treat intersex kids. Parents are dissatisfied with a kid who was made into a little girl, while all along saying, "I'm a boy; I want to be a boy. I want my penis; I want my penis back—I want a new penis!" They want to wear short hair. They won't have long hair, they won't wear dresses, and they won't play with dolls—it's obvious that is a mistake somebody made because they didn't look at all the facts. When the hypocrisy of the female circumcision condemnation came out in Congress, we activists ran into a debate about religious traditions and were told Congress couldn't make it illegal to do genital surgery on infants.

Sociologically, the artist community has for a very long time been the place for people who are counter-culture and sexually different than the mainstream. Whenever people who are different are looking for a place where they will be accepted (as opposed to receiving prejudice, being kept down, refused privilege, or kept from being able to advance), they go to these fringe communities. Lesbians and gays have won a lot of recognition in Western society. We are at a place where lesbians and gays have a significant political force. Queer others and sexually different others do get value out of associating themselves with these groups. The lesbian and gay communities have been willing to accept people who are sexually different. There is power in numbers. Already established political organizations that have their in-roads to the various powers-that-be (as well as to corporations that can monetarily support political pursuits), gain from inclusion of other communities.

Cultures like to define groups by their perceived commonalities. Is that a good or a bad thing? I can't be sure. Regarding sexuality in culture, homosexuality is "the bad thing," right? But if I am intersexed (and I do identify as intersex), when is it that I am homosexual? Am I homosexual when I sleep with a male partner because I happen to look male, or am I homosexual if I sleep with a female partner because I am really intersexed? Am I only homosexual when I sleep with another intersexed person, and how do we define that? How do we make sure that it is really an intersexed person? From the standpoint of the gay and lesbian movement, are intersexed people just more homosexuals jumping on the bandwagon? What if they don't identify as male or female? We must look at these definitional questions when we try to make sense of how we are going to arrange our prejudices, since sexuality is culturally constructed. It is one of those things we made up, and we want to believe it.

There are, of course, differences of opinion within our community. Some, like me, feel that intersex is an accurate term that represents the way we want to knock down the binary. It isn't just one; it isn't just this or that—it is all this and between. We are the intersex people. The ones who are in between. That makes sense to me if you look at pulling apart that word.

A trans activist in Norway—Esben Esther Pirelli Benestad—talks about being trans as having a "talent" that needs to be enacted and performed. For example: I pass as male really well. I keep my hair really short and keep my body muscular and lean. I have this big square jaw, grow hair on my face, and I am a doctor. I get a lot of cultural privileges for being a white male doctor with a hyper-masculine appearance...so I perform this male gender stuff really well, and it is fun. I know it's a joke, because of the effect that it has. When somebody has seen me on some TV show or something and I say I am not male, they look at this image and they think, "That is not male?" They have to make some sense of that and they ask questions of themselves like: "Well, what does that mean if that is not male? I don't look anything like that; I am supposed to be a real man.... What do I do now? If I can't measure up to that appearance, and he is not male, and I am, what does that mean?"

The answer is simple: sexuality is a cultural construction that is about what we want to believe through our eyes, how we make things look. We have agreed that this appearance is masculine, gender is masculine, and sex is male. But "true" for me would be a nice intersex presentation. I wouldn't have to be this heavily muscled or have to act out all the typical male behaviors in order to have power. But the fact is I get a better chance at success if I act out all the heavy male stuff; that is the truth. I dare anyone to refute it.

That said, I don't care how privileged you are, you are still going to have rejections and limitations. But we can make individual choices about how far we want to go. As I got more power as a result of my education, my degree, my experience, it was much safer for me to come out and say the things that I am saying. Previous to my having all those degrees, I could have been doing myself a lot of harm by saying this stuff, but because I did the work to have this position of power, I can defend myself much more effectively than other people who don't have these privileges. They take a lot more risk. If I want to go out into the job world to become an executive in a corporation, and they saw me on TV saying I am not a man, it would be hard to get hired. I chose a life where I am in charge of my office, work for myself, and see my own clients. They come to me, and thank goodness they pay me enough to be able to pay for my life.

I think we have to be careful about how we represent ourselves depending on the kind of success we want to have. People who are gender outrageous, politically rebellious, and radical in their gender presentation, I applaud them. I need them to be out on the street, to be organizing. As long as they can afford to do it, I need them to continue to do gender politics with their physical appearance and outspoken views. I know not all of them are going to be able to find a way to make a living where they can maintain that identity and appearance, and many have to tone that down in order to be able to survive—and that is too bad. What I'm hoping is that enough of this kind of work will make it possible for those people to be acceptable in the work place.

Meanwhile, our terminology is going to be changing. Nevertheless, there are people who are intersex who don't want to be called transsexual. That is a bad word to them, and they don't like that association. But I think there is strength in numbers. I think we are fighting for many of the same things and are stupid not to associate. I think we need to be able to bring the rights of gender and sexually different people forward, and I don't care if you identify as intersex or trans sex or queer or gender different. I think, as a group, we need to be able to work together to make this change happen within a larger society.

That said, we are gender different; we are not equal. I don't want to be like heterosexuals ever. I don't want to have the rights that heterosexuals have. I want to have the rights that other human beings have. We are different, but we are not different meaning that we should be subjugated, separated, destroyed, discriminated against, or the objects of prejudice—none of that. We are good human beings, and rights have to be extended to all human beings, not just heterosexuals.

The fact is that that difference is never going to go away. Saying that we are equal or that we are the same is silly. Change is not going to happen that way. I think what we are looking for is equal access to the privileges and laws that people who are married get: that is what we really want. The rest of it has nothing to do with identity, nothing to do with gender, nothing to do with biology, nothing to do with science; it just has to do with taxes.

Interviewers have often made statements about...some kind of advancement that will change everything, making us all into equals so that we won't regard ourselves as male or female and won't see ourselves as having hierarchy or power on that basis. There is an interesting utopian idea behind that, but I don't think we are moving toward a great leavening. I don't think we are moving toward a great sameness. I think we are really going to learn to celebrate difference in all of its forms. I don't see differentness reducing. I see difference increasing and being given space to be expressed as opposed to suppressed and eliminated.

∞∞∞∞∞∞∞∞∞∞∞∞∞∞∞∞∞∞∞∞∞∞∞∞∞∞∞∞∞∞

The text of this article, rewritten by Tiger Howard Devore for this book, was first presented as an interview with Carlos Motta for *We Who Feel Differently* in 2011. AB

∞∞∞∞∞∞∞∞∞∞∞∞∞∞∞∞∞∞∞∞∞∞∞∞∞∞∞∞∞∞

Chapter 24

A Hero in Search of a Myth: The Navajo Journey of Jack C. Jackson, Jr.

by Max Wolf Valerio

The room is filled with young Navajo women, gathered in a house on a remote area inside the sprawling Navajo Nation, the largest Native American reservation in the United States. Jack C. Jackson, Jr. is visiting the house with his boyfriend, a young man he met in Washington, D.C., where he has been working and continuing the legacy of public service established by his father, Jack C. Jackson, Sr.—a State Senator in the Arizona state legislature. Holding hands with his boyfriend openly in that house, Jack searches the faces and forms of the women surrounding him. Slowly, Jack feels overcome with a dawning apprehension—the bodies and faces of the women reveal a hidden dimension. These women, dressed in feminine clothing and holding themselves with grace (and a seemingly inborn intuition of their own female being), are actually biological males.... They are, apparently, living as women, and (as Jackson, Jr. was to discover later), they are not taking estrogen and have not had surgery to alter their biological sex. Jackson, Jr. finds himself and his boyfriend suddenly alone, starkly masculine in a small sea of feminine energy. He feels unsure.... Should he even be at this house, visiting this gathering? Then, one of the women emerges from the others; she approaches the couple in a beeline, her face set in a serious expression. She admonishes Jack: "We are very offended by how you guys are acting toward one another. We don't show affection to another male." She points to his clasped hand, which is gently holding his boyfriend's. "We don't do that here."

Jack would later recall and describe these unusual Navajo women as "young ladies," because they were indeed feminine and only detectable as biologically male after a long, intent look across the group at their forms and faces. They were not by any measure gay men in their culture, and they were also not transgender in any modern, western sense, since they were not following a western medical paradigm of therapy, sex hormones, surgery, and reintegration into the world as women. These young women were holding the traditional Navajo role of "*Nádleehé*," or biological males who lived in the traditional female role. *Nádleehé* dress as women, and essentially live their lives as women—marrying heterosexual men and performing the traditional Navajo role of cleaning, cooking, and supporting their husband as his wife. In order to integrate his strong identity as Navajo and his experience as a gay man, Jack sought a traditional role for a Navajo man attracted to other men, but he was not to find it. He would have to continue his search on his own, both part of and, yet, apart from his people's traditional view of gender and sexuality.

Instead, Jackson learned about being a gay man in the larger American society of the mid-seventies after he left the reservation. During that time, he went to university and lived in Phoenix, where he experienced gay life in the bars, events, and gatherings there. Like most Americans of his generation, his experience was fraught with anxiety, confusion, and the intrepid joy of discovery as possibilities unfolded and acceptance of gay life escalated in the changing social landscape of the seventies and into the present. Because he is also Navajo, Jackson's journey is nuanced with the backdrop of his life as a Native American. His journey is all of ours as LGBT Americans, attempting to find clarity and acceptance in our families, hometowns, or religions, and also uniquely Native American, as Jackson searched for ways to understand being gay in the context of his tribal traditions.

Like many postmodern Native Americans, Jackson, Jr. is an amalgam of many contrasting, competing, and culturally diverse influences and intuitions. Jack was baptized as Catholic, but did not practice Catholicism growing up; instead, he took part in the rites of his Navajo tradition, as well as those of the Native American Church, which uses peyote as a sacrament in its rituals. Jackson, Jr. was born from his mother's

Tó'áhaní clan, the "Near the Water" clan. He was born from the clan of his father, *Kinyaa'áanii* (Towering House) clan, and from the clan of his maternal grandfather, *Tábąąhá* (Water's Edge) clan, and finally, the clan of his paternal grandfather, the *Áshįįhí* (Salt) clan. Relationship is of utmost importance for the Navajo, like many Native American tribes, and the tradition of answering the very important question, "Where are you from?" is through recitation of one's specific clan history, as stated in the order above. And while people of his generation are not usually fluent in the Navajo language, this way of situating themselves in the world persists, and is still used today as an introduction when coming upon an occasion to introduce oneself to another tribal member.

Navajo traditions and language are not intact, although the tribe is large, at 332,000 persons, and is situated in an area that echoes with tribal legends—a dreaming place saturated with beauty. The landscape is vast, stretching to a vanishing at the edges of a long horizon. The reservation is called "The Navajo Nation" and is the largest Native American reservation in the nation, covering part of three states—Arizona, New Mexico, and Utah—encompassing 27,673 square miles. Powerful desert rock formations, forged in the earth's interior inside ancient cauldrons, thrust up into a cloudless, sunny blue sky. At night, the angularity of the rocks is accentuated with a watchful resting attentive quality—under a sweeping panorama of stars.

Domes, sudden cliffs, deep canyons, and sloping sandstone formations—created by millions of years of wind, water, and heat—adorn the land. Colors are everywhere, drenching the eye with pleasure. Traveling through this vast area, one can be overwhelmed by the natural and evocative beauty. Like many desert regions, there is a starkness, a feeling of walking into an ancient place: a stillness and grandeur. The sky tumbles with bright stars at night; one can easily feel a whisper of spirit powers, imagine an echo of sacred chants.

The people who live here—the Navajo—who also have called themselves Diné, are the keepers and denizens of this beauty. They are a young population overall, whose median age is 24. Like most Indian tribes, their traditions have been tested and sometimes broken, or changed by the weight of conquest and the subsequent alcoholism, disease, and poverty. Median household income is $20,005, and unemployment is currently at an astonishing 42%, while 43% live below the poverty line. On the reservation, 40% are without running water or electricity. High-school diplomas are held by 56% of the population, and 7% hold a college degree. Mining, taxes, and tourism are the tribe's main sources of revenue—with mining and taxes being the most important.[1]

The tribe has endured the vicissitudes of assimilation with dignity, strength, and some defiance. While the Navajo language is experiencing a renaissance in their schools—where Native children are now taught their mother language—most of Jack Jackson, Jr.'s generation (including himself) cannot actually speak Navajo, although they may understand a lot of it. Native religious beliefs are still existent, even if many are also baptized into Christianity and live some mixture of the two. In this world of lost, fragmented, and somewhat extant Navajo culture, as well as in the changing social norms and conditions of the greater American society, Jackson, Jr. has forged a career of public service serving both his fellow citizens of Arizona and the United States, in addition to the members of his own Navajo tribe.

Jack, Jr. graduated from law school in 1989, earning his J.D. degree at Syracuse University of Law in New York. Then he traveled to Washington, D.C., and started work as a Legislative Associate, advancing to become Deputy Director for the Navajo Nation Washington Office. Jackson, Jr. also worked as a Legislative Analyst at the National Indian Education Association and as the Director of Governmental Affairs at the National Congress of American Indians. He has worked in other capacities, culminating in a run for the Arizona State House of Representatives, where he would serve one term from January 2003 to January 2005. His father, Jack Jackson, Sr., was also a State Senator in Arizona (from 1985 to 2004), and Jackson, Jr. served concurrently with his father in 2003 to 2004, becoming the first father-and-son team to serve together and create a continuing family legacy of public service. In 2010, after serving as Executive Director of the Arizona Commission of Indian Affairs, Jackson, Jr. ran for and was reelected to his father's seat in the Arizona State Senate. Jackson, Jr. has also served by appointment on both President Bill Clinton's and President Obama's Advisory Council on HIV/AIDS.

His latest appointment was by President Obama for a newly created position, located in the U.S. Department of State: Senior Advisor and Liaison for Native American Affairs. This position gives Jackson, Jr. a special capacity working for the interests of Native American people as he helps Indian tribes protect their cultural resources that could potentially be affected by proposed federal projects. In the past, State Senator Jackson, Jr. worked hard in Arizona's State Legislation to create a bill that would redirect a percentage of the transaction privilege tax revenues collected on Indian reservations within Arizona back to each Indian tribe to help fund their governmental services. Arizona tribes currently do not receive any portion of the annual forty million dollars made by non-Indian businesses using their land. This legislation continues to inch its way through the legislative process in Arizona and, if enacted, will bring much needed money to tribes for added infrastructure.

The lack of infrastructure and dearth of small business inside the borders of the Navajo Nation is responsible for a continuing lack of jobs and subsequent government dependence and poverty. With foresight and conviction, Jack Jackson, Jr. has worked to enable small businesses in the Navajo Nation to be established and flourish, helping to establish Indian casinos while working as a member of the Navajo Nation Gaming Enterprise Board. Believing in the power of small business to transform the economic landscape of Navajo country by creating jobs, Jackson, Jr. is a small business owner himself, partnering to create a business that transports patients by plane out of the vast reaches of Navajo land to local clinics and hospitals for higher levels of health care. A continuing inspiration to Native Americans, to LGBT Americans, and to all Americans in general, Jackson, Jr. has advised young Native Americans in Arizona to understand that they are citizens of Arizona, the greater United States, and of their own nations or Tribes at the same time: "You are also citizens of the state and we do pay state taxes. Get the best education possible, but know your family and your land."[2]

In 2005, the "Diné Marriage Act"[3] was passed by the Navajo Nation Council. It defines marriage as between one man and one woman, outlawing polygamy, unions between family members, and same-sex unions. The law has held up through successive attempts to repeal it. Jack Jackson, Jr. believes that this anti-same-sex-marriage sentiment and anti-gay and lesbian feeling remains the product not of Navajo culture, but of the influence of Christianity. While the cross-gendered role of the Nádleehé persists—in spite of any Christian influence—the majority of Navajo, apparently, have yet to embrace enthusiastically the emerging gay and lesbian community in their midst and nationwide. Clearly, there remains work to be done and hearts and minds to change.

In 2008, before Proposition 8 in California, Jack Jackson, Jr. and his husband David Bailey were married in a "Sunset Ceremony." Navajo weddings are called this because they are held when the sun is setting, as night is considered sacred. They chose an area in Del Mar, near the beach, just north of San Diego. Jack's nieces attended, but his parents did not. Jack did not invite them, partly because he knew that the travel might be prove too difficult (they are elderly), but mostly he knew that his father was still having difficulty accepting his homosexuality.

In his quest to find Native traditions that are accepting of LGBT people, Jackson, Jr. has investigated and found inspiration in the idea of "two spirit": an idea and tradition which has become Pan-Indian, enabling LGBT Natives to celebrate their lives the country over and bring to them some measure of community and peace.

Jackson, Jr.'s father had once admonished his son many years ago, upon his first coming out as a gay man, "You need to have a female to have your life continue. That's all I am going to say to you about this." He explained that, in Navajo spiritual life, everything is male and female; there is the "male wind" and "female wind." Years later, his father would begin training as a Medicine Man, delving more deeply into ancient Navajo rituals and beliefs. He would remind Jack, Jr. to always recognize the sacred four elements and four directions, all the deities (including their Father Sun and Mother Earth), and the four sacred mountains. Now, with his own deepening spiritual knowledge and understanding of his son's place in the world (and a recognition of the leadership his son has shown), Jackson, Sr.'s disapproval has softened, and, in time, he has become more supportive of Jack, Jr..

Jackson, Sr. has told his son a story about when he was small and he took him to a ceremony of the Native American church. The presiding Medicine Man looked at Jack, Jr. and noticed a quality that set him apart. After reflection and prayer, the Medicine Man told his father, "Your son is special," and claimed that he was destined to "go on and do good things." Certainly, this observation has been proven true—Jack Jackson, Jr. has shown himself to be a blessing to his Navajo tribe and for Arizona. And he is certainly an inspiration for LGBT Navajos, who seek to live true to themselves, giving back to others as they discover and live out their most authentic selves.

Chapter 25

Interview with Judy Shepard: Remembering Matthew Shepard

by Adrian Brooks

AB: What do you want people to know about Matthew?

JS: I think people may have lost sight of the fact that Matthew was a person: a human being with foibles and special qualities that made him fun and smart. He loved people. He loved interacting with people, exchanging ideas. He was obsessed with politics, world events, current events. He was constantly reading about them. Very well informed. He was especially offended by people who took advantage of other people. Empathy was a big quality for Matt. Empathy—caring for other people and how they felt. He was very good at listening. People felt comfortable talking to Matt, because he was a listener. Matt was not somebody who tried to solve the problem for them, but who listened and discussed possible solutions or maybe just how to interact in a better way.

AB: I know that he was physically small—a beautiful, slender blond boy. Would you say he was an extrovert or an introvert?

JS: He was absolutely an extrovert. He would come into the room and right away look to try to be a part of whatever was going on. On the other hand, I was the person who would immediately go into the corner and try to disappear. So Matt and his dad, in our family, are absolutely the extroverts.

AB: Did his empathy for other people include empathy for racial minorities, persecuted religious minorities, the poor, or the elderly? How far did his scope expand?

JS: He had empathy towards anyone that he felt or saw was made to feel less-than, anybody who was a victim of a bully or a victim of a system—whatever that system might be. He just thought everybody should be treated equally, to be [treated] the same in understanding and even [in the] benefits that everyone else was getting.

AB: How did you hear about the attack?

JS: Dennis and I were living in Saudi Arabia. Dennis worked for an oil company there. And we got a call, really early in the morning, like dawn. And we thought it was just Matt, because time zones were kind of an issue for Matt—a little too much math going on there. He always called in the middle of the night, so it was not a surprise to get a call at an odd hour. At the same time, it was sort of mixed in with *oh my gosh there really [is] something terrible happening at home.* We both had families (other than Matt) living in the States, including friends. So there is always a little trepidation you have when you answer the phone, just like anybody else. It was the hospital in Laramie, calling us—it was nighttime there, probably eight o'clock—letting us know that Matt was there and that he was seriously injured. They had no details on how it had happened, just that he had serious head injuries and that we should come home.

AB: When you heard the term from the hospital, "serious head injuries," did you have an early indication on how serious they were or were you left in doubt or suspense?

JS: No, we were pretty sure for them to say we need to come home, and even asked them "Will he survive?" and the doctor was very non-committal. He just kept saying that the injuries were very serious and that [we] should come home. We assumed that it was a car accident, and he was not all that specific as to what happened. Maybe he even didn't know; I'm not that sure, because we never met that doctor in Laramie.

AB: When did you actually get the real facts? Did you call your other son, or did you have to fly back to the States and still not know what had happened?

JS: Because we were in Saudi, there was a long delay in actually leaving the country. We had to go through paper work—it's a bureaucracy. The company controls your passport; you have to have permission to leave; you have to make arrangements about work. We called the hospital back, but by then Matt was in the process of going to Colorado, because the Laramie Hospital couldn't treat his injuries. So there was really no one to talk to. Logan was [in] Minnesota in high school; he knew nothing. There wasn't anybody to call. We did get in touch with Dennis's brother (who lived in Denver) to go to Fort Collins and see what he could find out. But that was the closest we could get. But our travel and their travel was intersecting, so there was really no way for us to find out anything until we got home in Minnesota. We had to fly to Amsterdam, and we had a long wait, and then we had a long fight to Minneapolis, and we picked up Logan and met my sister there. And then we knew: It was all over the news. But even the specifics were not in the news yet, other than he was in the hospital fighting for his life and that he was a victim of an attack. That was pretty much all we knew until we got actually there with him and we could speak with the police and the doctors.

AB: He was still alive at that point?

JS: Yes, yes he was. He had been in Fort Collins since Thursday early morning. You lose almost a day, flying from Saudi to Colorado. It was Friday afternoon when we got there. Dennis's brother had been in to see Matt, and Logan heard that Matthew's godparents—who lived in Laramie, whom they had called to identify Matt—had seen Matt. Maybe one of Matt's friends was there as well. Those details are fuzzy for me. He was still alive, but we had met with doctors who were certain that Matt would not survive his injuries to the brain stem.

AB: How long was it between the time of your arrival and when he passed?

JS: We got there Friday afternoon, and he survived until just after midnight on Sunday. He was declared dead Monday, October 12th, at 12:53 a.m.

AB: How did his death affect you and your family?

JS: We had left instructions at the hospital to not resuscitate him if he started to go downhill, because we knew that would be what he wanted... to not be in a vegetative state, [or] to be kept alive on the machine. So when his condition started to worsen, we had the ventilator removed. We were very [much] with him when all of that happened, so there is a sense of relief among all of us, and I know it is all of us because we discussed this: that he wasn't suffering anymore. There was no sense of artificial life or pain or any kind of awareness he might have. We were relieved that time was over, but then it dawned on all of us that now our suffering was just about to begin. So it was a mixed bag. Anybody in the same situation is going to feel the same way.

AB: What did you feel at the trial when you saw his killers?

JS: Revulsion, confusion. I didn't feel any anger by that time. I was just kind of numb. Repulsed that they thought they could get away with it, because that's absolutely what we were beginning to understand: that they thought there [weren't] going to be any consequences to what they did. So it was a sense of just wanting it to be over. Well not over—just the whole thing over. We didn't want to have to keep reliving it, and seeing them, and being confronted with it in the news. We just wanted it to be over.

AB: As I recall, the two men got life sentences, and one complicit girl got a long term of imprisonment, though I think not as long as it should have been; what did you feel about the sentence meted out?

JS: The girl was imprisoned for a little while until she turned in state evidence, and then she got probation. So I think that she was in there for less than six months, maybe. We were satisfied with the sentencing for Henderson—who changed his plea from not guilty to guilty—who had no trial. He was sentenced to two consecutive life sentences. At the time, I think we knew that he was not complicit in the actual beatings. But the law states that if you do nothing to stop it, then you are as guilty as the person who actually does the crime. So we were fairly sure he didn't do anything to stop it, though he said that he tried to stop it. You're never really sure what goes on there. That was good with us. When McKinney was sentenced, we knew that was going to happen, because we were involved in a discussion for removing the death penalty, removing the sentence so that he would get the same as the other young man. But it was never appealed, which was the best part. It was over. He would never be out. He would never have another trial. He wouldn't be able to talk to the press. And that was the best. Logan would never have to see them, ever; we would never have to see them again. It was just done.

AB: Did you ever speak to them directly?

JS: No. We did have an incident were we came into face-to-face contact with Aaron McKinney in the courthouse. We were both being brought into the courthouse through an underground access. And we unexpectedly ran into him, and the police were very embarrassed and conscious that that should never happen. [They] hurried him back onto the elevator to go up to where the courtroom was and kept us in the hallway waiting for the next elevator. That was the closest we ever came to one of them.

AB: Why did you create the Matthew Shepard Foundation?

JS: A lot of people began to write to us. And sent us money: five dollars, ten dollars, just to get a cup of coffee. A lot of people said use this money to help Matt's hospital bills or any legal fees you may incur, and we just thought that this was not at all their responsibility. So we had this money and we thought, well, we could use this for something positive out of something so terrible. We talked to a lawyer, a family friend, and an accountant and thought this would be the best way to disseminate this money, and would be the best way to help out young people in particular.

AB: What are the goals of the Foundation? What does it do?

JS: The statement is to replace hate with compassion, understanding, and acceptance, and we just want to change people's hearts and minds. To try to understand what people of the gay community were being denied, and how they were being treated in a general sense. Because of all the correspondence, we began to get the definite feeling that the straight community, in particular, had absolutely no clue as to what was happening in the gay community. People weren't out, and unless you had a connection to the gay community, it just wasn't on your radar. You just had no understanding beyond the AIDS pandemic. That was pretty much all people knew about the gay community. In gay pride parades, all they saw were the more exotic members; they didn't understand that their next-door neighbor could be gay, their doctor, or whatever, because people just weren't out. So there was a high level of ignorance and fear, and we just thought as parents losing a gay child in this way may cause people to rethink their position and try to learn more.

AB: How does the foundation try to do that through education or outreach? I know you did the Laramie Project, the play, as an educational tool...

JS: We weren't directly involved in the Laramie Project, but we certainly are taking advantage of the discussions that have come from that. We support them in every way possible. It's one of very few projects that we officially support. We are largely a presence; if you are looking for information, we are not a direct service provider—never wanted to be that. I speak at colleges. Dennis and I work with the Department of Justice and the FBI on educating the people on the Hate Crime Bill. We have educational programs; we collaborate with much larger organizations that have more manpower and more money and lend our names in what they do and [provide] our own expertise and experience. But we are very small; we are six people, about, with less than a-million-[a]-year budget with offices in Denver. We are very small, and we try to engage people primarily through the Internet—young people in particular.

AB: How do you see the Foundation's effectiveness?

JS: It's one of those things that is really hard to quantify. We have no tools to measure, besides how many people visit our site and how long they stay. Those kinds of numbers mean nothing to me. But we get letters from people who thank us for the work that we do, especially when Dennis and I go out and speak. It's just a matter of keeping the story alive. To remind people what happened—because it should never happen again. It's just, coming from us—from parents—the people who aren't members of the [gay] community other than through Matt and the work that we do, we can get away with so much more.

AB: Do you think that you reach parents of gay and lesbian children whose understanding is expanded through your experience or the foundation?

JS: Well, yes and no. I think, in the beginning, we reached parents that were our age at the time. But we have reached people—who are now parents—in a way that we were not able to reach them fifteen years ago.

AB: Has the Foundation helped you and Dennis and Logan deal with your loss?

JS: It has certainly kept us busy and engaged and made us feel like we are part of Matt's life, community, and friends. So yes, it's been my grieving process, and I think Dennis's as well. And it has kept Logan in the community. All of us just trying to make things better for a person in the community, and that's where we should be going all along.

AB: How do you feel about Federal Hate Crimes legislation, which came as a reaction to this crime? Did the law go far enough? Matthew's death really gave propulsion to include gender as a hate crime.

JS: The movement was already existed. I think everyone knew that the Hate Crime legislation needed to be expanded. To try to include sexual orientation and gender identity expression was the part that was holding it up. And it was due to organizations, like the ADL (Anti-Defamation League), for example, or the Human Rights Campaign, that had all been lobbying for that, but it was really Matt's story that...many organizations had been working to expanding different laws, but Matt's story really helped the straight community at large understand what was happening to the gay community, and for some reason that I still don't understand.

AB: I think that it was effectively and symbolically a crucifixion.

JS: But it had been happening so often before and...

AB: But it wasn't seen...

JS: I guess the media did take it, and it kind of took a life of its own. So if that's what it sort of ended up being, yes, it was the first time that sexual orientation and gender identity had been acknowledged by any law on the federal level. And it was the beginning of a domino effect of many other things involved. I didn't think it was going to go in the order that it did. But great changes are happening.

AB: What do you want to say to the parents of LGBT kids or to the kids?

JS: For the parents, it's so important to understand that they took on responsibility when they had these children to love and respect them no matter what. And if you love them five seconds before they said they were gay, why do you not love them? This is not a choice; this is who they are, and you have loved them since the beginning. Why are you allowing someone else to tell you that this is wrong? You didn't do anything wrong; your kids are who they are, and you should love them no matter what. You could lose them at any time—gay or straight—but to voluntarily give them up is just wrong. That's wrong.

AB: And to LGBT kids, what do you want to say?

JS: Everyday is a brand new day, and don't ever, ever give up. Every day is a brand new day; something is going to happen tomorrow that will make yesterday seem like nothing. And growing up is painful; it never gets easier; it just becomes a way how to cope with who you are and to cope with the people around you and who they are, and you will find the people who will make your life wonderful. You will be the best that you can be, no matter what.

AB: How has Matthew's death affected the U.S., or the world, for the better?

JS: I think it's an open book discussion, and we don't get anywhere unless we talk about it. Fifteen years ago, I could not imagine that sexual orientation and issues of gay equality would be in a public forum. I just never would've thought that could happen. But here it is: I mean, judges striking down state constitutions that define marriage and coming to realize that it's a matter of equality straight across the board—it's a civil rights issue. If you have a religious conviction that being gay is wrong that is all right with you, but you cannot impinge that on someone else's civil rights. I think the younger generation is understanding that this is just the case.

AB: What are your goals for the future?

JS: I'm not sure I have any. Dennis, Logan, and I will do this as long as people ask us to, as long as there is a need for our story or for our input; the foundation will exist as long as it needs to. Of course, the ultimate dream is that this issue will become a non-issue, and it won't be. I don't think that will ever happen actually, but I'll keep my fingers crossed. Dennis and I do stuff at the State Department, which includes international things, which ha[ve] been really interesting for us to see, really, how different and yet the same these issues are worldwide.

AB: What kind of "international stuff"?

JS: We've been to several Central European countries: Poland, Latvia, and Hungary, to talk about gay equality, because it's become a mandate in the State Department since Obama has been in office that we should help nations come to terms with lesbian and gay populations. So the State Department works with local organizations wherever they are, if it's at all possible to bring about equality from their point of view and from their work. To introduce—just to talk about it—to show support for organizations in those countries to talk about the issue and try to make changes in their own country.

AB: As you know, the treatment of the LGBT people in Russia is a worldwide concern. Have you come into any direct contact with organizations in Russia?

JS: No. We have worked with countries that used to be a part of the USSR, and we totally understand the mindset that is there and now that it has become law, it has become all the more heinous. The mindset is already there, so...things are changing, I mean—

AB: Is it safe to assume that if you are invited to help LGBT people in Russia that you will show up?

JS: Yes. I'll gladly go. But we will not go where we are not invited; that is the number one rule. We will not go where we are not invited. That is not my personality. I will go help, but I will not chain myself to a fence.

AB: Frankly, I think you are doing such splendid work, and I support you and endorse you, and can't wait to find out opportunities to help your foundation.

JS: We appreciate that very much, and we do have a board member that lives in Santa Rosa and is in San Francisco quite a lot, and so maybe we can figure something out to do something together.

AB: I'd be honored. Your son's death shocked me. I don't know what to say; it absolutely shocked me, and I've seen an awful lot. I'm sixty-six, and I'm honored to have you in this book, since the whole point of this book is that there is an interconnectedness and an interrelated quality to social and political progress that is taken by brave people by all genders, racial backgrounds, and sexual backgrounds to embrace human liberty. I don't think we will ever see the Golden Age, where such issues disappear, but I sure think the pivot is changing, and I think your work is a testament to that.

JS: You are very kind to say that. Thank you.

Chapter 26

Interview: Barney Frank

by Brenda Knight and Adrian Brooks

AB: Would you tell us about your life and how being gay influenced you and your career choices?

BF: Very interesting. I'm writing about this in my autobiography; when I was fourteen...I realized I was gay when I was thirteen, and when I was fourteen I realized I wanted to go into politics, but I also knew that that was very unpopular, being gay. So the first part of my life I tried to figure out how I could go into politics and hide being gay, and then politics was decided: I'm still going to have to hide being gay, but it would be dishonorable not to be a fighter for gay people. And then, interestingly, as time went on and it became more and more possible, because by 1987 (about twenty years into my political career), I was able to come out and survive, and then there was the gay stuff, but then, as my life went on, by the time...being gay was probably more popular than becoming a politician, and what I tried to do at first was use the prestige of being a politician to help gay rights, but then, instead of fighting harder for gay rights, I tried to fight harder for all the recognition and support in the government.

AB: What were the surprises in Congress for you during your career?

BF: One, it was thirty years ago, and it's not as true today as it was then. There were no other high level members. I served at the State Legislature and as a member of city council, and to give the public credit, they tended to vote people in Congress that were generally very intelligent. I was impressed; when I was in the State Legislature, if I was trying to explain something complicated, I would often have to stop and be careful about how I do it. And Congress much less so: I was able to take for granted a level of much higher thinking, and, also, there was this interest in public good. In the past couple of years, this right-wing group comes in, and I hope that it goes back to the way it used to be.

AB: How does the Tea Party and the polarization right now endanger the country, and what are the echoes of the McCarthyism involved?

BF: Well it's not so much the McCarthyism.... They just reject the whole notion of a civil society in which we work together. And it's very frustrating to me for this very reason. I think we need to have a private sector that creates well-being and a public sector that does what the public sector needs to do. They are so angry that they keep the public sector from functioning by their influence. What then happens is what's very frustrating again for me. Instead of blaming the people who are screwing up the government, a lot of people blame the government for being screwed up by that, claiming to be the victim. And then they get angrier and angrier at the government. It's a big, huge struggle. I keep trying to say it's not the government's fault that these people shut it down. It's not our society's fault that they look to these people, so they do basically threaten our capacity to improve the quality of our life by working together.

AB: What do you think they are angry about?

BF: Really interesting. A large part of it, frankly (and it's true for a lot of Americans), is that America's face in the world has eroded through no fault of anything. In the immediate post-war period, we were the only main economy that had survived World War II, so if you were an American going to work, you could go to the auto plant, steel plant, rubber plant, and make a good living. And what then happened was that the rest of the world caught up with us, and it's now not as easy for some people to make a living. Like for white guys—it's not as easy to make a good living just by hard work, and that's a problem.

BK: Isn't this the first generation that children now are going to have fewer opportunities?

BF: Some people will, unfortunate as that situation [is].

BK: Test scores, number 39.

BF: But the other problem is the anger sticking with white guys. Forty years ago, white men had a lot of preference, and then women and racial minorities caught up. And some white guys don't like sharing the world as equals with white women and minorities. So some are angry with this erosion and this situation they are in, and then some of them are angry because gay people are being hired, and some of the things that they [the white men], grew up believing actually had the effect of advantaging them [the gays]. You were no longer more likely to be well off if you were a white guy compared to women, blacks, gay people, etc.

BK: What do you see for America's economic future, in the short term, like 2015?

BF: We'll still be a very popular place, but we can't stop being competitive. In the *Economist*, they're all "America hasn't accepted the fact that in ten years China will have a larger economy." Well, China has four times as many people, why should I begrudge China? I don't like the Chinese government. But why do I have to look to Chinese people to teach me the economy? It doesn't hurt me that we aren't number one. I mean this notion that we are not overwhelmingly number one in the world and somehow losing is a bad idea. I think what we need to do is take the great prosperity that we have now and share it less unequally.

BK: Do you have any concerns about the fact that America's test scores came out for high school students last week and we were ranked number 39, and we had the number 1 up until the early 90s?

BF: Well, we were number 1 in terms of other countries until very recently.

We also have done a much better job than other countries in assimilating a larger immigrant population.

BK: Yes.

BF: And I'm not so much surprised as looking for a solution. I think that our educational system does a pretty good job in general, but we have a hard time assimilating children who live very bad lives through no fault of their own, and I think that major role should be to improve the living condition of poor children—particularly minority children, but others as well.

AB: My brother said that in 1960, this country had 50% of the world's wealth and it now has 25% of the world's wealth. How does that—

BF: And that's not a bad thing. The reason is that the rest of the world is no longer as poor as it used to be. That's exactly what I was saying, when a very small sliver of the world has 50% of the wealth. We have more money than when we have to share it all with people. And that's why private property people are so angry.

AB: But when the country had 50% of the world's wealth, it was more expansionist in terms of social policies: Medicare spending, civil rights, and Medicaid. And now that it has less percentage of the wealth, we see more selfishness. What do you think about that?

BF: I'll just have to disagree. We didn't do Medicare until '65. I think it's been more mixed. But there is this argument: the less individuals have, the less everywhere you share.

AB: Yes, that's what I meant.

BF: And then you have a vicious cycle. But on the other hand, let's go back to our topic. Better country? If I'm a twenty-year-old gay man, I'm a lot better off than if I was in 1960, than being gay then. A lot of kids are better off than they were then. Women have a lot more opportunities than they had in the 1960s. Overall, the economics may have eroded some, but the degree of discrimination against people based on certain "qualifications" has gone way down. Some of the white men may have resent this.

AB: Barney, given the progress on Marriage Equality, what do you think the next big thing on the horizon—socially or politically—in this country will be?

BF: A national program for job protection. It hasn't gone national yet. At that point, we will have re-forged marriage, and we will have pretty good legal equality in almost all the country. Except for that, maybe half the population or 40% agree on that. But I think that will be the last major national effort. At some point, I think the courts will decide to make marriage legal everywhere, but that may take awhile, and it'll be a problem for some people who live in those states, and they will have to move. But if you live in New York or California or any of those states, you will have full legal equality thanks to the National Gay Rights Movement.

AB: Harris Wofford is working with the Aspen Institute right now, hoping to bring in something which I'm wondering is even possible to happen: a national two-year mandatory public service.

BF: I don't like coercion. And what would they do? What I'm afraid of is: you pick people to do public service and it's not useful and valuable; they wind up and angry. Plus, I doubt that we have the national capacity to take millions of people everywhere and give them useful things to do.

BK: You need to be inspired to serve.

BF: Why inspire them to do menial work? What would they do?

AB: That brings me to my next question. How does grassroots organizing and protest motivate government?

BF: That's a very good question. Here's why: Grassroot activities help, but protest often does more harm than good. The National Rifle Association is the most greatly effective group in America. They do not have sit-ins or die-ins—they lobby, they call their members of Congress, they write. The most effective activity is sustained grassroot activity. Let your elected officials know what you think; vote primaries; tell them how you are going to vote. Protests and demonstrations do more to serve as an emotional release for the participants than in swaying politicians.

AB: I beg to differ, because when you look at Bayard Rustin and his influence on the Civil Rights Movement, and the 60s protest against the war in Vietnam, we saw a major pivotal shift back then. So how do you explain—

BF: When did the war in Vietnam end?

AB: 1975.

BF: When were the demonstrations at their height?

AB: Until Kent State, 1970.

BF: In other words, the demonstrations did not stop the war. What about—

AB: But a majority of people were against the war.

BF: But one: it's not the majority in the war. And two: Richard Nixon just won a big election. They were not helping in stopping the war, because they did not put enough pressure on the members of Congress. As for Bayard and the Civil Rights Movement, yes—what they did was like Gandhi. Martin Luther King and Gandhi engaged in massive protest until they got the right to vote. Once they got the right to vote, they organized themselves politically. You had fewer demonstrations after '65, when the Voting Rights Act passed, and people began to use their political pressure. Members of Congress don't care about demonstrations and marches; they don't even know who is in their own district. They care about people saying, "I'm in your district and I'm not going to vote for you."

AB: Would you say therefore that things like the ACT UP, to draw attention to AIDS funding, were counterproductive?

BF: No. That's a very good question. They were helpful in one area, and not very helpful in another. They played a major role in putting major pressure on the drug companies, because private corporations aren't used to being yelled at. Politicians are not only used to being yelled at; if the right people are yelling at you, it's a good thing. When ACT UP puts a condom on Jesse Helms's house, that was counterproductive. How they did that made him a hero. When they demonstrated, demonstrations helped with regard to the corporations. But no, marches and the gay and lesbian march on Washington did nothing to help, but in some cases they can hurt. Look at the March on Washington by the blacks in '63, very disciplined. Bayard Rustin censored what John Lewis had to say. People say, "Oh, we are going to speak out; gays and lesbians have the right to say." In the March on Washington, John Lewis had to submit several drafts of his speech to Bayard Rustin.

AB: Well, he was a real firebrand back then. He was very young.

BF: Yes, and so were some people in the gay and lesbian marches. The difference was they were allowed to say whatever the hell they wanted to, and in the black situation, they were forced to be more disciplined, which had a much better political effect.

AB: Then what is your message to young gay and lesbian kids, and intersex kids today?

BF: If you want to continue to fight for your rights, register to vote, join an organization, and make sure everybody who you can vote for makes sure they know you care about this, and then make sure your friends and relatives do the same thing.

AB: Then what I'm hearing you say is that you really still believe in the system in this country, and you don't think it's been fatally corrupted by things like the Supreme Court decision—

BF: Well, what's your alternative? It has been weakened in some way, but that's the only system you got. I don't believe in the system as you see it. If you are asking me if I think political pressure on members of Congress by their constituency is effective? You bet I do. That's what the NRA understands; it's the only thing that works. What else would work?

AB: I'm just thinking Winston Churchill saying, "Democracy is the worst system, except for everything else that's been created."

BF: And I agree with that. But you have to consider what would be in place, instead of democracy.

AB: I was just curious about your views. Aside from young people today registering to vote, not being intimidated and disenfranchised by the Republicans.

BF: Organizing, and letting people know that if they don't vote for your rights, you're going to vote against—

AB: What's the difference, then, between organizing and protesting?

BF: The purpose in organizing is to get people to result in communicating to your officials what you want. Protesting is just expressing yourself so you feel better.

AB: Fair enough.

BK: I know we only have a little time left; do you have any advice for young LGBT aspiring politicians?

BF: First of all, make sure you live in a place where there is not too much prejudice, because you can't win if there is. Don't worry so much about being out, because, these days, in places where people would vote against you if you voted for same sex marriage (or whatever), they would vote against you anyway. So don't worry about being out. Try to get some degree at college. Secondly, make sure you have a way to make a living in case you lose, because most people lose. There aren't enough places to go around; there is an element of winning. Third, if you live in a place where you can win, get a good job, start getting involved with meeting other people, go to work at other people's campaigns, and join an organization. Working at other people's campaigns is a good way to meet other people who will eventually help you win.

AB: Barney, my last question is: how do you define success and a life well lived, because you are a civil servant and have done amazing things?

BF: For me, in my public life, it was to ensure that I was doing everything I could to improve other people's rights. Particularly from the standpoint of reducing discrimination and economic insecurity, I want to make the world less unfair. Privately, there is a lot of turmoil, because I didn't come out till late, and there was damage in some way because of it. But it was to live a life in which I found emotional fulfillment, and I pray that the best way for that was to share my life with one other person in particular and to emotionally fulfill that way. I'll give you a rule: if you care deeply about a cause, and if you are engaged deeply in that cause that makes you feel unrestrainably good and enthusiastic and emotionally happy, you are probably not helping.

AB: Say that again. I didn't understand.

BF: If you believe in a cause, and engage in activity that makes you feel really good and warm, you are probably not helping. You are just cheering people on; you are not having any affect whatsoever.

BK: You have to be uncomfortable?

BF: Yeah, you have to get outside your own comfort zone, because the purpose of this is to try and influence people who don't agree with you. So if what you are doing is just cheering each other on until people agree with you, how do you expand your numbers?

AB: I don't know. I'm an artist, so I had to commit entirely to certain kinds of [creative] work.

BF: Right. That's fine. But I'm talking about what you do to bring about change in the political sector. There's positive culture change; artists can affect a person's way of thinking in the longer term of life. But in terms of political change, everyone's on stage just cheering each other—

AB: Right, one hand is just washing the other hand.

Chapter 27

Black, Gay, and Muslim

by Sultan Shakir

I am a gay, black Muslim. My family chose Islam out of the power it held for black people, out of the hope it gave and the power it demanded black people take from a society that devalued us. My parents shed their "slave" names of Parker and Gunter, going from Jeene Parker and Eddie Gunter to Nabeehah and Asim X, eventually choosing to be called Nabeehah Shakir and Asim Shakir. And I was Sultan Abdus Salaam Shakir, the second of two boys, whose name means "leader, servant of peace," and "thankful." I took part in the Jawalla Scouts in Philadelphia, participated in Muslim youth groups, prayed five times a day, and fasted during the holy month of Ramadan. I was as involved in the practice of being a black Muslim as one could be at that age.

When I think about the power and purpose of personal story, I think of what Bayard Rustin has meant for me. As one who is also a gay, black man, but who was raised as a Muslim, I find parallels not just in our biographies but also in how we both have made sense of the world and the progressive movement, and our place in both. To be so consistently both an insider and an outsider is an unusual position. As such, I follow in his footsteps on a path that people like he and I must "make by walking." I am writing this brief essay to offer my support as you make your own way.

Although the gulf between King and Malcolm X has certainly been exaggerated in the popular imagination—particularly, the archetypes they embody—the very reason these archetypes have power in the first place is because they match a sort of preconceived notion of what it means to be a progressive leader or activist in the United States—be it Malcolm, with his fiery speeches, penchant for violence, and radical, defiant critique of white supremacist culture, or Martin the minister, the aspirational orator who eschewed violence and whose tactics were marked by negotiation and compromise. Both men knew the role they played. As Malcolm said, "At one time the whites in the United States called [Martin Luther King] a racialist, an extremist, and a Communist. Then the black Muslims came along and the whites thanked the Lord for Martin Luther King."

As a young black Muslim, I would spend hours memorizing the Quran, a practice that many devout Muslims take part in to strengthen their faith and understanding of the religion. I was on track to memorizing the whole Quran, a practice undertaken by only the most devout of Muslims. I spent hours kneeling on tightly knit industrial carpet. It was a tan color with specks of blue. I spent hours with my head down, repeating the sounds over and over; repeating words and phrases until their cadence was stuck in my head. I learned about the peace that Allah calls for but also the punishment that is called for of those who were Kafirs, those who wouldn't enjoy heaven in the afterlife.

As I grew up, I often heard stories of those who started off as I did, as young Muslim leaders, who slipped too far away from other Muslims. The stories were about how it was important to "stay close" to others who were Muslim and to stay away from people who weren't: the Kafirs; hearing stories of the one who went off, who didn't find a Muslim community in "enter city here" when they moved away for college, and who now...were no longer Muslim.

In addition to the oft-mentioned warnings to stay close to other believers, one of the common themes in the repeated stories of the men around me was a harsh opposition to homosexuality. One involved the appropriate action to take when encountering a gay person, which was to take him to the highest roof you could find. And quickly throw him off. The story was usually told with a smile and always raised a strange sense of alienation in me that, to this day, I can't understand in the context of everything else the Quran teaches, for Islam teaches peace and compassion. The stories seemed born in an obsessive hatred of people whom I had yet to meet and who, unknowingly, I would turn out to be. Both then and now, I had a great respect for the deep history of the religion and the vast achievements of the Islamic culture. These were not only limited to art, architecture, science, astronomy, poetry, mathematics, and other forms of one of the great foundational cultures of the human race, but also for the purity of following what I took to be words from God—especially words that hadn't been smudged by the hands of man. But in being a devout Muslim, I was a minority. I gladly suffered the consequences of being such. I'd often go to my neighbor's house to play, neighbors who were very religious as well, but Christian. I'd eat dinner in their TV-less living room, then the boys would go downstairs. Play time and even sleepovers became a game of "Save Sultan" while they took turns telling me how much Jesus loved me and finally asking me if I'd accept him into my heart. I wondered why they weren't okay with me being Muslim and them being Christian. To me, that seemed to work out just fine. It not only seemed fine to me, but acceptance of differences, particularly religious differences, is how we—a Muslim and a Christian—even got to remain in the same space. We were both the beneficiaries of bloody battles and feuds that went back hundreds of years in Protestant/Catholic strife and a thousand years in terms of the West's conflicts with Islam, which had pushed the country down a path towards religious freedom from inception on. And yet, if race is always the eight-hundred-pound gorilla in the room in the United States (as some commentators have said), the issue of religious perceptions and the assumptions made about American Muslims was a ticking time bomb in that same room—one set to explode on 9/11.

Before the 9/11 attacks and the subsequent wars, Muslims didn't have to worry (as much) about being visible or being identified with or confused with terrorists, at least in day-to-day life. Middle Easterners were certainly the easy targets for the FBI and media outlets immediately following the 1995 Oklahoma City bombing, with the FBI issuing an all-points bulletin for Middle Eastern suspects, the *Wall Street Journal* calling the bombing a "Beirut-style car bombing," and many Arab Americans facing verbal and physical attacks, all for an act perpetrated by a white, Catholic-raised (though self-proclaimed agnostic) American. The 9/11 attacks tilted the playing field to a much greater degree. Suddenly Islam—a religion of peace—was construed as a monolithic enemy by right-wingers and knee-jerk reactionaries. Like most discrimination, those who bore the brunt were those perceived to be the enemy in the eye of the beholder, whether that be a Middle-Eastern man who may or may not be a Muslim, or an African-American Muslim woman, who, like my sisters, wear a *khimar* or hijab—the female head covering. For me, not being of Middle Eastern descent nor wearing any clothing or markers that identified me as a Muslim, my interaction with the post-9/11 reality for Muslim Americans was largely limited to experiences with TSA, who always randomly selected me for additional security screening for years, always marking my boarding pass with "SSSS" in what every agent called a random occurrence. But for me, it would be even more complex. As I grew older, a constant pressure to change weighed on me: the pressure from Christians to leave Islam and convert, the pressure from my Muslim friends to not be gay, and, while there wasn't pressure to "not be black," there was plenty of pressure because I was all these things. Any one of these made me a minority. The combination of all three made me a walking, talking, living, breathing example of the challenges that America faces in living up to its own original promises of "life, liberty and the pursuit of happiness" for all of its citizens. And I was one of those.

The internal struggle caused by that pressure resulted in an internal drive for something different. Years before I ever allowed myself to don the term "activist," I had a deep-rooted feeling that there's a basic principle that should drive life, and that principle is simply that everyone should be allowed to live and do as they pleased, as long as no harm was done to others in the process of living one's life. Over and over, I saw evidence of this being true—evidence that, if we were all free to be ourselves, we would likely all reach that place we're searching for and striving to achieve: a place of freedom and acceptance. It's a place that even our founding fathers sought to build, working to enshrine religious freedom in an effort "to create a more perfect union." Even as our forefathers fought to create a country free of religious oppression and intolerance, the definition and the ideal of that more perfect union continued to evolve. We fought wars that led to "the founding fathers" finally granting rights to "my fathers," who were slaves and descendants of slaves. All through that struggle, we evolved in our understanding that if we are to ask others to be tolerant of us, we must be equally (if not more) tolerant of them.

One important turning point was the election of JFK. Until 1960, Catholics were viewed with suspicion. After that, no one thought about it. Similarly, Obama's election is a parallel to that, racially, speaking. Yet anti-Semitism continues in some right-wing hate groups; various Protestant denominations split in their views of the acceptability of LGBT people, and while the Catholic Church is beginning to sound less discriminatory, the verdict is still out.

As we move forward, I struggle to find a home as a gay black man but find comfort in Rustin's example. A gay black man raised in a faith community, he was constantly working to navigate his insider-outsider status. I have often imagined him sitting in church while the preacher decried the evils of the homosexual, imagined him listening to the early civil rights conversations where communists were dehumanized. I think of how alone he must have felt, surrounded by those he loved and admired—surrounded by his community—as they degraded core parts of his identity. And, finally, how he, himself, was stigmatized and driven out of the civil rights leadership because of his homosexuality, a stain on a powerful movement and on the legacy of a great man only partly assuaged by the recent awarding of the nation's highest civilian honor: the Presidential Medal of Freedom (by an African-American President, no less).

I remember sitting as a child with men I loved and admired—men I had come to think of as part of my family and leaders in the community—who taught me what my faith commanded of us when we discovered a homosexual. He was to be thrown from the roof. I remember the cold feeling in the pit of my stomach each time the story was told with a rueful smile—the sort of humor one can only find confidence in when speaking about strangers. And later in life, working in the gay rights space, I recall sitting in a room of almost exclusively white, upper-middle-class gay men—my colleagues—people I love and respect—and listening to commitments to increase diversity—not just inside our organization, but in the types of work our organizations undertakes—commitments only to be followed quickly by, "but probably not in this budget year."

Today, I sit in a place of immense privilege. I'm the son of former slaves who fought for their freedom, the son of two people who chose their own names. I sit at a place where I can choose what struggles to take on, or to not to take on. I can be at ease in spite of the fact that the more perfect union has not yet fully embraced me, knowing that the union will never fully embrace all of me unless I show myself as I am and choose to be seen and be embraced. No one ever said the union would ever be perfect, or close to perfect. The only thing that was guaranteed was the ability to fight forward.

Being a gay black man raised Muslim in the United States can be painful. Yet it is also a gift. The mother who cried out that there was something wrong with me when I first came out is the same woman who rocked me to sleep each night as a baby and who now always tells me she loves me before we hang up the phone. Those men that talked so callously about throwing boys like me from the roof were also men I had seen do great acts of charity and courage—they are men who had often treated me with tenderness and kindness. Those colleagues who continue to hem and haw about truly committing to changing the lives of black and brown gay men like me are also individuals with whom I have worked 16-hour days for weeks on end united against attempts to slow the progress of equality. The ease with which distance grants the ability to simplify these people as simply homophobes or as indifferent white supremacists is not an option for me.

Instead, the complexity of my own identify grants me access to the undeniable complexity of others. Rustin once wrote, in one of the most succinct expressions of his pragmatisms, to be afraid is to pretend the truth is not the truth. As FDR said, "The only thing we have to fear is fear itself." The same could be said about hate. My insider-outsider status, this complex identity, grants me the ability to see and care for those different than myself, to imagine what the world looks like through their eyes and to have—though it is often pressed—both the faith and patience that they will and can come along.

When I was coming up in the movement, it was hard for me to find others that had similar worldviews as my own. The idea that the only alternative to allowing ideology to define strategy and tactics was selling out was communicated explicitly and implicitly. Yet I have learned that this is simply not true. While the world needs Malcolms and Martins, the world also needs Rustins. People whose worldviews are pragmatic, guided by effective action. My experience has taught me that people are immensely complex and multi-dimensional and as such—to be as effective as possible in changing hearts and minds—requires a complex and multi-dimensional approach.

The success of America as a heterogeneous society committed to equality for all will not only be measured by how it treats blacks or LGBT people. That will surely be one test. As set out and delineated in the First Amendment of the Constitution, religious liberty and the honorable according of respect to all people of all faiths, including Muslims, will be another key bellwether on the success of this nation, one that has been prescribed for but takes active and conscious involvement to fulfill.

Chapter 28

Bullying

by James Gilliam

Imagine walking down a long hallway lined with green lockers multiple times a day while being called names like "faggot," "sissy," or "dyke." Imagine a long bus ride to and from school each day, where the bus driver never stops to do anything about the endless taunts and objects lobbed from behind you once you've left the safety of your own home. Imagine going through an entire school day—every day—in fear of what may happen to you for daring to step inside the bathroom to use it. Imagine having your glasses knocked off your head, your books knocked out of your arms (apparently I carried mine "like a girl," whatever that means), being bumped into deliberately, repeatedly, and being subjected to catcalls and jeers, simply for being who you are, or, possibly, for who others imagine you to be. Imagine being so scared and lonely and frightened and confused that you obsess about (and engage in) ways to end the misery and pain.

Unfortunately, I know firsthand what this is like. Because it happened to me. And it has happened—and is happening—to so many children every day. More than 160,000 students stay home from school each day because they are afraid of being bullied—they stay home, not to avoid doing their homework or taking a test, but to escape the constant fear they face each time they board the school bus, or walk down the halls, out onto the playground, or into the locker room, or a restroom, or even the cafeteria.

My mom made me go to school most days, so my survival tactic focused on avoiding the locker room, where—at least for me—the bullying was the worst. It got so bad that, when I was in the seventh grade, I purposely slammed my foot into a wall to create an excuse not to participate in PE. I ended up breaking my big toe and having to wear an open-toe shoe with Velcro straps for six weeks. No one knew I meant to do this, and if they did, they wouldn't have understood. And I certainly didn't feel like I could tell anyone what was going on. That would have been too risky. And I was still trying to figure it out myself. But despite all the bullying, I endured back in my small hometown. I consider myself one of the lucky ones. Thankfully, I finished high school, went to college and law school (though, admittedly, a bit delayed), and ended up landing my dream job at the ACLU of Southern California ("ACLU SoCal").

But I will never lose sight of the fact that some LGBTQ youth who are bullied throughout school don't get to achieve their dreams; many are haunted by the thought of attending more years of school, resulting in LGBTQ youth having the lowest academic aspirations of any student demographic. In fact, my desire to create better experiences for future generations of LGBTQ youth drove me to law school.

Though it's been more than twenty years since I graduated high school, it seems little has changed for LGBTQ students. Survey after survey point to the continued bullying—in many different forms—these youth experience. The impact of such harassment can be devastating to the students, to their families, and to the entire school community. And the cost of lost job effectiveness, individual suffering, illness, or blocked creativity can't even be estimated.

LGBTQ students experience the school day differently than most other students. As the LGBTQ students themselves report—and based on my own firsthand knowledge as a victim of what one scholar has labeled "hostile school violence"—bullying is the typical experience so many of the LGBTQ students in America face in their schools. Across this country, they face unthinkable circumstances every day. Many of these students "spend an inordinate amount of energy plotting how to get safely to and from school, how to avoid the hallways when other students are present so they can avoid slurs and shoves, how to cut gym class to escape being beaten up—in short, how to become invisible so they will not be verbally and physically attacked."[1]

Most troubling, the instruments of harassment against LGBTQ students are not limited to their peers; in many instances, LGBTQ students report that members of the school administration and/or teachers also bully them. Such conduct not only violates a school's affirmative obligations to protect all of its students, it also sends a message throughout the entire school community that such behavior is acceptable.

Schools have legal obligations to take affirmative steps to protect the rights guaranteed to LGBTQ students under the United States Constitution, various state constitutions, and the statutory protections that exist in a limited number of states. These rights include, for example, their right to be themselves and to freely express their sexual orientation, gender identity, and/or gender nonconformity; their right to be safe at school and free from harassment; and their right to be treated the same as every other student. Despite these well-established, longstanding protections, LGBTQ students frequently face challenges seeing these rights fully realized, particularly in the context of prom dates, school dress and attire, through the struggles they face with the formation and treatment of support groups like gay-straight alliances ("GSA"), and with persuading the administration to stop the bullying they are experiencing.

With so many LGBTQ students discovering and proclaiming their sexual orientation, gender identity, and/or gender nonconformity at younger and younger ages, schools must prepare now to confront these issues. The time has come (and is long overdue) for schools to examine and improve the lived experiences of their LGBTQ students, and for schools to ensure that the administration addresses appropriately the harassment and bullying so frequently meted out against this vulnerable group of students.

Shortly after I started working at ACLU SoCal we were reminded—in the grimmest of ways—of the horrific price bullying exacts. In September 2010, Seth Walsh, a gay teen in Tehachapi, California, died by suicide after enduring years of bullying at school. Having survived such bullying myself and being driven to law school to stop it, I was honored to advocate alongside Seth's mother after his death to find ways to not only hold his school accountable, but to also protect other LGBTQ youth from suffering like Seth had.

I'll admit that I was a bit nervous at first about working on the Walsh case. I had no idea what to say to a woman who had lost her son in such a tragic way. Had I taken any classes during law school to teach me how to interview such a client? Prior, had I worked on any case in private practice that was similar to this one? What I realized was that, although I had no idea what it felt like to lose a child to suicide, I certainly knew what it felt like to be Seth.

But there was obviously one big difference between Seth and me, one his grandfather stressed during our interview at the end of a long day: I had survived being bullied as a gay teenager, and I had grown up to become an adult. Seth didn't, and won't.

His grandfather wanted to know why. Why had I survived when Seth didn't? I was left to ponder that question during the long drive back home that night.

Although I had never thought of myself as a "survivor" before being called that, as I reflect back on the years of bullying I endured, and as I think about all the LGBTQ youth I've met and whose stories I've heard, I realize how much that label resonates. We have survived being bullied for being different. We've made it through some of the toughest years of our lives.

As so many of the stories in this book illustrate, many advocates and activists dedicate their lives to ensuring that the memories and spirits of those who are no longer with us still survive, too.

For example, California passed a law (named after Seth) that requires teachers to intervene to stop bullying when they see it. Seth's mother was instrumental in making that happen. One out of every eight public school students in our country attends school in California, so that law will impact a significant number of students.

And the federal government investigated the Tehachapi School District, leading to the first use of the federal law prohibiting sex discrimination against a school for failing to protect a gay student bullied based on gender nonconformity.

Seth Walsh is not the only young LGBTQ student to have succumbed to death by suicide. In fact, after several young LGBTQ (or perceived) students died by suicide in the fall of 2010, it seemed everyone's attention was focused on the bullying of these youth. The White House held the first-ever "Summit on Bullying." At least one rock band released a song dedicated to those youth. Columnist and author Dan Savage launched the "It Gets Better" Project, an online video campaign in which thousands of individuals have shared their stories of "coming out" and survival. Even the United Nations held its first-ever international consultation addressing anti-gay harassment in schools.

Since then, the discussion about how to stop bullying and how to protect LGBTQ students has been ongoing. Without doubt, what schools and school administrators can do to protect these students at the school-site level is an important part of that dialogue. As Human Rights Watch noted, "The systematic failure of the public school system in the United States to protect these students means that they are left to choose between struggling in isolation to survive the harassment as they seek an education or escaping the hostile climate by dropping out of school."[2] No student should face such a terrible choice.

After working on the Walsh matter, we founded an anti-bullying project at ACLU SoCal with the mission of stopping unlawful harassment and bullying in California schools and creating school communities that promote safety and respect for all students. The project often hears from students who are being bullied yet who face judgmental teachers, unsympathetic principals, and ineffective superintendents. To help address this challenge, the staff of the project spends a significant amount of time researching evidence-based interventions to address anti-gay bullying in schools. The staff then uses these research findings to teach schools how to address the anti-gay climate that may exist on their campuses.

Our project staff also teaches LGBTQ youth, parents, and school personnel about the rights of LGBTQ students. The project strives to educate and empower students to use the law in their favor to protect themselves and their peers. We also have lawyers to hold accountable those who allow anti-gay discrimination to go unchecked. Admittedly, the project's goals are lofty, but they are made more attainable by the strong anti-bullying laws we have in California, including explicit protections for LGBTQ students.

If only every LGBTQ student lived in California. Seth's case is so important because so many LGBTQ youth attend schools in states where there are no laws on the books to specifically protect them. In such places, many of these youth will be able to turn to the federal government now for help when their schools refuse to address bullying.

Not every instance of anti-gay bullying will fall within the federal government's jurisdiction, though.

We need anti-bullying legislation in each state and at the federal level.

And ensuring enforcement of these laws will require constant monitoring.

The national dialogue may not be as focused on the issue these days, but the bullying continues, as do its horrific effects. At the time of this writing, communities like Des Moines, Iowa, are reeling from the recent death by suicide of a high school student who was bullied relentlessly after coming out as gay. The family and friends of a 15-year-old sophomore in La Grande, Oregon, who is no longer with them are going through the same torture. It's time that the bullying stops here.

10 Steps Schools Should Take to Change the Anti-Gay Climates on Campus

1. Educators need to acknowledge the anti-gay environments that exist in their schools and stop blaming LGBTQ students for the bullying they experience.

2. Schools should educate students, parents, teachers, administrators, and education support personnel about the legal rights of LGBTQ students.

3. School districts should pass comprehensive, district-wide, and school-specific nondiscrimination policies with enumerated categories that include sexual orientation and gender identity, and should train everyone in the school community about such policies.

4. School districts should conduct professional development training on a regular basis for everyone in the school community to learn how to protect LGBTQ students, including training to intervene and stop bullying when they witness it.

5. Schools should ensure that students know where to go for information and support related to sexual orientation and gender identity, including how to find supportive teachers and other members of the school administration.

6. School districts should promote the formation of gay-straight alliances at every middle and high school.

7. School districts should adopt curriculum that includes positive portrayals of LGBTQ people, history, and events.

8. School districts should support events that celebrate and high-light the diversity of the LGBTQ community.

9. School districts should develop a system to facilitate increased reporting of bullying and harassment.

10. School districts should adopt reasonable accommodations to protect LGBTQ students who continue to experience bullying and harassment, such as assigning a monitor to the bullies (or to the bullied student).

∞∞∞∞∞∞∞∞∞∞∞∞∞∞∞∞∞∞∞∞∞∞∞∞∞∞∞∞

ENDNOTES

1 *Hatred in the Hallways: Violence and Discrimination Against Lesbian, Gay, Bisexual, and Transgender Students in U.S. Schools* (New York: Human Rights Watch, 2001), 2.

2 Ibid., 3.

Chapter 29

A Conversation with Evan Wolfson: Freedom to Marry Leader

by Angela Dallara

AD: How did you become interested in marriage?

EW: I was born in Brooklyn and grew up in Pittsburgh. I came from a household with very loving parents who have been together for a long time. They put the kids first and taught us the importance of family. Their love and partnership made them role models for marriage. Watching them, I knew I always wanted that for myself. But as a kid, even before I knew what gay was, I also knew that something was different about me, and I wasn't sure how their example could apply to me. I didn't see a place for me in the images of marriage society gave me.

I spent two years in the Peace Corps, which played an enormous role in shaping me and my life. I was young—twenty-one years old—and had not yet come out, had not yet figured out what it meant to be gay, to live a life as a gay person. In the Peace Corps, I began to explore relationships. I began to have a deeper understanding of the power of societies to shape behavior. In my experiences with friends there—who, had they lived in a different country, would probably have come out as gay, but in Togo never would—I saw that the vocabulary that a society gives us informs the choices we make and shapes, in part, who we are. I realized that a big part of our identity, and thus our ability to fulfill ourselves, comes from the opportunities created or limited by society, its institutions, and its laws.

When I returned, I attended Harvard Law School and began living my life as an openly gay man—something that, unlike my friends in Africa, I could do in America. My great passion then, as throughout my childhood and now, was history—and it was in law school that I read the history book that changed my life: John Boswell's *Christianity, Social Tolerance, and Homosexuality*. Boswell showed that the treatment of homosexuality and gay people had varied widely across societies and throughout the first two millennia of Western history. And I concluded that if it had once been different, it could be different again.

AD: Your Harvard Law School thesis in 1983 put forth a constitutional argument for the freedom to marry. What did it say, and what kind of reaction did it receive?

EW: I wrote my thesis—"Same-Sex Marriage and Morality: The Human Rights Vision of the Constitution"—from my perspective as a recently returned Peace Corps volunteer and inspired young law student. I believed then, as ever since, that marriage matters, that we can learn from history, and that change is possible, and I believed that by claiming the resonant vocabulary of marriage—love, commitment, connectedness, and freedom—we could transform non-gay people's understanding of who gay people are and explain why exclusion and discrimination are wrong. The paper is a 140-page manifesto that makes the argument that marriage is a civil right guaranteed under the equal-protection clause of the Constitution. It later served as a vision for my 2004 book and for Freedom to Marry's national strategy, the Roadmap to Victory.

At the time, people generally thought the idea of marriage for same-sex couples was either implausible or unimportant, and many faculty declined to serve as advisors on the paper. The freedom to marry movement today is a far cry from the much more silent and lonely circumstances surrounding marriage and gay people thirty years ago. At the time, Ronald Reagan was president; people were ignorant about HIV/AIDS; there was no country—or state-level—legal recognition of same-sex couples, let alone marriage itself; and courts had, a decade earlier, rejected the first wave of freedom to marry cases brought by couples in the immediate aftermath of Stonewall.

Even though there was little support for the idea at that time, I believed there was a power in aspiring to make a difference and a power in ideas. As more gay and non-gay people have engaged, the freedom to marry for loving gay couples is an idea whose time has truly come.

AD: What was it like being a part of the historic Hawaii case?

EW: Unlike the first wave of litigation in the early 1970s brought by gay couples challenging their exclusion from marriage (all of which were rubberstamped away), the second wave—most importantly, Hawaii—transformed the world. The 1993 Hawaii Supreme Court decision in a case I co-counseled launched the ongoing global movement for the freedom to marry (and led to our progress today—17 states and DC, including Hawaii, and 18 countries on 5 continents, where gay people can now share in the freedom to marry).[1]

Knowing I was the lead voice within the movement for pushing forward to win marriage, I was approached by the plaintiff couples in 1990, asking me to represent them. At that point, I worked at Lambda Legal, which, like the ACLU and all other gay rights groups at the time, declined to take the case (though I was allowed to help behind the scenes). That refusal led the couples to a non-gay attorney in Hawaii—Dan Foley, who signed on as attorney. Dan and I bonded over the next couple of years and worked closely, first with me behind the scenes, and then as co-counsel.

In 1993, the Hawaii Supreme Court held that excluding same-sex couples from marriage is clearly discrimination, presumptively unconstitutional. The court stopped short of ordering marriage licenses, but instead said to the government: "If you want to deny something as important as marriage to loving and committed couples, you have to at least show a good reason." That chance to show there is no good reason was a game-changer. I was cleared of all my other cases but one (the Boy Scouts case, which I won in the New Jersey Supreme Court in 1999 and argued before the United States Supreme Court in 2000), and focused on working with Dan to prepare for the world's first-ever trial on the freedom to marry. And I began speaking around the country, preaching the need for political organizing and public education alongside the litigation; one newspaper at the time dubbed me "the Paul Revere of marriage."

While we began rallying our movement on marriage as never before, so did anti-gay forces that did not want a national conversation about marriage. They pushed anti-gay measures in many states, denounced gay couples and the "threat" our love allegedly posed to marriage, and stampeded through Congress the so-called Defense of Marriage Act (DOMA) in 1996, excluding same-sex couples from more than 1,000 federal protections and creating a federal system of first—and second-class—marriages.

Meanwhile, Dan and I appeared before Hawaii state court judge Kevin Chang and squared off against the state's attorneys over the question of whether there is a sufficient reason to deny gay couples the freedom to marry. We mounted weeks of witness testimony and cross-examination, calling in national experts in adoption and child raising, who testified that the role of same-sex couples as parents, their ability to care for their children, and the well-being of their children is strengthened with the freedom to marry. After extensive briefing and argument, on December 3rd, 1996, Judge Chang ruled in our favor. For the first time in the history of the world, we won the freedom to marry.

The decision was appealed by our opponents, but even worse, they mounted a political attack to block the courts from finishing the job. Pouring millions into Hawaii, they led a campaign to amend the constitution exempting marriage from the Equal Protection Clause. The amendment passed, and the Hawaii Supreme Court held that its hands were tied.

AD: You served as the marriage director at Lambda Legal and then went on to launch Freedom to Marry in 2003. How did the focus shift over time?

EW: Although a destructive amendment had passed in Hawaii, the work for marriage had begun. I went on to contribute to the legal battles in Vermont, which led to civil union; and I argued at the Supreme Court in *Boy Scouts vs. Dale*. I was then granted an opportunity to explore the next steps for the marriage movement and seek out new strategies, resources, and voices. As Lincoln put it, it was time to "think anew" about how to best advance a sustained campaign to win the freedom to marry.

Building on the lessons I learned in Hawaii and in Vermont, I worked to shepherd a national strategy, and in 2003 launched Freedom to Marry to pursue that strategy to victory through a sustained, affirmative campaign, a new model for our movement. Freedom to Marry has grown from a handful of staff at the time of its launch to over 25 full-time staff today strategically situated around the country, growing from a budget of just over $1 million to a budget of more than $10 million and still aiming higher to get the job done. Freedom to Marry drives the marriage movement, providing leadership in messaging and public education about why marriage matters, creating groundbreaking organizing tools through strategic digital action, fueling the campaign to win as the largest funding engine of marriage work in the country, and guiding partners and funders on the strategy to win.

We've learned from our stumbles and turned them into successes. We learned, after Hawaii (and again, California with Prop 8), that political organizing must accompany and defend the gains we make in litigation. We learned how to overcome barrier after barrier—how to win in courts, in legislatures, in the heartland, among Republicans as well as Democrats, and at the ballot box. We learned that what moves the persuadable middle is not a discussion of rights and benefits, but the understanding that gay people want to marry for similar reasons as non-gay people: love, commitment, and family. We learned the importance of sparking the conversations that are the single most important engine of change.

AD: How has working on marriage affected you personally?

EW: My life and future changed when I met my now-husband, Cheng, in 2002. We bonded from the start, and in the twelve years we've been together, we've been there for one another through the good times and the bad. He became my longtime fiancé in 2008, before Prop 8, while we still couldn't marry in New York. Once we won the freedom to marry in 2011 here in New York, we got married in front of family and friends, in the city where we've built our life together—the pinnacle of joy in my life, both personally and professionally.

Being married has solidified our commitment for each other—and we still feel its glow. We've traveled the world together—from the Pyramids to Machu Picchu, the Great Wall of China to the Western Wall in Jerusalem, from the Serengeti in Africa to the continental ice sheet of Antarctica (for our honeymoon, no less). Having finally been able to stand before our now combined families, our closest friends, and so many movement colleagues to celebrate our love, Cheng and I wish that same freedom to marry for everyone, and are working to finish the job.

AD: What has been the most memorable moment in marriage work for you?

EW: This year, I had the privilege to attend the bill signing in Hawaii—our fifteenth freedom to marry state, twenty years after I served as co-counsel in *Baehr*. As long as I have been doing marriage work—and although Freedom to Marry staffers who do field work on the ground often attend—I've never chosen to celebrate at one of the signings. It was a long time coming in Hawaii, and an especially sweet victory. It also shows how far we have come. The same legislature that in the 1990s passed the first of the anti-gay constitutional amendments voted resoundingly for the freedom to marry. It was incredibly touching to watch these state lawmakers sign the bill into law, and to see them weeping, touched by the moment, and by history, knowing that they finally did the right thing.

Another of one of my most memorable moments—besides my own marriage—was Election Day 2012, when we won four out of four ballot measure battles in Maryland, Maine, Washington, and Minnesota. It was a late night (though a lot better than the all-nighters I spent to find out we had lost the first ballot battle back in Hawaii in 1998), and I spent it (working) at home with my husband Cheng. Every time we saw another state win, we leaned in and gave each other a kiss. It was the ideal way I could have asked to spend such a transformative night.

AD: Where do you get your inspiration for your work?

EW: The waves of personal thanks and stories people share with me—and, still a passion, history. I study and gain encouragement and inspiration from the lessons of other movements—the defeats, the resilience, and the turmoil—and the heroes behind those victories. I read a lot of history, from civil rights struggles and the women's movement to biographies. On my wall hang pictures of Abraham Lincoln, Franklin Roosevelt, and Martin Luther King, Jr.

AD: What is the current marriage landscape and what is the strategy going forward?

EW: As of today, we've won the freedom to marry in 17 states and the nation's capital. Through the Supreme Court, we struck down the core of DOMA, and we have built historic levels of public support for marriage. We've racked up wins at an unparalleled pace, reflecting and accelerating the momentum we have worked so hard to build over so long.

But we still have to finish the job. As we look ahead, we will see a new pace and some new challenges, but the Roadmap to Victory national strategy that brought us to this point of progress is the same strategy that will bring it all home. The Roadmap to Victory says that we must create a climate demonstrating that America is ready for marriage, so that when we again reach the Supreme Court, the justices are encouraged to bring the country to national resolution, ruling in favor of the freedom to marry and full respect for marriage nationwide.

The Roadmap strategy is based on the history of other social movements and says that we create this climate by working simultaneously on three tracks: winning more states, growing the majority for marriage, and ending federal marriage discrimination. Through the Roadmap to Victory, Freedom to Marry has set specific targets for building the critical mass needed for victory at the Supreme Court. By 2016, we aim to secure a majority of Americans living in a freedom to marry state, grow public support to higher than 60%, and ensure that all legal marriages are respected equally across federal programs, even in states that for now discriminate. These are ambitious targets, but attainable—in years, not decades—if we do the work.

ENDNOTES

1   At the time of publication this number has grown to 37 states, plus the District of Columbia. In January 2015 the Supreme Court granted review of a ruling from the U.S. Court of Appeals for the 6th Circuit, which ruled in November 2014 against the freedom to marry in Kentucky, Michigan, Ohio, and Tennessee. Arguments will be heard in spring 2015 and a ruling from the Supreme Court, which can legalize marriage equality nationwide, is expected in June 2015.

Chapter 30

Diana Nyad

by Rita Mae Brown

There are people who smile at you, and you have to smile back. Even at Pine Crest High School in Ft. Lauderdale in the mid 1960s, Diana Nyad could make you smile just by looking at you.

From August 31st, 2013, to September 2nd, 2013, she swam from Cuba to Florida—the first person to do so. Moreover, she accomplished it without being protected by a shark cage. It took fifty-three hours. She'd tried the heroic feat four times before, beginning in 1978. High winds with swells ended that attempt after she'd gone 76 of the 110 miles. Then, in 1979, she swam from the Bahamas to Florida, 102 miles, and though she set the world record for both women and men, she declared that was it: no more competitive swimming for her. But despite her stated intention, she began swimming again 30 years after that and just 3 years later was back in the Gulf water for the "impossible" Cuba-to-Florida haul.

Between 1978 and 2011, she hadn't been idle, however. From 1979 on, she played squash so well that she was ranked #13 nationally. She also embarked on a media career at a major network, interviewing athletes. Sometimes she slipped someone in who wasn't quite a professional. Her manner—that smile again—always disarmed the subject, so often she got more from the interviewee than another reporter.

While her victories piled up in whatever she turned her hand to, her ego remained stable. She was confident, but not conceited. She's gone through life pretty much as she swam to Florida: one more yard, one more mile.

At 64, looking fabulous and undaunted by age, she's lived long enough to know adversity is not shy. He has knocked on all our doors and the doors of our friends. He has taken our friends, our parents, and he has even taken some of our children. He can wipe out your life savings in a heartbeat. But one of the wonderful things about Diana is that she has always had a strong sense of proportion. And the way in which she achieved what was thought to be undoable is a metaphor for facing any and all challenges: persist; go on; take one more stroke, one more breath.

I'm not passing myself off as one of her best friends, but I've known her for five and a half decades. That's a long time to take someone's measure. Even if we did attend rival high schools, I can "forgive" her for attending Pine Crest. (I graduated from Ft. Lauderdale High, Class of 1962, so I'm five years older.)

All the jocks, in what was then a small town, more or less knew one another. Brian Piccolo graduated from Central Catholic High School in 1961, going on to Wake Forest and then the Chicago Bears. Chris Evert—the top tennis player in the world—also went to Central Catholic, by then renamed St. Thomas Aquinas. More glory for little Ft. Lauderdale, a town of 30,000 people—if you stretched it. The best athlete of all (again, from Central Catholic), Betty Rinehart, became a Dominican nun—otherwise, I believe she'd also be a household name.

Why so many of us happened to be around at the same time, I have no idea. Many of us started out at the Naval Air Station from which the famous Lost Squadron took off. Our schoolbooks had "Naval Air" printed inside, and from there we filtered to the public high schools, the one private school (Pine Crest) and the Catholic School. Dillard High was the African-American school, for those were the days of segregation. I often wonder how much our generation lost by being kept apart. Still, what we all learned no matter where we went to high school was discipline, sportsmanship, and respect for others. Seems quaint now, but one way or the other it was drummed into us.

Years later, every time I ran into Diana in New York, she still exemplified those qualities. We could blast each other hammer and tong on the squash court, but, when it was over, we'd sit down, have a Co-Cola (never called a Coke by Southerners) and catch up—not on gossip, as neither of us cared about that. We'd talk world events, politics, and especially the women's movement or what we were reading. She never grilled me about what I was writing, and I repaid the compliment by not digging into her career. In that sense, we were like any two people who'd known one another for a long time. What interested the outside world about either of us wasn't what interested us as friends.

Of course, I was impressed with her athletic ability, but I was far more impressed with her sensitivity to other people. She didn't judge people by what they had or even by what they'd accomplished. She valued honesty, discretion, and loyalty. She understood that all oppressions are linked: a simple fact still ignored today when many "leaders" of the outcast groups are loathe to jeopardize their lofty position to make common cause with others. Not that we would dwell on such things, but, even so, we made note.

Being a Southern lady, Diana does not call attention to her good works any more than to her insight into how oppression really works. Such sensitivity is rare. Athletes are tremendously self-centered. In many ways, they have to be in order to master their craft. But focused as she was, I never caught a whiff of that heavy odor of self-regard. Now that she has publicly discussed being sexually abused as a child,[1] it makes sense that she saw beyond her nose, felt the suffering of others, and managed to use that anger to fuel her work. That in itself is extraordinary. But when we were young, I had no idea of what she was going through. I don't think any of us suspected.

When Diana started swimming in 1967, a woman was supposed to be silent. And be grateful. A few years later, Billie Jean King blew down the patriarchal doors in tennis. Other sports work at it, but many still remain behind. For all the good that Title IX has done, women haven't crossed home plate. But Diana's life was her proof. She won. She kept winning, in one way or another, and she was smart enough not to call attention to male fragility when she beat their times, as in the Bahamas to Florida swim. Commentators might pound the drums but Diana wasn't out to drive anyone down, male or female—she was just out to excel. Or, as she put it herself with characteristic understatement, "Got to be my best self."

In the late seventies and eighties, Diana was one of the few professional athletes willing to be seen with someone identified as being gay.

Me. She never mentioned it. We never talked about it. Nor did we discuss her private life. Still, she never avoided me in public only to then apologize in private about fearing losing endorsements, as others did. And for her integrity, I was, and will always be, grateful to her. Put simply: she was never a coward. And never a hypocrite.

Diana's swim, those grueling 53 hours, makes us realize that not all the sharks are in the water. For every person marginalized by age, gender, color, who they love—for every LGBT person abused, discarded, their pain ignored—her swim is a victory. The message is: go on. Just go on. You can do it.

Nyad credits partner/coach Bonnie Stoll, as well as members of her team, for her success, saying, "It looks like a solitary sport but it takes a team." Sandy Armstrong—Executive Director of California's Marin Rowing Association—is the Recipient of the 2013 Ernestine Bayer Award, formerly "Woman of the Year." During her tenure as coach, MRA women's varsity eight has qualified for the Youth National Championship every year but one since 1991. Her junior women's eight holds the Southwest Regional Championship record. Armstrong says:

The strength of knowing that someone is behind you, a coach, a friend, a partner, a teammate, even a stranger who, in their core, believes in your potential; who believes in their heart that you can do it; that you can—one step at a time-persevere, [helps] you [to] end up believing and trusting more in yourself. All of this, while teaching integrity, humility, respect, and confidence without arrogance, is what women like Diana bring to all of us, as well as benefit from themselves. Diana is successful because of who she is, not just for what she has accomplished. It's not just what she's done, it's how she's done it. That is what my athletes look up to in her life— and take with us as we embark on achieving our own goals, whether to win a race, find our way in the world, or in allowing ourselves to find self-confidence in who we are.

What I have found in my coaching is that women and girls have the natural ability to be there for one another, and *the need to be part of a bigger team. We prefer to be one of many, not just the One. Indeed, we want to succeed as individuals, but it isn't really worth it if no one comes with us, or if we have left others behind. And in the end, we know we are better for bringing others along with us, even our competitors and our doubters, as they make us stronger.*[2]

Diana once likened marathon swimming as "the loneliest sport in the world." Perhaps those who feel alone can find courage in her endeavor? I always liken it to writing a novel: you are totally alone…but Portuguese man-of-war jellyfish are out there, too. Still, she and I never felt a reason to talk about our loneliness. It was just there for both in different ways and for different reasons. But when Diana touched Florida's shores and smiled, the world smiled back. I'm still smiling. And I hope her vision of her epic swim, as if her odyssey were a film she pictured, will make you smile:

You're going to be able to see the palm trees during the day. I have this fantasy that I'm seeing the lights. It's that third morning. I've swum through Saturday night and Sunday and Sunday night and now it's Monday. Every time I come into that boat for a feeding, there are more and more lights, and then the sun rises and you start seeing actual things: planes flying and buildings and trees. The world looks green instead of just blue. And then I'm there.[3]

ENDNOTES

1   Elizabeth Weil, "Marathon Swimmer Diana Nyad Takes On the Demons of the Sea," *The New York Times Magazine*, December 1, 2011.

2   Sandy Armstrong, interview by Adrian Brooks, March 19, 2014.

3   Weil, "Marathon Swimmer."

Afterword:
Our Lives, Our Words: Newspapers, Bookstores, and Gay Liberation

by Victoria A. Brownworth

"We needed to write about ourselves—no one else was doing it," said gay publisher Mark Segal when he was inducted by the National Lesbian & Gay Journalists Association (NLGJA) into the LGBT Journalists Hall of Fame in 2013.

Segal began publishing the *Philadelphia Gay News* (now *PGN*) in 1976. Not yet 25, Segal had been a gay activist since his teens and was one of the organizers of the first gay pride marches in New York City in 1970. Segal was also known for his "zaps" as a Gay Raider, an activist group he founded in Philadelphia. Zaps were hit-and-run political actions infiltrating mainstream media—notably TV—and demanding attention for gay rights. Segal did the first of these in 1972, after being ejected from a dance competition for dancing with his male lover when he crashed the evening news broadcast of WPVI-TV in Philadelphia. These activist statements were repeated by Segal during many other television broadcasts, including, most famously, the national evening news with Walter Cronkite.

As newsworthy as these zaps were, Segal wanted more attention to gay issues than this. Immediately post-Stonewall, there was still no news coverage of gay men or lesbians in mainstream media unless someone gay committed a crime. On January 3rd, 1976, Segal published the first issue of what would be a monthly, then bi-weekly, then weekly publication: the *Philadelphia Gay News*, now *PGN*, which is still in publication. Segal touts the newspaper as the most award-winning LGBT publication in the country, and Segal himself has won several awards for his weekly newspaper column.

On the West Coast, gay activists Bob Ross and Paul Bentley were older than Segal, but also living in the heart of America's gayest city: San Francisco. On April 1st, 1971, they founded the *Bay Area Reporter* (known locally for years as *BAR*), the nation's first continuously publishing gay paper. Like *PGN*, the paper found its initial distribution throughout the gay scene in the city, notably in the gay bars South of Market, the Castro District, and Polk Gulch. *Bay Area Reporter* is the country's oldest continually published LGBT paper. Ross died in 2003, but was inducted into the LGBT Journalists Hall of Fame in 2013, along with Segal.

The *Bay Area Reporter* would become one of the most vital of America's LGBT newspapers as gay men started to fall victim to AIDS in the 1980s. The paper published more than 10,000 obituaries during the first wave of the AIDS crisis. Where it had begun as a nexus for gay men and lesbians to read about each other's lives, it was soon the focal point for San Francisco's gay men to record the devastation of the epidemic.

The importance of an emerging gay media post-Stonewall cannot be overstated. Gay men and lesbians had rarely seen themselves in print before. Newspapers dedicated solely to their community's issues and concerns were an essential tool in spreading the gay liberation message and keeping the activism born out of Stonewall in the forefront of the budding community's consciousness. These papers were also the place to explore issues related to the community, from problems with police to how to build social networks.

Following the suit of other minority publications in the black and Jewish communities, these newspapers and others (which would spring up throughout the country, among them the *Washington Blade,* Chicago's *Windy City Times,* and *The Advocate* magazine, as well as a plethora of lesbian-feminist publications like *off our backs),* would serve to reach closeted gay men and lesbians nationwide who had no other access to gay community. Stories on gay issues focused attention on the breadth of the LGBT community, as well as on the deep need for connection between and among people who were living in a kind of hidden diaspora. In the early days, personal ads in these papers linked men and women with each other in a world where the closet was the norm.

Concomitant with the growth of the gay press was the spread of gay and lesbian bookstores. In the Stonewall era, the thirst for books and anything else gay or lesbian was tremendous. But going to the local library to seek out books about homosexuality and homosexuals again presented the problem of revealing one's self to be gay or lesbian. And coming out was still far from the consciousness of most gay men and lesbians.

Bookstores provided alternative meeting places, especially for men and women who didn't want to go to the bars, either because of the risk or because they didn't want to drink. Oscar Wilde Bookstore in New York's Greenwich Village opened in 1967 as the Oscar Wilde Memorial Bookshop. Craig Rodwell sold only books by lesbian and gay authors and also used the shop as an organizing and meeting place for the gay liberation movement. Rodwell and Segal were among the organizers of the first gay pride march in New York in 1970.

In Philadelphia, Giovanni's Room Bookstore (named for James Baldwin's iconic novel) became the world's largest purveyor of gay, lesbian, and feminist books in 1973 and grew to have an inventory of over 100,000 titles. Founded by a small group of gay men and lesbians, it has been run since 1976 by Ed Hermance, who built the then tiny one-room store into a vast five-room, two-story bookstore in the heart of Philadelphia's Gayborhood. Giovanni's Room has a special space for kids to read LGBT picture books with their lesbian moms and gay dads and a comfy area upstairs for the weekly book groups, author readings, signings, and community meetings that have evolved over the years at the store.

The *Different Light* bookstore chain opened in 1979, with stores in Los Angeles, San Francisco, and New York. As Edmund White said of Giovanni's Room in its earliest days, "The gay bookstore is so important. It's a non-alcoholic place for cruising. There are so few places to meet other gay people than bars. I think people who are looking for bookworms are not immediately obvious in a bar."

Armistead Maupin stated the importance of the gay and lesbian bookstore succinctly—it was a place for the marginalized to be recognized. Maupin noted, "If you want to know who the oppressed minorities in America are, simply look at who gets their own shelf in the [mainstream] bookstore. A black shelf, a women's shelf, and a gay shelf."

The gay bookstore, like the gay newspaper, gave a marginalized community a voice that was all its own.

Acknowledgements

Doing a book is always an unusual process, but I'd like to describe the one involved here in the hope that it inspires other struggling writers.

The Right Side of History came of my friendship with Brenda Knight. That fact can't be overstated for the background of that friendship is central to the book's existence.

In 2011, I submitted a novel to Cleis. At the time, Brenda was the editor, not the publisher. It took a year for a decision to come. When it did, my book was rejected. But something positive about communicating with Brenda led to an exchange of emails. Over time, we met and became friends. That said, I didn't feel that Cleis was the right home for my work, so I made no further submissions. Still, something else was in play.

In late 2012, another of my nonfiction books was accepted by the editor of a well-known San Francisco publishing house. But the promised contract never arrived. Throughout the months of confusion that ensued, Brenda offered wise counsel and patience. Ultimately, "there was no there" with the aforementioned editor. But by then, Brenda and I were sharing off-the-wall ideas, simply having fun, and indulging in the inspired madness of divine play.

In May 2013, she returned from a trip to New York with high praise for Christopher Bram's *Eminent Outlaws*. As we discussed his anthology, the concept arose of a wholly different slant on how the United States has been affected and shaped by LGBT radical activists.

I thought Brenda planned to tackle the book and encouraged her. I had no idea that she saw me as its editor. When she urged me to do it, I was stunned. As such, *The Right Side of History* evolved out of a creative dialogue with a quality which has virtually disappeared from U.S. publishing: a publisher willing to take risks. So it is to Brenda that I owe my primary thanks.

The collaboration born of longer-established friendships was further enhanced by the book's first contributors: Patricia Nell Warren, Jonathan Katz, Neeli Cherkovski, and Tiger Devore. Once they jumped in, approaching Barney Frank and Evan Wolfson seemed less daunting. But from the start, everyone understood that I was after gutsy, non-academic, forthright truth telling, so we steered clear of the cerebral.

If there was a guiding principle, it was this: at a time of increased visibility, when LGBTQI youth are more visible yet more persecuted, and when suicide rates are appallingly high, we wanted each chapter to be one which might give heart to troubled youngsters and help them grasp the fact that they have a heritage to be proud of; they belong to a community waiting to welcome them; they're precious and valuable, and that men and women of every race, creed, sexual preference, and faith have gone to the wall to secure fundamental human rights and make life better for them.

Clearly, no single work can deliver on such promises by itself, but our intention with this book was to promote that non-negotiable belief and place it firmly in the historical line of American values. Given such goals, the process by which this book manifested is due to individual contributors. But the good will wasn't limited to those who submitted essays, although every participant merits my gratitude. Brandon Logans provided insightful scholarship and criticism, as did Paul Gabriel and Kelly Hill. I'm also thankful to Mark Segal for his generosity; Susan Burk, at the Matthew Shepard Foundation, was a delight and was instrumental in arranging my interview with Judy Shepard; Jennifer Bass at the Kinsey Institute offered wise feedback. Denton Smith generously shared memories of Harvey Milk. At Cleis, Felice Newman, Frederique Delacoste, Samantha Kornblum, Sara Guisti, Cat Snell, Robin Miller, and Amanda Kreklau all helped the book along. Deb Beck took the photo of me, for which I'm grateful.

As the project rolled forward, it became a bandwagon since people got the point: we were firmly attaching LGBTQI equality to the foundational ethos of the nation without equivocation or tiptoeing around what basic human rights should be. Or what the force field is, which unites causes into one integrated, inter-generational dynamic of just and inclusive positive social change.

Everyone involved grasped a larger truth, which bears special emphasis: we represent a fraction of the millions who went before, people who took stands in support of individual freedom, oftentimes when it could be fatal to fight for liberty. As such, while it might be easy to overlook their sacrifices given the indisputable glamor of Josephine Baker and Bayard Rustin—to whom this book is proudly dedicated—unsung, forgotten multitudes merit equal thanks and praise. We stand on their shoulders, for *The Right Side of History* is as much about them as its own creators.

Finally, I thank William Hodsoll for his love and support.

Adrian Brooks

About the Contributors

JEAN-CLAUDE BAKER was born in France in 1943. At 14, he met the legendary entertainer Josephine Baker, who became his unofficial adoptive mother. On his 20th birthday, Jean-Claude hitchhiked to West Berlin, where he worked for four years. After reuniting with Josephine Baker, he became the spokesman for the Rainbow Tribe, her 12 adopted children of different races, nationalities, and religions. They toured the world as a symbol of Baker's utopian dream. Josephine Baker died in 1975; Jean-Claude remained in New York. In 1983 he began working with Chris Chase on the biography *Josephine: The Hungry Heart.* In 1986, on 42nd Street's Theater Row, he opened the bistro Chez Josephine, which became a favorite of theatergoers. In recognition of his many achievements, Jean-Claude was made a *Chevalier des Arts et des Lettres* by the government of France. He died in 2015.

RITA MAE BROWN (b. November 28, 1944) Birth was the search for the library. My natural mother, however, dumped me in an orphanage. Such beginnings create an independent spirit, good for me, upsetting for those hagridden by the status quo. I graduated from New York University during times that rapidly became tumultuous. The Vietnam War was escalating, no reason ever being given for risking American lives then and this silence remains. Everything came into question and I was only too happy to be one of the questioners. My motto then and now is, "If you can't raise consciousness, raise hell." In this I have richly succeeded. For the last forty years I have farmed as well as written novels. I write this in my library looking out at horses in the pasture. Truly, I am home. I hope you have found your heart's home, too.

VICTORIA A. BROWNWORTH is a journalist, editor, and writer. She has won the NLGJA and the Society of Professional Jo urnalists awards, the Lambda Literary Award, and has been nominated for the Pulitzer Prize. She is a regular contributor to *The Advocate* and *SheWired,* a blogger for *Huffington Post,* and a contributing editor for *Curve* magazine, *Curve* digital, and *Lambda Literary Review.* The author and editor of nearly 30 books (including *Coming Out of Cancer: Writings from the Lesbian Cancer Epidemic* and *Restricted Access: Lesbians on Disability*) her collection *From Where We Sit: Black Writers Write Black Youth* won the 2012 Moonbeam Award for Cultural/Historical Fiction. She lives in Philadelphia with her partner, artist Maddy Gold.

CHARLOTTE BUNCH, Founding Director and Senior Scholar at the Center for Women's Global Leadership at Rutgers University in New Jersey, has been an activist, writer, and organizer for women's, LGBT, civil, and human rights for over four decades. She is a professor in Women's and Gender studies at Rutgers, and is the author of numerous essays and books such as *Passionate Politics: Feminist Theory in Action* and *Demanding Accountability: the Global Campaign and Vienna Tribunal for Women's Human Rights*. Bunch was inducted into the National Women's Hall of Fame (1966). She is also the recipient of the Eleanor Roosevelt Award for Human Rights (1999) and the "Women Who Make A Difference Award" (2000) among many other awards and prizes.

NEELI CHERKOVSKI is the author of many books of poetry and prose. His most recent publications are *Fallendes Licht* (*Fallen Light*), a bilingual collection of poems from Austria; *L'Amore Comunque* (*Love Always*); *Manila Poems;* and *Lucent Feather in the Sky*. He is also the author of the poetry collections *Leaning Against Time, From the Canyon Outward*, and *From the Middle Woods*. He has written a critical memoir, *Whitman's Wild Children*, and biographies of Charles Bukowski and Lawrence Ferlinghetti. A recipient of the PEN Josephine Miles Award for Literary Excellence, Neeli lives in San Francisco. Currently, he is completing a memoir of his life in poetry.

JEANNE CÓRDOVA's activism began as Los Angeles chapter president of the Daughters of Bilitis in 1970, and as founder/publisher of *The Lesbian Tide*, the largest national newsmagazine for lesbian feminists. After being a key organizer of the first National Lesbian Conference in 1973, she worked on the campaign to defeat Prop 6—the Briggs initiative—and was Media Director for STOP 64, the statewide AIDS quarantine ballot measure. One of the first openly lesbian delegates to the National Democratic Convention, she was also president of the Stonewall Democratic Club in the early 1980s. Her memoir *When We Were Outlaws* won the Lambda Award, a Publishing Triangle Judy Grahn Award for Lesbian

Non-fiction, a Golden Crown Award, and a Stonewall Book Award. As well as writing for many publications, including the *L.A. Free Press* and *The Advocate*, Córdova has contributed to many anthologies. She lives in the Hollywood Hills among other outlaws, artists, and authors.

JOHN D'EMILIO is a pioneer in LGBT studies and the history of sexuality. Emeritus Professor of Gender and Women's Studies and History at the University of Illinois at Chicago, he is the author or editor of almost a dozen books including *Sexual Politics, Sexual Communities: The Making of a Homosexual Minority in the United States, 1940-1970; Lost Prophet: The Life and Times of Bayard Rustin; Intimate Matters: A History of Sexuality in America*, coauthored with Estelle B. Freedman; and, most recently, *In a New Century: Essays on Queer History, Politics, and Community Life*. His awards include the Brudner Prize from Yale for lifetime contributions to gay and lesbian studies, and the Roy Rosenzweig Distinguished Service Award of the Organization of American Historians. His biography of Bayard Rustin was a finalist for the National Book Award.

TIGER DEVORE, PhD, has been an Intersex activist and advocate for over 30 years. Born with genitals that did not conform to physicians' standards of male or female appearance, between the ages of 3 months and 53 years, he suffered 22 surgeries to attempt alignment with those standards. Along with many others, Tiger works to get a moratorium on medically unnecessary cosmetic surgery on infant genitalia. A clinical psychologist and certified sex therapist, he was the first Intersex person to come out publicly during a 1984 interview with Oprah Winfrey. He is routinely sought out as an expert within the scientific disciplines and by the media. Tiger works in private practice, as a consultant to care providers, and to affected individuals around the world.

MATT EBERT is an American writer currently living in rural Pennsylvania. He is committed to social justice issues, politics, labor, and healthcare, and writes a blog for the Huffington Post.

BARNEY FRANK, b. 1940, was a Congressman from Massachusetts from 1981 to 2013. In that capacity, he served as chairman of the House Financial Services Committee and co-sponsored the Dodd-Frank act to reform the financial industry. A driving force to repeal the "Don't Ask

Don't Tell" laws restricting gays and lesbians in the armed forces, Frank was also one of the most prominent Democrats to confront the conservative Republican agenda. One of the first members of Congress to be out about his own sexuality, Frank came out publicly in 1987. Throughout his storied career, he proved to be one of the staunchest defenders of individual liberty, civil rights, the environment, and fundamental human equality in the country.

PAUL GABRIEL is an educational therapist in San Francisco, assisting children and teens with learning and processing differences. He was the Exhibits Director of the GLBT Historical Society in Francisco, served on its Board of Directors and co-chaired its Oral History Project. A community historian whose primary area of research is how the community in San Francisco formed between WWII and the early 70s, Paul has served on the American Alliance of Museums (AAM) and the Western Museums Association (WMA) Program Committees, the WMA Board of Directors, and on the steering councils of the Diversity Committee and the Alliance for Lesbian and Gay Concerns for AAM. He helps museums use insights from neuro-diverse populations to transform exhibition design, interpretation, and education to enhance cognitive comfort for all visitors.

ANAHI RUSSO GARRIDO is the Allen-Berenson postdoctoral fellow in Women's and Gender Studies at Brandeis University. She holds a PhD in Women's and Gender Studies from Rutgers University and an MA in Cultural Anthropology from Concordia University, Canada. She has been a visiting scholar at PUEG/UNAM in Mexico City. Her research currently focuses on gender and sexuality in Latin America, change, space and place and queer and feminist theory. She has worked with women's rights organizations in Mexico, Canada, and the United States. She is the co-editor of *Building Feminist Movements and Organizations* and has published articles on queer Mexico City in Women Studies Quarterly, NWSA Journal and the Journal of Postcolonial Cultures and Societies.

JAMES W. GILLIAM is the deputy executive director of the ACLU of Southern California and founding director of the organization's anti-bullying project. He is also an adjunct professor at Loyola Law School in Los Angeles and a featured contributor to "Understanding and Addressing Bullying," an online course offered by California State University, Fullerton's Extended Education Department specifically for school administrators, staff, and teachers. The views expressed herein are his own and do not reflect the positions of ACLU SoCal, Loyola Law School, or California State University, Fullerton.

ERIC A. GORDON is an independent scholar and writer with an undergraduate degree from Yale University and a doctorate in history from Tulane. He is the author of *Mark the Music: The Life and Work of Marc Blitzstein*, and co-writer of *Ballad of an American: The Autobiography of Earl Robinson*. He is Southern California Chapter Chair of the National Writers Union (UAW/AFL-CIO). From 1995 to 2010, Eric served as Director of the Arbeter Ring (Workmen's Circle) Southern California District, a national progressive secular Jewish organization. He earned *vegvayzer* certification, authorizing him to conduct secular Jewish life-cycle ceremonies. He currently volunteers to conduct marriage ceremonies for Los Angeles County. Eric is presently co-producing a CD of rare Soviet Yiddish songs by Samuel Polonski. He is a frequent contributor to People's World online. He is now shepherding into print two more books: an autobiography, and a translation from Yiddish of a history of the Jewish anarchist movement in America.

MISS MAJOR GRIFFIN-GRACY was born in Chicago in 1940 and was assigned a male identity at birth. In the 60s, she moved to New York where she was a sex worker and dancer. At Stonewall, she led the charge against the police, but got knocked out and jailed. Behind bars, an officer broke her jaw. In 1978, she moved to San Diego and organized a food bank for women who were incarcerated, suffering from addition, or homelessness. She moved to San Francisco in 1990 and served on the Tenderloin AIDS Resource Center. In 2002 Miss Major began working at the Transgender Gender Variant Intersex Justice Project. The program supports transgender women of color who have survived incarceration and brutality in men's prisons. Miss Major was the Grand Marshal of Pride in San Francisco in 2014.

JONATHAN D. KATZ curated *Hide/Seek: Difference and Desire in American Portraiture*, the first queer exhibition mounted at a major U.S. museum, which opened at the Smithsonian National Portrait Gallery in 2010. *Hide/Seek* received the 2011 Best National Museum Show award from the International Association of Art Critics and its accompanying book was voted the best LGBT nonfiction in 2011 by the American Library Association. Katz directs the doctoral program in Visual Studies at the University at Buffalo and is presently completing a new book, *The Silent Camp: Jasper Johns, Robert Rauschenberg and the Cold War*. A pioneering scholar, in 1990 he was the first full-time American academic to be tenured in the field of gay and lesbian studies, and founded the Harvey Milk Institute. As an associate professor at Yale University (2002-2006), he was founding director of its Lesbian and Gay Studies Program. He co-founded Queer Nation San Francisco and the Gay and Lesbian Town Meeting, the organization that successfully lobbied for queer anti-discrimination statutes in the city of Chicago. He is the president of the Leslie Lohman Museum of Gay and Lesbian Art in New York City and curates many of its exhibitions.

HAYDEN L. MORA serves as Director of Strategic Relations at the Human Rights Campaign. His focus is on long term strategic planning, systems design, and program integration. Earlier, Hayden worked in the labor movement for 11 years, as the Deputy National Political Director of the Service Employees International Union. In that position, he increased SEIU's Political Action Committee fundraising by 60%, building the largest PAC in the U.S. with an average annual revenue of $21 million, funded entirely by working people. Hayden is an out transgender man and uses male pronouns.

JULIE RHOAD has been the President and CEO of the NAMES Project Foundation since 2001. Under her leadership, the foundation has expanded the AIDS Memorial Quilt's outreach to ever-growing communities in need, starting key programs such as "Call My Name," which works to encourage panel-making and HIV prevention in the African-American community, as well as programs for middle and high schools to reach our new generation of youth with prevention and other educational messages. She oversees the work of making Quilt panels available to organizations throughout the country and around the world for educational programs and community-based fundraisers, as well as the ongoing care and upkeep of all of the 48,000+ Quilt panels hand sewn by family and friends who have lost loved ones to AIDS.

SULTAN SHAKIR is the Executive Director of SMYAL (Supporting and Mentoring Youth Advocates and Leaders) which works to support and empower LGBTQ youth in the DC metro area. SMYAL works to provide the tools, resources and support for young leaders to create positive change in their schools and communities. Prior to this, Sultan worked as the Director of Youth & Campus Engagement at the Human Rights Campaign and even earlier as a Regional Field Director at HRC as the Campaign Manager and Political Director for Marylanders for Marriage Equality, the campaign that successfully passed and defended marriage equality in Maryland. Sultan has worked on a number of national, state, and local HRC campaigns, including the effort to oust former Senator Rick Santorum and helping state and local partners in Gainesville, Florida, to preserve the city's non-discrimination protections covering sexual orientation and gender identity.

JUDY SHEPARD lost her 21-year-old son, Matthew, to a brutal murder motivated by anti-gay hatred in October 1998. To save others a similar fate, she and her husband, Dennis, turned grief into action, establishing the Matthew Shepard Foundation to advance the causes Matthew championed: to replace hate with understanding, acceptance, and compassion through educational resources, outreach, and advocacy. As the founding president of the Board of Directors, Judy travels the globe urging audiences to act individually and collectively to make the world more accepting for everyone regardless of race, religion, ethnicity, sex, and gender identity. As an LGBT activist, she became the most recognized voice in the fight for a more inclusive federal hate crimes statute. In 2009, The Matthew Shepard and James Byrd Jr. Hate Crimes Prevention Act was signed into law. Judy's memoir, *The Meaning of Matthew*, explores the family's journey, Matthew's life, the prosecution of his murderers, the ensuing media coverage, and the family's continuing work to advance civil rights. The Shepard family lives in Wyoming.

MAX WOLF VALERIO is a poet, a writer, and a long-transitioned man. An American Indian (Blackfoot Confederacy—Blood/Kainai band) on his mother's side, his father is Hispano from Northern New Mexico, descended from Conversos and crypto-Jews of the Sephardic diaspora. Max began his medical transition from female to male in 1989. His memoir *The Testosterone Files* was a Lambda Finalist for 2006. Recent works include: *Exile: Vision Quest at the Edge of Identity*, a long poem set to ambient music; a collaboration with photographer Dana Smith, *Mission Mile Trilogy +1*; poems in *Troubling the Line: Trans and Gender-queer Poetry and Poetics*; and essays. Max is currently writing a novel set in San Francisco where gentrification impacts three trans men. His book of poems, *The Criminal*, will be published in 2015.

PATRICIA NELL WARREN was born in 1936 on the Grant-Kohrs Ranch at Deer Lodge, Montana, now a national historic site. An author of fiction and nonfiction, she has published 10 books, including the *New York Times* bestseller *The Front Runner.* She has also written for magazines, both mainstream and LGBT. She blogs at Bilerico.com and SBNation, and has written a column on the politics of AIDS for *A & U Magazine* for the last 12 years. She owns her own independent publishing company, Wildcat Press. Over the years, she has been a human rights activist. During 1996-1999, Warren served as a commissioner of education in the Los Angeles Unified School District, and worked with at-risk LGBT youth in LAUSD programs. She has received the Barry Goldwater Human Rights Award (2000), the New York City Public Advocate's Award (2003), a Literary Pioneer award from the Lambda Literary Foundation in 2013, and a Bonham Centre Award (U. of Toronto) in 2014. Her 1982 *Reader's Digest* article about the ranch won the National Cowboy Hall of Fame's Western Heritage Award in 1982. Several of her novels, notably *One Is the Sun* and *The Fancy Dancer,* are set in Montana.

EVAN WOLFSON is the founder and president of Freedom to Marry, the campaign to win marriage nationwide for same-sex couples. Prior to founding Freedom to Marry in 2003, Wolfson served as co-counsel in the historic *Baehr* case that launched the ongoing global movement for the freedom to marry. Wolfson is the author of *Why Marriage Matters: America, Equality, and Gay People's Right to Marry.* He graduated from Harvard Law School in 1983. In 2004, *Time* magazine named him one of the "100 most influential people in the world," and in 2012, he won the Barnard Medal of Distinction alongside President Barack Obama. *Newsweek*/the Daily Beast has dubbed him the "godfather of gay marriage."

MERLE WOO is a socialist feminist poet, activist, and retired lecturer in Women Studies, San Jose State and San Francisco State University. She also taught in Asian American/Ethnic Studies at UC Berkeley. When unjustly fired, she fought and won three multi-discrimination and free speech battles against them. She is the author of a poetry collection, *Yellow Woman Speaks: Selected Poems.* In 1994, she received the humanitarian award from the Northern California Lesbian and Gay Historical Society.

About the Author

ADRIAN BROOKS (b. 1947) is an activist and traveler, a poet, play-wright, performer, novelist, journalist, nonfiction writer, and spiritual teacher. Raised in the Philadelphia art world/establishment, he began writing when attending Friends World Institute (FWI), a radical international Quaker school designed to produce lifelong agents of social change. He volunteered for Martin Luther King in 1968. After Dr. King's murder, Brooks went to Mexico and Africa with FWI. In 1970, he became part of New York's SOHO avant-garde where he knew Andy Warhol and appeared in one of his films. In 1972, Brooks moved west. From 1974 on, he was an out front gay liberation poet, as well as scriptwriter-star of San Francisco's "Angels of Light," the iconic underground free theater and lightning rod of the city's vanguard gay culture. At this time, he met and appeared at events with Harvey Milk. He retired from the Angels in 1980. In 1985, he left the U.S. In Europe, he performed with the "Amsterdam Balloon Company," a forerunner of Burning Man. In India, he studied Siddha Yoga and Ramana Maharshi's Path of Self-Inquiry before returning to California in 1995. His novels include: *The Glass Arcade, Roulette,* and *Black and White and Red All Over,* and he has also written a theater memoir about his years with the Angels of Light: *Flights of Angels.* Brooks lives in San Francisco.